FOREWORD.

The present Deacon has shown the great interest he takes in the affairs of the Incorporation, not only by the attention he has given to the ordinary work of his office, but by his researches among the old records of the craft. As the handwriting of these records is in the characters to be found in ancient Scottish documents, and now difficult to decipher, their contents were necessarily available to very few, and to these only after much labour. With the aid of an expert in such writings the Deacon had a number of the old documents transcribed, and on the results being shown to the Master Court it was resolved that it was in the interests of the Incorporation that the transcriptions should be printed in book form.

The Deacon kindly consented to see the proposed volume through the press, classifying the transcriptions and writing explanatory and connecting notes, but without attempting to produce a formal history of the Incorporation.

In placing the result before the Incorporation, the Master Court trust that this glimpse of its past history will stimulate an interest in its present affairs, and that the members of to-day will emulate their predecessors in doing what they can to promote the continued prosperity of this old Incorporation.

IN NAME AND BY AUTHORITY OF THE MASTER COURT.

C. J. MACLEAN,
Clerk.

115 ST. VINCENT STREET,
GLASGOW, *1st September, 1905.*

PREFACE.

The matter available has not been such as to make a continuous record possible. For facility of reference it has been thought advisable to classify the extracts, necessarily somewhat arbitrarily, in Chapters, and to dispense with a detailed Index. With few exceptions the extracts have, in each chapter, been arranged chronologically.

The Minute and other Books now awanting were first missed in 1849, as is shown in an acknowledgment then granted by a new clerk for other books.

It may add to the reader's interest to have the following Chronological Table for reference:—

1488—James IV., King of Scotland.
1513—Flodden. James V. succeeds to the throne.
1542—Queen Mary.
1550-60—Reformation.
1567—James VI.
1603—James succeeds to English throne.
1611—Glasgow made a Royal Burgh.
1625—Charles I.
1649—Commonwealth in England.
1651—Charles II. crowned in Scotland.
 Scotland United to English Commonwealth by Cromwell.
1660—Charles II. restored and Episcopacy revived.
1685—James II. and VII.
1689—William of Orange. Re-establishment of Presbyterianism.
1702—Queen Anne.
1707—Legislative Union of England and Scotland.
1714—George I.
1715—First Newspaper published in Glasgow. First Jacobite rising.
1727—George II.
1745—Second Jacobite rising.
1746—Culloden.
1760—George III.
1820—George IV.
1830—William IV.
1837—Queen Victoria.

The writer desires to acknowledge much kindly help received, especially from the Clerk, Mr. C. J. MacLean; and from Mr. Robert Renwick, Depute Town Clerk of the City.

PREFACE.

There were many documents and articles available for illustration, of which comparatively few members were able to examine the originals. Such of them have been chosen for reproduction as are most likely to be interesting to the wider circle which this book is intended to reach.

If any apology is needed for including the plate of the present members of the Master Court, it has been done entirely on the writer's responsibility, believing that had portraits been available of those who were in a similar position fifty or a hundred years back it would now have been of surpassing interest, and that, should this volume survive, our sons and grandsons will have a similar interest. Every effort has been made to avoid errors; it is, however, hardly possible but that some have been made and that others have escaped the eye of one who is not only an amateur, but a novice, at such work.

ROBERT D. M'EWAN.

22 MONTROSE STREET,
GLASGOW, *1st Sept., 1905.*

NOTE TO SECOND EDITION.

The want of an Inventory detailing all the very interesting books and papers found to be in the possession of the Incorporation in the course of preparing this book was felt by many members to be a serious omission.

The writer had not sufficient antiquarian knowledge to prepare this list, but Dr. George Neilson, F.S.A., etc., has been good enough to give the Incorporation the benefit of his great experience, and there is now included in Appendix VI. a complete Inventory.

At the same time it has been thought advisable to include a copy of the last revision of the Continuous Roll, having in view that entries there might disclose to present members that the immediate forebears of men now living had been members, and the Master Court invite the help of present members to bring such within the membership of the Incorporation.

R. D. M'E.

June, 1908.

INDEX.

Chapter	Page
I.—Origin and Early History,	1
II.—Constitution,	12
III.—Apprenticeship and Freemanship,	22
IV.—Trade Privileges,	35
V.—Relation to Trades' House and Care of the Poor of the Craft,	42
VI.—Supervision of Tradesmanship,	47
VII.—Meetings and Places of Meeting,	59
VIII.—Discipline,	62
IX.—Money Matters,	73
X.—Legislation and Litigation,	86
XI.—Relations with Gorbals and Bridgend Weavers,	95
XII.—Relations with Calton and Blackfaulds Weavers,	107
XIII.—Social Matters,	115
XIV.—Property held by Incorporation,	118
XV.—Burials and Mortcloths,	122
XVI.—The Weaver in Public Affairs,	126
XVII.—Later History,	131

APPENDIX.

I.—Master Court, 1904-5,	136
II.—Laws and Regulations, also Table of Entrance Fees,	137
III.—Tabulated Statement,	149
IV.—List of Deacons and Clerks,	150
V.—Names of Present Members,	154
VI.—Inventory of Old Minute Books, Documents, etc.,	167
VII.—Copy of Roll Revised in 1863 and Continued till June, 1908,	191

ILLUSTRATIONS.

PLATE		PAGE
I.—PAGE OF MINUTE BOOK, 8TH FEBRUARY, 1658, SHOWING A REFERENCE TO THE INCORPORATION HAVING BEEN IN EXISTENCE IN 1514,		*Frontispiece*
II.—SEAL OF CAUSE, 1605,		to face 1
III.—TITLES OF GORBALS LANDS,		96
IV.—TITLES OF EDDLESTON MANSE (IN LATIN),		120
V.—DEACON'S BOX, SNUFF-BOX, BELL, AND SHUTTLES,		8
VI.—COLLECTOR'S BOX, HORN, AND MALLET,		16
VII.—SEALS ON DOCUMENTS REPRODUCED AS PLATES III. AND IV.,		112
VIII.—GROUP OF PRESENT MASTER COURT OF INCORPORATION,		136

OLD GLASGOW WEAVERS:

BEING

RECORDS OF THE INCORPORATION OF WEAVERS.

I.

ORIGIN AND EARLY HISTORY.

The records of the Incorporation have had a varied fate, some of the earliest having survived while the history of the middle age of the craft is a complete blank. All records for sixty to seventy years in the middle of the eighteenth century have disappeared, and from 1683 till 1793 there are no minute books extant. It has always been believed that the Incorporation owes its existence to a "Gift or Seal of Cause by the Magistrates and Town Council of Glasgow, with concurrence of the Archbishop, dated 4th June, 1528." Mr. Crawfurd so states in "A Sketch of the Trades' House of Glasgow," published in 1856, and in a small pamphlet published by this Incorporation in 1888, the preamble of the Act of Parliament passed in 1681 (given on a later page), is quoted as the actual wording of the Seal of Cause granted by the Magistrates of Glasgow, on 4th June, 1528. No copy of that document has been preserved.

A small minute book, commencing in 1591 and concluding in 1611, and a larger minute book, dated from 1611 till 1683, have

ORIGIN AND EARLY HISTORY.

been preserved. In this latter, on 8th February, 1658, the following appears:—

Octavo Februarij 1658.

The haill old actis extractit out of the buikis for the yeir 1514, and sen syne, war red and allowit and approvine and farder it is statut and ordanit, with consent of the haill bodie of the calling, that quhat prenteis sall fie himself heirefter to serve his maister on his awin meit, sall have no benefeit of the calling thairefter, and the maister to pay in to the calling twentie pundis Scottis; as also that ilk brother quhais staikis sall be fund wrang, sall pay in to the craft twa markis ane half, extending to xxxij s. iiij d. for ilk fault.

The page of minute book from which above is extracted is given as Plate I. There is every reason to regard the date as genuine, because were it supposed to be a blunder for 1614, the same book has within itself the records for 1614 and would not be referred to as 'old actis extractit out of the buikis." The Incorporation has therefore had an existence of nearly four hundred years. The Provost and Magistrates granted a Seal of Cause on 16th February, 1605, which document exists in a good state of preservation and is reproduced as Plate II. The wording of it is as follows:—

SEAL OF CAUSE by the Provost, Bailies, and community of Glasgow to the Incorporation of Weavers, dated 16 February, 1605.

To ALL and sundrie To quhome it effeiris To quhais knawledge thir presentis sall com. The proveist, baillies, counsall and communitie of the burght and citie of Glasgow greiting in God ewirlasting. Witis yowr Wniversitie that the day and dait of thir presentis compeirit befoir ws the deikin, heidismen and maisteris of Wobstercraft and presentit to ws sitand in judgement our counsall gadderit, thair petitioune and supplicationne makand mentionne. That quhair thay had grantit wnto thame ane Lettere of deikenheid for the weill of thair craft and commoune weill of this burght and all and sindrie our soverane lordis leigis duelland and repairand within the samine haveing to do withe thame in thair calling and ocupationne. In the quhilk thair Lettere of deikinheid was conteinit certane liberties and priviledgis of certane penulties and wnlawis applyit of auld to certane superstitious usis quhilkis now cannot be applyit thairto be ressounc of the reformationne thairof. Thairfoir desyring that thair said Lettere of deikinheid may be reformit and renewit keipand the effect and substance of thair said former Lettere of deikinhead and the saidis penulties applyit to the said former superstitious usis to be applyit to sick guid and godlie usis as ar underwrittin. Quhilk thair desyre and petitionne We the proveist, baillies, counsall, and communitie of the said burght findand expedient and ressonable hes grantit and consentit lyk as be the tennour heirof, grantis and consentis that the said Lettere of deikenheid grantit of auld to the said wobstercraft be renewit and reformit in manir and forme wndirvrittin : First that all manir of prenteissis to be taine bund be ony of the said craft sall remaine prenteis be the spaice of sewin yeiris and na les without dispensatioune of the said principall maisteris of the said craft and speciallie an burges soneis that salbe ressaveit prenteis in the said craft. Secundlie that ilk prenteis that salbe bund to the said craft (burges soneis of the said craft being exceptit) sall pay at thair entrie to be prenteis fourtie schillingis money to the help and confort of thair decayit brethereine of the said craft and uther godlie and guid workis as the deikin and maisteris of the said craft sall think expedient burges craftismen soneis of the said craft payand onlie thretteine schillingis four pennyis conforme to auld use and wount and that na prenteis nor uther persoune of the said craft unfrieman be suflirit to set up ane boithe within the said burght without he be fund ane sufficient expert craftisman of the said craft and admitit be the deikin and maisteris of the said craft beand first admitit burges and frieman of the said burght. And give he be ane owtintownis man not learnit prenteis within the said burght sall pay for his upset to the deikin and maisteris of the said craft the sowme of tuentie pundis money; and give he be ane learnit prenteis within the towne sall pay tuentie markis money of upset; and give he [be] ane burges sone of the said craft sall pay four pundis of upset conforme to auld us and wount quhilk salbe applyit be the deikin and maisteris of craft to the weill and support of the decayit brethreine of thair said craft. And that na manir of persoune frieman of the said craft resaife in serveice with him ane uther manis prenteis or servand to work with him in the said craft without he obteine licence of his maister or utherwayis that he be frie at his maisteris handis and haife comptit with and quhatsumewir persoune of the said craft dois in the contrar the samine being tryit be the deikin and maisteris thairof sall pay to the said deikin and maisteris of the said craft ane wnlaw of saxteine schillingis. Ferdlie that ilk frieman of the said craft hauldand buithe or hows within this burght sall pay oulklie twa pennyis to the help and supplie of the new erectit hospitall erectit be the craftis within this burght, and that na craftisman of the said craft tak na man nor womanis work upone hand without he have sufficient and guid worklumis and sua fund and tryit be the said leikin and maisteris of craft quhairby the said work may be sufficientlie wrocht and not spilt : And quhasoewir spillis ony man or womanis work throw wnsufficient worklumis sall pay ane wnlaw of saxteine schillingis to the said deikin and maisteris of craft to thair commoune box : And it salbe leasum to the deikin and maisteris of craft to sicht the samine, and give it beis fund wnsufficientlie wrocht be the craftisman worker thairof it salbe leasum to thame to compryse the same in the craftismanis handis and the pairtie to be satisfiet and recompensit according to the skaithe. And siclyk that it sall not be leasum to na man of the said craft to tack ony uther manis work that is warpit of befoir without loife of the deikin under the paine of saxteine schillingis to be payit to the deikin and maisteris of craft. Item, give ony owtintownis wobsteris takis work out of this burght to work without the samine being apprehendit with himselfe sall pay to the said deikin and maisteris of craft for the tyme twa pennyis money how aft and sa oft as thai tak work furth of

ORIGIN AND EARLY HISTORY.

the towne with ane frie denner to the said deikin and maisteris of craft or ellis the sowme of tuentie sax schillingis aucht pennyis thairfoir togidder with sax schillingis aucht pennyis as for ane pund of waix conteinit in thair auld lettere of deikenheid to be applyit to the commoune us of the said craft and help of thair decayit brethreine; and give ony owttintownis wobster beis apprehendit bringand in work sall pay onlie tua pennyis how aft he beis apprehendit with the samine to be applyit as said is. And farder give ony owtintownis wobster presentis or bringis to the markat of the said burght ony wobis wrocht be thameself without the said burght, to be sauld as thair awin work sall pay for ilk wob the sowme of tua pennyis money to be applyit to the commoune use of the said craft as said is: And for exerseising and observeing of the statutis abovewrittin it salbe leasum to the heidismaisteris and remanent of the said craft yeirlie to elect and chuise thame ane deikin and maisteris of the said craft quhome the proveist baillies and counsall of the said burght for the tyme, sall approve and defend in all thair leasum actis and statutis for the commoune weill of this burght and weill of the said craft, and give ony brother of the said craft dissobeyis the said deikin in using and executing of his said offeice sall pay to the deikin and maisteris of craft the sowme of fourtie schillingis money with ane wnlaw of saxteine schillingis to the baillies; And for inbringing of all and sindrie the sadis onlawis to the effect and us foirsaid it salbe leasum to ane officer of the said craft chosin and admitit be the deikin and maisteris thairof accompanyit with ane of the officeris of the said burght to pas and poynd all and sindrie persounis of the said craft for the saidis wnlawis. Quhilkis haill heidis, statutis, and priviledgis abovewrittin :—We the proveist, baillies, and counsall of the said burght undersubscryveand for ws and our successouris in offeice ratifies and appreifis and interponis our authoritie thairto in all tyme cuming: In witnes quhairof to thir presentis wreitin be Williame Fleming at command of Archibald Heygait, cowrt clerk of our said burght subscrivit be our handis and be our said clerk at our command the commoune seall of our burght is to hung. At our said burght the saxteine day of Februar the yeir of God j^m vj^c and fyve yeiris.—Signed by Sir G. Elphinstoun, provost, Thomas Muir, baillie, Johne Andersoun, baillie, William Anderson, baillie, Robt. Stevin, William Stirling, Johne Nisbit, James Fischer, James Bell, Wm. Robisoune, Robert Rowat, Mathow Trumble, deane of gild, Wm. Petersone, William Wallace, James Lyonis, Johne Rowat, Thomas Pettegrew, Johne Woddrop, H. Conynghame, W. Fleimyng.

[P.S.] Ita est Archibaldus Heygait scriba dicti burgi de mandatis Joannis Diksoun et Joannis Scot duorum virorum consiliariorum scribere nescien signavit.

(City's Common Seal in good preservation).

It will be observed that here the seed is sown of the charitable work of the Incorporation, which then was only an incident, but now has become the principal reason of its existence. The earlier deed of 1528, made in time of James V., shows that the country was then under Roman Catholicism, while the later, made in James VI.'s reign,

ORIGIN AND EARLY HISTORY.

shows that a better use could be made of the funds of the craft than consuming them in wax candles. The minute of meeting on 30th March, 1605, shows how the cost of obtaining the letters of Deaconhood was liquidated:—

Die xxx Marcij 1605.

The quhilk day, the haill bretherene of craft condiscendis that every ane of the fremen of the craft pay thair awin pairtis of the xl. mark borrowit fra William Woderspoone in obteinyng of thair lettir of deakinheid, and that betuix and Witsounday nixt.

In 1681 a further Charter was granted by the Archbishop of Glasgow, and ratified by Act of Parliament on 17th September, 1681:—

CHARTER by Arthur, Archbishop of Glasgow, in favor of the Incorporation of Weavers, Glasgow, dated 19 July 1681.

Be it knoun to all men be thir present letteris Ws Arthur by the mercy of God Archbishop of Glasgow Lord of the Lordship barrony and regality therof: Forsameikle as the deacon masteris and remanent bretheren of the Incorporatioune of the weavers within the burgh of Glasgow Be their supplicatioune given in to ws hes desyred our ratificatioune and confirmation of ane former Gift granted to them be the magistratis and counsell of Glasgow with consent of the Archbishop of Glasgow for the tyme, with the alteration of some small dewes formerlie used to be payed be the said trade for the service of alters and utherwayes thairinspecifeit the tyme of superstition and poprie: Whilk supplicatioune maketh mention:—That wheras his Majestie conform to the laudable custome of all weill governed nations, hes for the benefeit of his leidges and his oun speciall service erected burghs royall within this kingdome not only with severall priviledges and authorities in themselves, bot also with power to establish particular Societies and Incorporatiounes for particular trades within themselves with severall immunities and liberties, conform quhairunto the Citie of Glasgow hes erected the Societie of the Weavers within their burgh, with consent ratificatioune and approbatioune of the most reverend father in God, Gawin, Archbishop of Glasgow, and hes impowered them to creat deacons to establish ordouris for regulatioune of their trade and impose fynes upon trespasseris of the samen as the said Gift and Chartour of the dait at Glasgow the fourt day of Junij $j^m v^e$ twenty eight yeirs at lenth beirs. Which particular fynes being either established as furnishing for the superstitions of the popish tymes and services or in such rates as are now inconsiderable by the act of parliament King James the sixt parliament eleventh capnt—Are extended ilk pund or penny of old unlaw to be now ten and proportionally. Lykas your grace being every way most competent both as superiour and patron of the burgh and as Archbishop of the Sea and province to make a conversion, innovatioune and destinatioune of the particular fynes of old superstitiously bestowed on their blind devotions—now to be applyed to the use of the poor of the said craft as

ORIGIN AND EARLY HISTORY.

your grace shall think fitt. As also that necessar it is that your graces authority be obtained for punishing of persons living without the bownds of the touns jurisdictions and authority and within the bownds of your graces regality conform to our former rightis granted and confirmed to ws. Therfor your graces petitiounneris humbly beggs your grace wold be pleased to signe a Chartor and grant containing your confirmation of our former rights with the conversion and destinatioune to pious uses as is thairin at length exprest. And in speciall Wheras incommers weavers taking out the stuff aff the toun to work or utherwayes incroaching within the burgh wpon their liberties and priviledges when apprehended are of old appoynted to be fyned in a pund of wax and a dinner to the maisteris of the craft which was occasion of needles expences without good to the poor your grace wold appoynt twentie pounds for the poor of the trade in place of wax and dinner. And quhairas by the said old gifts ilk prenteis was to pay fyve shilling Scotis your grace wold allow conform to the said act of parliament fyftie shilling Scotis, and where ilk new wpsetter payes this to be conform to their old richts. Item Who takes work and does not compleitly doe the same were formerly to pay a pund of wax, and who did take another mans work ower his head to pay a pund of wax. Item, disobeyeris of the deacon to be fyned in a pund of wax and als much to the magistrats whilk are all but mean fynes and inconsiderable. Therfor your petitioneris also humbly beggs your grace to allow for ilk pund of wax as aforsaid the soum of foure pundis Scotis and accordingly to authorize the said trade to exact the samen having your graces authority interponed thairto as the said supplicatioune in itself beirs. Whilk supplicatioune being taken to our serious consideratioune, and finding the desyre therof most reasonable We have not only ratified allowed and approven as we heirby ratifie allow and approve the said old gifts and priviledges granted formerly to the said weaver calling in the haill heads clawssis priviledges and immunities therincontained in favouris of the said trade but also conform to the desyre of the said petition Allowes them to exact the fynes in manner and conform as is therby requyred of us Wherunto we have interponed and interpones our authority be thir presentis, the said fynes being allwayes applyed for the use of the poor of the said trade, and hes converted destinat and appoynted the forsaid small fynes now augmented as said is conform to the said act of parliament and formerly payable to alters to the use of the poor of the said calling as we heirby convert destinat and appoynt them to be payed to the said poor accordingly. In witnes quhairof we have subscrivit thir presentis att Glasgow the nynteenth day of July j^m vj^c eightie ane yeirs befor thir witnessis Mr William Nimmo comisser clerk of Glasgow, William Guthrie, our servitour, and James Muir, wryter in Glasgow and wryter heirof Our seall is heirto appended.

WIL: NIMMO, wittnes   (Signed) ARTH: GLASCUEN.
WILL: GUTHRIE. wittnes

RATIFICATION BY PARLIAMENT, dated 17th September, 1681.

Att Edinburgh the Seventenith day of September One thousand Sex hundred Eightie one years Our Soveraigne Lord with advise and consent of Estates of

ORIGIN AND EARLY HISTORY.

Parliament of this his Majesties ancient Kingdome of Scotland Hes Ratified approven and confirmed and be thir presents Ratifies approves and confirms to and in favor of the Deacone Masters and remanent Bretheren of the Incorporation of the Weavers within the Burgh of Glasgow and their successors ane Gift or Seal of Cause made and granted by the Provost Bailzies Councill and Communitie of the Burgh and Cittie of Glasgow with consent of the Archbishop of Glasgow for the time in favor of the weavers of the said Burgh of Glasgow of the date the fourth day of June one thousand five hundred twentie eight yeares Bearing that the Maisters of the webstercraft within the said Burgh and Cittie had presented ane Supplication to the Magistrates and Councill of the said Burgh of Glasgow making mention that the said Craft was misguided and destroyed in the fault of good rule and reformation of the Craft and good statutes to have been made therein for the common weill of the Realme and the King's Leiges of the said Cittie and Town and therefor they desyred for their profeit, the Loving of God, augmentation of the Burgh, and to the honor of St.——— to be their Patron these points and articles after following—They are to say that seeing all encreasement of virtue practick and knowledge stand in good beginning and from then'forth To continue in rise and persevere to finall end That frae then'forth all manner of prentese fees to have been taine at the said Craft should stand in prenticeship for the space and termes of fyve years and no less, without dispensation of the principall maisters of the said Craft and speciall favour of the commons of the said Craft Secondlie Ilk prentice to pay to his entrie to the reparation and upholding of divine service at their alter fyve shilling of money and that na thir prentice nor na other persone of the Craft be suffered to sett up ane Buith within the said Burgh and Cittie without he be found sufficient and worthy thereto in Practick and admitted by the sworn masters of the Craft and thereafter to be made a freeman of the Good-Town Thirdlie If any man sett up a Buith within the said Burgh and Cittie that he should pay for his upsett two merks money To the reparation and upholding of devine service at the said alter and that na maister of the Craft-house harbour or resett any other man's prentice or servant And if any does sicklyke should pay ane contribution or taxt to the said altar at the discretion of the principal Masters of the said Craft and the cause thereof to be reformed by them Fourthlie That ilk man or woman having buith within the said Burgh and Cittie should pay ane weekly penny to the reparation and adorement of the said alter ay as it should come about and that no Craftman of the said Craft take no man's or woman's work upon hand without he have good workloomes and that the said work be not spoyled But at the Masters of the Craft's sight shall be made sufficient and who falzied thereintill should pay a pound of wax to the said alter, and that nae man take another man's work that is warped of before without leave of them that warped it under a pound of wax of paine sicklike and that ilk servant of the said Craft exceptane prentice shall pay a hapenny in the week to the reparation of the said Alter and it shall be lawfull to the haill Craft to choise ane Deacon once in the year for the inbringing of all their statutes above expressed—To the honor and reparation of the said Alter of St.——— and where any persone or persones disobays the Deacon that bees chosen for the tyme shall pay a pound of wax to the light of the said alter and ane unlaw of Eight Shilling to the Provost and Bailzies of the said Town and any certain of the Principall Maisters of the said Craft that shall happen to be for the tyme may have full faculty leave and priviledge with ane Officer of the Town (if need bees To pass with them to poynd and distreutzie for the taking inbringing and receivin of the duties foresaid To the sustentation and upholding of Gods Service and St.———as said is but any let stop or impediment wherefore seeing their rationable desyr and Simple Petitions conforme to equitie and consonant to honor and policy accordin to the use and custome of Great Towns of honour in other Realms Desyred tha the samen might be Ratified approved and confirmed by the said Provost Bailzie and Councill of the said Burgh with which desyres articles and points above expres and every one of them maturely and diligentlie advyzied considered and fand th same to the honor of God their mother of Holykirk The augmentation of God' service the comon well of the Kings leiges The good Town of Glasgow and Inhabitant of the samen and Therefore all and Sundrie the saids desyres points and articles i form manner and effect above expressed The saids Provost Bailzies Councill an Community of the said Burgh and Citty of Glasgow with consent authority an approbatione and confirmation of ane most Reverend Father in God and Specia Lord and Regale under the Kings grace Gavine Archbishop of Glasgow for all tym to come in perpetuall memorie Approved Ratified and confirmed and because th commnnity of the Websters' Walks wards stents and bear all the common charge of the said Town That if ilk outintoune Webster or Landward that comes withi the said Towne and takes the stuff thereof shall pay ilk tyme they are tane an pound of wax to the light of the said alter Together with ane free dinner to th Maisters of the said Craft and this to be done with consent of the haill Craft a the said gift or Seal of Cause having the Archbishop and Towns seal appende thereto of the dait foresaid at more length proports And in like manner our sai Soveraigne Lord Hes Ratified approven and confirmed and by thir presents Ratifie approves and confirms to and in favours of the said Deacone Maisters and remanen Bretheren of the said Incorportion of the Weavers of the said Burgh of Glasgo and their successors ane charter of confirmation made and granted by ane Reveren Father in God Arthure by the mercy of God now Archbishop of Glasgow Lord o the Lordship Barony and Regalitie thereof of the date the nyneteenth day of Jul last by past mentioning forasmuch as the Deacone Masters and remanent Bretherer of the Incorporation of the Weavers within the said Burgh of Glasgow by thei supplication given into the said Archbishop his Grace had desyred his Ratificatio and Confirmation of the said former Gift granted to them by the Magistrates an Councill of Glasgow with consent of the Archbishop of Glasgow for thetyme Wit the alteration of some small dues formerlie used to be payed by the said Trade fo the Service of Altars, and otherways above and therein specified the time of Super stition and Popery Which supplication maketh mention That whereas His Majesti conform to the laudable custome of weill governed Nationes Hes for the benefit o his Leidges and his own speciall service erected Burghs Royall within this Kingdom not only with severall priviledges and authorities in themselves But also with powe

PLATE V.

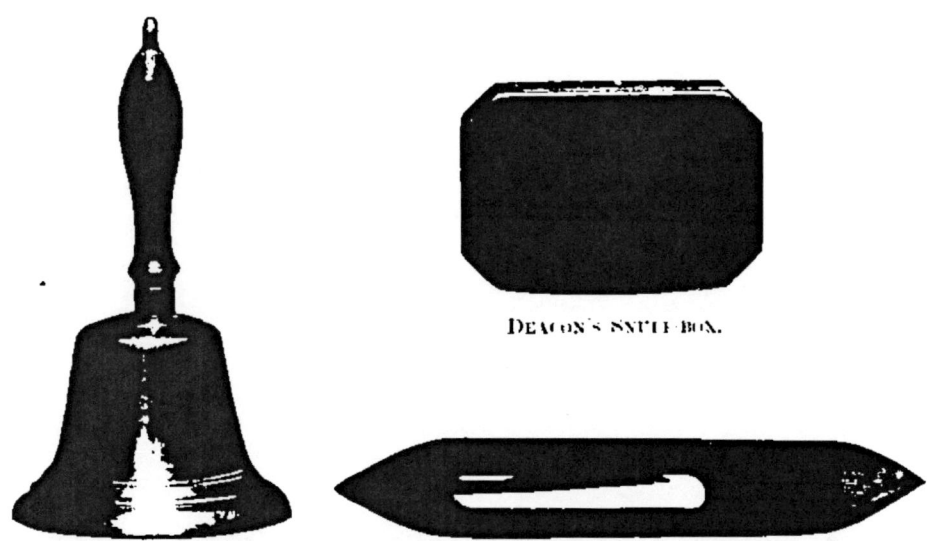

DEACON'S BELL.   DEACON'S SNUFF BOX.

FIRST FLYING SHUTTLE.

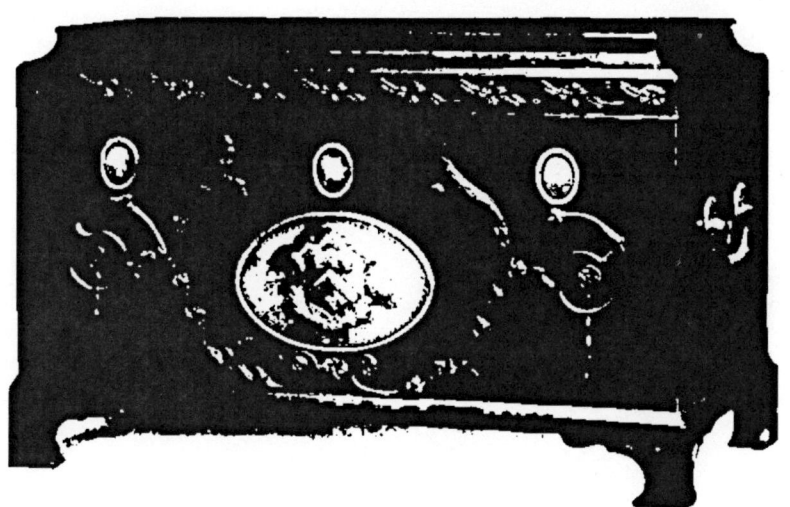

DEACON'S BOX.

THE OLD WYND SOCIETY THROWING SHUTTLE SNUFF GUN.

to establish particular Societies and Incorporations for particular Trades within themselves with several immunities and Liberties conforme whereunto the City of Glasgow has erected the Society of the Weavers within their Burgh with consent Ratification and Confirmation of the said most Reverend Father in God Gavine Archbishop of Glasgow and hes impowered them to create Deacons to establish orders for Regulation of their Trade and to impose fynes upon the Trespassers of the samen As the said Gift and Charter of the date the said fourth day of June One Thousand Five Hundred Twentie-eight years at more length bears Which particular fynds being either established as furnishing for the superstition of the Popish tymes and services or in such rates as are now inconsiderable by the Act of Parliament King James the Sixth Parliament: Eleventh cap.: are extended ilk pound or penny of old unlaw to be now Ten and proportionally Likeas the said Archbishop his Grace being every way most competent both as superior and patron of the said Burgh And as Archbishop of the see and province to make a conversion innovation and destination of the particular fynes of old superstitiously bestowed upon their blind devotions now to be applied to the use of the poor of the said Craft as his Grace should think fit As also that necessary it is that his Graces authority be obtained for punishing of persons living without the bounds of the Towns jurisdiction and authoritie and within the bounds of his Graces Regalitie conform to the Petitioners former Rights granted and confirmed to them Therefore the Petitioners humbly craved that the said Archbishop his Grace would be pleased to signe a Charter and Grant continuing his confirmation of their former Rights with the conversion and destinatione to pious uses as is therein at more length exprest and in special whereas incomers Weavers taking out the stuff of the Towne to work or otherways encroaching within the Burgh upon their liberties and privileges when apprehended were of old to be fyned in ane pound of wax and a dinner to the Maisters of the craft which was occasion of needles expences without good to the poor His Grace would appoint Twentie punds Scots for the poor of the trade in place of wax and dinner And whereas by the old gifts ilk prentice was to pay five shilling scots His Grace would allow conform to the said Act of Parliament fyftie shilling scots And that ilk upsetter pay conform to their old rights Item who takes work and does not complethe doe the same were formerlie to pay ane pund of wax and wha did take another mans work over his head to pay ane pund of wax Item disobeyer of the Deacone to be fyned in ane pund of wax and als much to the Magistrates which are but mean fynes and inconsiderable Therefore the Petitioners also humbly craved That the said Archbishop his Grace would allow for ilk pund of wax as aforesaid the soume of four punds scots and accordinglie to authorize the said Trade to exact the samen Having his Graces authority interponed thereto as the said supplication in itself bears Which supplicatione being taken to the said Archbishop his Graces consideration and fynding the desyre thereof most reasonable He has not only ratified allowed and approven by the said Charter The foirsaids old Gifts and priviledges granted formerly to the said Weaver calling In the haill heads clauses privileges and immunities therein contained In favours of the said Trade But also conform to the desyre of the said Petition allowed them to exact the fynes in manner and conforme as is

ORIGIN AND EARLY HISTORY.

thereby required of the said Archbishop his Grace whereunto he has interponed his anthority by the aforesaid Charter The saids fynes being always applyed for the use of the poor of the said Trade and hes by the said Charter converted destin^{at} and appointed the aforesaids small fynes thereby augmented as said is conforme to the said Act of Parliament and formerly payable to the Altars To the use of the poor of the said calling in all tyme coming As the said Charter of confirmation of the dait foresaid Having the Bishops seal appended thereto at more length proports, In all and sundrie the heads articles clauses provisions alterations and conversions above mentioned therein contained and after the forme and tenor of the samen in all poynts And His Majestie with consent foresaid of the said Estates of Parliament by these presents alters changes and converts the old penalties and unlaws above specified contained in the said first Gift and Seale of Cause In and to the particular soums of money and penalties above mentioned contained in the said last confirmation granted by the said Arthur Archbishop of Glasgow ordaining the samen to be exacted uplifted and applyed for the use and in manner therein specified And that this present Ratification thereof shall be als valid effectual and sufficient to all intents and purposes as if the said respective Gifts and Seales of Cause were herein particularly exprest Whereanent and with all defects and imperfections that may be moved or objected thereagainst or against this present Ratification of the samen His Majestie with consent foirsaid has dispensed and by ther presents dispenses for ever Extracted furth of the Records of Parliament by me Sir Thomas Murray of Glendook Knight and Baronet Clerk to his Majesty's Councill Register and Rolls.

(Signed)   THO: MURRAY, Clk. Reg.

Eating and drinking had long been a weakness of the "Maisteris of the Craft," as we find that a condition which does not appear in the document of 1605 has been imposed, and they are now to save the needless expense "for the good of the Poor of the Trade." There is in the 1681 deed a stronger note of exclusiveness than in the earlier time, when the anxiety seems to have been rather to secure good workmanship by having only well-trained apprentices and careful journeymen.

The minute of 1st October, 1681, shows that the Incorporation was then in funds to meet the outlay in procuring the Archbishop's Charter and the Parliament's ratification:—

1 of October 1681.

The whilk day, the deacone, maisteris, and remanent bretherin of the calling being convenit in the craftes hospitall all in ane voyce bothe now and of befor, allowes and approves what the tred hes deburst and barrowit for the new chartour

ORIGIN AND EARLY HISTORY.

grantit be the archbishop, and the parliamentis ratificatioune theirof, and of the old gift in the callingis favouris; all put in the box.

R. FYNNISONE.

The records of the years following are lost, but in the concluding chapter the history of the last hundred years or so is briefly dealt with.

II.

CONSTITUTION.

From the earliest records the head of the Incorporation has always been known as the Deacon, and there have been associated with him a varying number of Masters whose mode of election or selection has varied from time to time. There has been a clerk from very early times—though not from the origin—as there occur intermittently casual references to the necessity for a clerk. Clearly the office of collector was not created until many years from the foundation of the Incorporation, and the records as regards this office read as if the appointment also had been intermittent. Below is given the earliest minute and roll of members which has been preserved. The outside of this book is marked as follows:—

JOHNE ESTERLING
No. 1.

Then the first page bears this entry:—

Quinto Maij 1593.

The names of the brether of the craft.

Johnne Glen, dekin
Williame Clerk ⎫
Johnne Young ⎪
Archibald Patersone ⎬ Maisteris of the craft
Patrik Walker ⎪
Matthow Blak ⎪
Finlaye Schankschawe ⎭
Williame Kirkland
Richard Kirkland
Johnne Porter
Robert Dobbie
Allane Winzett
James Blair
Robert Aikein

Archibald Thomsone
Andro Wetherspune
Henrie Relstoun
James Scott
Johnne Patersone
Andro Gemmill
Andro Kilpatrik
Charles Snyip
Johnne Wilsoun
Nichell Cudbert
Bartie Mure
Alexander Gemmill
Robert Andersone

Upone the xxj daye of September the yeir of God j^m v^c four scoir allevin yeiris.

The quhilk daye, be voittis prevaleand of the brethrene, Johnne Glen is electit dekin of the wobsteris for the yeir nixttocum.

ELECTIT MAISTERS OF THE CRAFT.

Williame Clerk,—Johnne Young,—Fynlaye Schankschawe,—Matthow Blak,— Patrik Walker,—Archibald Patersone.
Charles Snyip,—Officiar

Vigesimo secundo Septembris 1592.

The quhilk daye, be voittis prevaileand Johnne Glen is electit dekin of the wobsteris for ane yeir nixttocum.

The dekin with consent of the craft hes continewit maisteris of the craft as of before.

And electit Johnne Wilsoun officiar

The above show that Deacon Glen occupied his position for at least two years, and the following minute shows that thus early we find record of the present custom that each deacon should bear office only for one year. There is also reference to the services of a clerk at the annual election meeting, as also to the service as officer of the craft.

Apparently the position of officer was not considered a desirable one, and this feeling was utilised to obtain funds for the benefit of the poor of the craft:—

Decimo tertio Maij 1598.

Quhilk daye, Bartie Muir, Robert Steuart, Finlay Allansone, Thomas Bryce, Thomas Gemmill, George Herbertsone, and George Clidisdale wnderstanding that gif thai salbe alyve successive eftir wtheris thai ar bund to serve yeirlie ilk ane of thame to be officiar to the craft for the space of ane yeir, and quhilkis wilbe ane burdein upone thame; and thai all desyrit earnestlie to be fred of the service, and submittted thame in the will of the maisteris of craft quhat the said maisteris wold ordour thame and ilk ane of thame to pay for thair fredome of the officiar servitor. The said maisteris remoivit, and advysit maturelie upone the said sevin bretheris submissioun in maner as said is, frethis the said sevin brether of craft of thair serving in the officiarschip, and for that cause decernis ilk ane of the said brether of craft to paye to the dekin xiij s. iiij d. betuix and the sevint daye of July nixtocum. And ferder statutis gif ony brother of craft sall desyre fredome of the serving in the officiarschip of thair craft, the saming brother, and everie brother of craft desyring fredome as said is, sall paye for his fredome as said is, xx s., unforgeven.

The dire penalties of canvassing for support of a candidature for the deaconship are thus set forth; the phraseology is particularly quaint:—

(13-2-1595)

Item it is statut and ordanit for avoiding of all superioritie and tyrannie in thair craft in all tymes to cum that he that sall happin to be dekin in thair craft be na langer continewit dekin in the said craft bot onlie for ane yeir, bot that he be changit, and sum wther brother of thair craft be electit and chosen to beir office as dekin in thair said craft.

Item the dekin and maisteris of the craft hes statut and ordanit, as be thir presentis statutis and ordains, that in all tymes comming the electioun of the dekin pas be woittis of the brethrene, burgessis, and fremen in thair craft, and that the electioun of thair dekin in tymes comming na woittis of wther dekinis in the said citie be requirit, bot the woittis of all wther dekinis in chesing dekin in the said craft be simpliciters dischargit; and in the chesing of the dekin at the Michalmes, yeirlie, thair be ane clerk present to tak up the woittis of the brethrene for election of the said dekin; and quhasoevir of the brethrene sall labour to contravein this ordinance, salbe deput mainsworne to the craft, and pay to the box of the craft foure lib. and xvj s. to the baillies, unforgevin.

Item it is statut and ordanit that na burges nor freman sone in the said craft serve officiar in the said craft sa lang as thair salbe ane outtintownisman quha hes enterit burges and freman in the said craft have first servit as officiar in the said craft.

CONSTITUTION. 15

Duodecimo die mensis Februarij 1603.

Quhilk daye, the dekin, maisteris, and haill craft convenit in thair quarter court, hes statnt and ordenit, as be thir presentis statutis and ordeins, for quietnes of thair craft in all tymes to com, that quhatsumever brother of craft sall solist be himself or ony wtheris in his name, ony of the brethrene of thair craft for thair woittis to mak him dekin of the craft, the saming persone or persones first nouen and imediat persone or brother mowit be thame to wott as said is sall never be ane of the maisteris of the craft thaireftir, bot salbe decernit to paye to the dekin of craft for the tyme ane new upset for the weale of the craft, and sall mak his publict repentatioun on the pillar in the kirk as ane persoune seditious and mowear of truble to the greit hurt and hinder of the craft.

It is necessary again, sixteen years later than the minute first quoted, to enact that the deacon shall only stand for one year:—

Secundo Novembris anno 1611.

The quhilk day, the deikin and haill craft, be pluralitie of woitis, hes ordainit the act beirand that the deikin sall onlie stand for ane yeir. Sall stand inviolabill in all tyme cuming.

The following is the earliest minute bearing on the method of electing maisteris, or "quartermaisteris" as they are here called; there is an indication that it was found undesirable to allow the deacon to exercise exclusive control of the affairs of the craft, and through the later years there is a continued desire to limit his power:—

ACT ANENT QUARTERMAESTERIS   Tertio Novemb. 1613.

The quhilk day, the deikin, maisteris, and haill craft, all in ane voice, upone consideratioun of the greit abuis hes oft fallin out in electioun of the maisteris, throw the deikinis chuising of the haill, have, thairfoir, concludit, statut and ordainit, for cleiding of the former abuis, that thrie of the four upone lyt to be deikin, with the auld deikin, sall stand still maisteris for that yeir, and the deikin to chois tua, and the craft uther tua, quhilk compleitis aucht.

The following gives an indication that the funds of the Incorporation have not always been used exclusively for the relief of the poorer members of the craft. The reference is a little mystical, but no doubt the "heidwasching" was not effected without considerable internal washings of strong waters:—

Septimo August 1616.

The quhilk day, the haill craft present, all in ane voice hes statut, concludit, and ordainit, that in all tyme cuming the new deikinis to be chosin, that hes nevir borne that office, sall pay furt of his awin purs for his heidwasching, and the commoun guidis to be disbnrdeinit thairof.

Apparently there had been frequent re-election of same deacon for a succeeding year, and then the Incorporation repents its action and re-enacts as follows:—

xxii Septembris 1618.

The same [day], it is statut and ordainit that nain be deikin bot for ane yeir, and quhaevir contraveinis, sall pay fourtie pundis to the deiken conveiner.

There are continual indications of difficulty in getting a craftsman to discharge the duties of officer. Evidently these were unpaid labours, and the burden fell on the latest comer:—

Decimo tertio Novembris 1624.

The quhilk day, it is statut and ordainit be the deikin, maisteris, and haill craft present, that all friemen that enteris frie with the craft heireftir, sall ather serve as officer to the craft, or ellis sall furneis ane officer to serve for thame, and sall nowayis be redeimit thairfra for money, with this conditioun, that friemenis sones enterand frie, sall nawayes serve sua lang as thair is anie stranger to serve befoir thame, and quhen thair is na stranger frieman to serve, then sall friemans sones serve as officer, or ellis furneis ane officer, ilk mann his awin plaice as he enteris, utherwayes sall nevir have the benefeit of ane frieman that servis not ains as officer.

The 3 day of November 1627.

The quhilk day, the deacoune and haill craft, hes statut and ordainit in all tymes cumming, that the last incomer of the craft sal be officer, and na wtheris sall serve for thame bot thamesellves, freemen sounes being excepit.

Mr G. STIRLING.

The following is the earliest reference to the office of collector:—

The 6. day of August 1628.

The [quhilk] day, the haill craft being convenit for taking ordour with the commoune guidis. It is statut and ordanit, be pluralitie of votis, that in all tyme cuming, thair sall be ane of the craft chosing, be the vot. of craft, for keeping of thair commun guidis fra yeir to yeir, quha sall deburs at the deaconis command, quha sall gif compt of his intromission yeir be yeir.

Mr G. STIRLING.

The two following minutes aptly illustrate the alternating tide in the affairs of an Incorporation as in those of an individual; 1640

Plate VI.

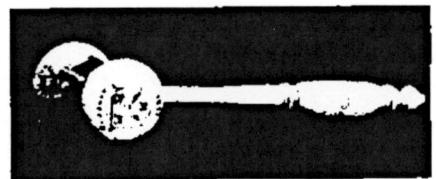

Collector's Mallet.

Collector's Box.

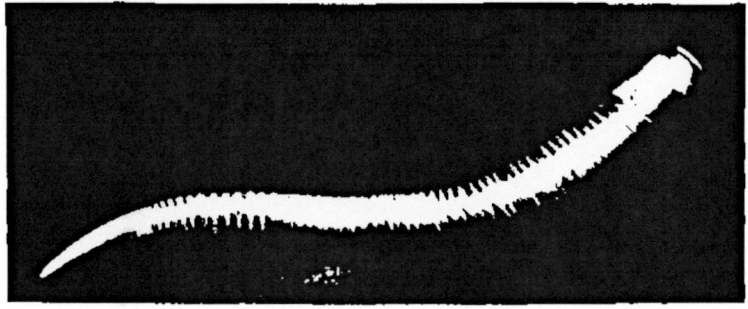

Collector's Snuff Horn.

minute indicates an excess of interest and stir at the election time, 1642 the reverse:—

Sexto Novembris 1640.

The quhilk day, the deacon and maisteris of croft, being convenit with the haill brethrein, at the leist, the maist pairt thairof, understanding the great abuse, contest and stryfe that hes bein in thair calling at the electioun of the deacon and utheris courtis; thairfoir, that the samen may be amendit, and peace intertanet, it is aggried and concludit amangst them, in all in ane voice, that na personne, not payit of thair qwarter comptis, nor keipels thairof, sall have ony voitt or voce the day of the electioun; and that na unfriemen sall compeir in court that day, nather servantis nor prenteissis, and that all the croft be silent, and evrie ane byde thir presents, and voitt as they ar callit.

21 September 1642.

The whilk day, the haill bodie of the craft being all present, some few exceptit, who war absent for certane guid caussis moving them, and speciallie becaus it is knawin to them that sundrie of the bretherine absentis themselfs the day of the electioun of the dekine, having lytle or na regaird of the guid of the calling; and thairfoir it is concludit, statut and ordanit, that if any of the bretherine of the calling, heireftir, beis absent the day of the electioun of the dekine, the yeirs heireftir, sall pay in to the box sextein schillingis, wnforgevin, to be gevin to the use of the poore; and they to be presentlie poyndit thairfoir if it be fund that they be in the toune and in healthe of bodie.

Here we have the first record of a collector actually being appointed:—

7 November 1645.

The said day, be pluralitie of voitis, Patrik Bryce is electit collectour to the craft, and he is to intromet and deburs all concerns the craft; and the dekin is to intromet with nothing; and the collectour is to be comptable to the craft.

Apparently the first collector had proved himself acceptable to the craft, for he is in 1650 appointed as a great exception to a second term of service as deacon:—

20 September, 1650.

The said day, the haill maisteris of craft and bretherine of the calling quhairof the most pairt war present all in ane voyce continwit Patrik Bryce dekine for the yeir to cum, quha being present, did (altho agnns his will) accept the said office in and wpon him and gave his aithe; and becaus of the trubles of the tyme, and maney wther guid and weghtie caussis knowin to the craft, they have continwit the said dekine in his charge all in ane voyce without lytting of him conforme to the commoun ordour of the craft. It is thairfoir statut and ordanit be the haill calling, that this forme sall mak no pratique, and that non sall be permitit to beir office as dekine heireftir bot snche as sall be lyttit, conforme to the ordour of the calling, and that non beir office as dekine bot for the space of ane yeir allanerlie, and no langir heireftir, conforme to the former actis sett doun thairanent.

The officer does not appear to have had any remuneration in cash, but the tear and wear of his duties was provided for as follows:—

21 August 1654.

The same day, it is inactit and ordinat that the officer sall have ane pair of schoone only the yeir which he serves, or then fourtie schilling thairfoir.

Apparently line upon line and precept upon precept were necessary to keep the power of the deacon within reasonable bounds, as repeated entries, such as the two following, indicate a constant seeking for continuance of power on his part:—

The third day of November 1662 yeris.

The quhilk day, the said deacone, and the maist pairt of the craft being conveinet, finding and tacking to consideratioune some prejudice susteinet be thame throw suffering of deacones formerlie to remayne and continwing in office moir then one yeir togither, and that the same be no preparative in tyme cuming eftir this yeir, they all in ane voice inact, statute, and ordaine, that none of the said craft sall remayne and continew deacone in all tyme heirefter more then one yeir together, and that wnder the paine of thrie scoir pundis Scottis money, to be payit be the personne quho sall happin to be continwit or chosin one yeir after another deacone as said is, to the box for the us of thair poore, by and attour that he sall be turnit out of his office for that yeir quhairin he sall happin to be continwit and fund incapable thairof; and this act to remayne and continow unalterable in all tyme cuming as aforesaid.

M. ROWAND, Clerk.

At the craftis hospitall, the aught of February, 1667.

The quhilk day, the deacone and maisters, with the maist pairt of the brethren of trade being conveined, having taikin to consideratioune the great abuis done be former deacones in puting on in lytis all thes whom they pleasit to be ellectit and chosin deacone out of the maisters without consent of the rest of the calling, being contrair to the laudable actis and statutis sett doune thairagainst. Thairfoir, to prevent the lyk in tyme cuming, the said deacone and remanent brethrin of craft all in ane voice inact, statute and ordaine that all deacones, in tyme cuming, sall onlie have power to chois out thrie of the tuell maisters to be putt on the lyt to be deacone, and the craft to chois uther thrie out of the nyne to be lykeyis on the lyt; and no mae to be putt thairon in all tyme cuming.

M. ROWAND, Clerk.

CONSTITUTION.

As als it is heirby statute and ordanet that the deacones sall have power to chois sex maisters for himself yeirlie, and he to nominat aughtein uther indifferent persones besyd out of whiche the craft ar to chois the uther sex maisters yeirlie in tyme cuming.

M. ROWAND.

The following entries show an increasing desire for regularity both in the conduct of the money and the business matters of the Incorporation, and here we have the first indication of a permanent clerk being appointed:—

At the craftis hospitall,
Septimo Novemberis 1670.

The quhilk day, it is inactit, statut and ordained, that the haill calling heir the collectouris compt yearlie in tyme comeing after the paying of the quarter comptis ellectioune of the new collectour and maisteris of tread.

The same day, be pluralitie of votis, it is concludit, inactit, statut and ordained that Patrick Clark, present clark to the said tread, continow and remaine clark therto, not only for this present year, bot *ad vitam aut culpam*, quhilk fault being instructit, he to be votit; and this to remaine unalterable in tyme comeing.

PATRICK CLARK. clericus.

Again there has arisen need for regulating the money matters of the Incorporation, as the following minute shows:—

At the craftis hospitall the eleviuth day of October 1672, convined John Patersone, present deacone with the maisters and tread the deacon conviner for the tyme and—

The same day, in farder corroboratioune of ane former act made anent the collectouris intromissioune with the haill treads geir to witt in uplifting and receaving the same and debursing thairof; it is aguine statut and ordained that in all tymo comeing the collectour of the said tread present and to come intromett with and receave the haill comoune guids and causwallities belonging to the calling and to debura the samyne accordinlie as he sall be ordred; as also that the collectour nor deacone distribuit to no poore in the calling for supplie above aughtine shilling Scotis and that the samyne sall be at sight and be the consent of soome of the maisteris; as also that ther be non of the treads geir spent at any tyme comeing in meiting bot out of ther awne proper money except at ane extraordinar caice with certificatioune the samyne sall not be allowit and the contraviner to be punished farder at the optioune of the deacon conviner.

PATRICK CLARK.

The accounts for this period are in a fairly good state of preservation, and, considering the degree of education then attained among tradesmen, they are exceedingly well kept. The minute books, of course, were the work of a professional man, and while his spelling as reproduced is, to our ideas, extraordinary, his phraseology is clear and pointed and the caligraphy in most cases very perfect; otherwise it would not have been possible to transcribe the records as has been done for the present volume.

The following entry fixes the remuneration of the clerk, and, by comparison with the freedom fines and other money items quoted, the sum paid was not an extravagant one. The same minute shows that the deacon personally benefitted by entering of journeymen on the roll. Possibly that made the office sought after:—

Octavo Novembris 1672.

The same day, be pluralitie of votis, it is statut and ordained that the clark of the weaveris sall have twelfe punds Scotis of yearlie fiall in all tyme comeing beginand at the dait of thir presentis; as also it [is] heirby statut and ordained that all servantis for farder instructioune or jurnaymen being strangeris sall pay ten shilling Scotis to the deacone at ther booking in all tyme comeing by and attour the fourtie shilling to the tread and the clark and officeris dewis; and this to remaine unalterable.

PATRICK CLARK.

There appear to have been two sets of records at this time, as the repetition of above entry in other wording shows:—

At Glasgow the aught day of November j^m jv^c and seavintie twa yearis.

The quhilk day, John Patersone, present deacone of the weaveris of the said burgh, his maisteris and most pairt of the calling being convined, it is statut and ordained that the clarkis fiall sall be twelfe punds Scots in all tyme comeing yearlie, and that in regaird his paines is muche greater then formerlie.

(Sigd.) PATRICK CLARK.

Apparently it was thought desirable that in a contest for the

CONSTITUTION.

deaconship the unsuccessful rival should be made sure of being one of his competitor's counsellors:—

> At Glasgow the seavint of November 1673. Convined the fornamit deacone conviner, Robert Flaikfeild, deacone with his remanent maisteris and breathrine of craft wha for the most pairt war present.

The same day, it is statut and inacted be commoune consent, that he who is nixt to the deacone in the numer of votts at the deacones cllectione sall be ane of the deacones sex maisteris for the inshewing year without any votte of tread.

(Signed) PATRICK CLARK.

The following shows that it was recognised that the officer's post involved loss to the holder:—

> At Glasgow the first of Maij 1674.

The same day, John Flaikfeild younger, weaver, is discharged and fred be the deacone and his maisteris fra serving as officer to the calling in respect of his povertie and inabeillatie to serve in the said office.

III.

APPRENTICESHIP AND FREEMANSHIP.

Five years seems generally to have been recognised as the period necessary to fit an apprentice for the position of journeyman, but frequently two years were added, during which he was paid in "meat and fee." There are several indentures preserved, but one will serve to indicate the obligations undertaken. This is drawn by the then Town Clerk of Glasgow, who at the same time was clerk to the Incorporation of Weavers:—

> INDENTURE of Johne Bryssoune as prenteis to David Arnot, dated 27 July 1658.

At Glasgow the twent seavin day of Julij j^m vi^c fyftie eight yeiris. It is apoyntit indentit and agried betwixt the persouns pairteis fallowing they ar to say David Arnot, Weiver burges of the said burghe on the ane pairt Johne Bryssoune sone lawfull to umquhill Johne Bryssoune, Weiver burges thairof with expres advyce and consent of Hew Cowane, Weiver, burges of the samyn his father-in-law and Cristine Wyllie his mother on the uther pairt in maner forme and effect fallowing, that is to say forswameikle as the said Johne Bryssoune is heirby became bundin prenteis with consent foirsaid to the said David Arnot in his said arte and craft of weiver trade and that dureing all the dayis space yeiris and tyme of fyve yeiris as prenteis and twa yeiris thairefter for meit and fie as they cane best agrie furth and fra his entrie thairto quhilk sall be and begane at the dait of thir presentis dureing the quhilk space the said Hew Cowane binds and obleissis him to move and caus the said Johne Bryssoune prenteis foirsaid to serve his said maister faithfullie honestlie leillalie and trewlie and not to divert himself out his said maisteris service at na dayis nor tyme without leicance askit and given and for ilk day he absentis himself out of his said maisteris service without leive askit and given as said is (health of bodie servand as God grant) the said Johne Bryssoune bindis and obleisses him to content and pay to the said David his said maister thrie schillings four penneis for ilk day absence and the saids absent dayis to be provin be the said David his aith of veritie allenerlie. Attour the said David Arnot binds and obleisses him to teach learne and instruct the said Johne Bryssoune his said prenteis in his said arte and trade of weiver craft and sall not hyd nor conceall no poynt nor ingyne thairof fra him knowin to himself, bot sall use his best and uttermost meins to mack him ane perfyt craftismane thairintill and sall furneis him in meit drink and bedding in household with himself dureing his said prentischipe honestlie effeirand to his rank and degrie and sall give him all sort of abulyrament necesser as becumes dureing the said tyme of prentischipe for the better enableing him to goe about his service. For the quhilkis premissis the said David Arnot grantis him to have alreddie receavit fra the bailleis of this burghe out of the fynes they have exactit fra ofendaris as justices of His Heighnes peace within this purghe the soume of twentie merkis Scottis in name of prenteissie with his said prenteis and discharges them thairof and the said Hew Cowane heirby for ever; and for performance of the said David Arnot his obleisment in the premissis James Rodger, weiver, burges of this burghe is heirby becum actit as cautionner for him and he is obleist to releive his cautiouner, and for the mair securitie the saids pairties ar content and consentis thir presentis be insert and registrat in the hie court bookis of justice comissar or toune court bookis of Glasgow that letteres and executions of horning poynding and wardeing may heirupone pas on sex dayis warneing and heirto constitutis.

Thar procuratouris writtin be Donald M'Gilcrist, servitor to Williame Yair, Notary in Glasgow and subscrivit be theim as fallowis att day yeir and place foirsaid befoir thir witnessis Robert Allane, servitor to the said Williame Yair and the said Donald M'Gilcrist.

I, William Yair, notar publict subscryvring for the saidis David Arnote, Johne Bryssoune, Hew Cowane, Cristine Wyllie, and James Rodger, at thair command, becaus they can not wrytt as they affirmed.

D. M'GILCRIST, Witnes.
ROT. ALLANE, Witnes.

The earliest entries referring to apprenticeship are as follows:—

(5-5-1593).

The dekin, maisteris, and haill craft statutis and ordains that na brother of craft tak ane prenteis for shorter space nor the space of fyve yeiris, according to the letter of dekinheid. And gif ony brother of craft sall put the said prenteis to taskwork during the space of the said fyve yeiris, the said brother, for sa doing, sall pay to the dekin and brether of craft foure pundis money unforgivin, and that, befoir the imbuiking of the said prenteis the said prenteis produce his indenture before the dekin and maisteris of craft gif the saming be sufficient; and the said prenteis entering in taskwork during the said space of fyve yeiris sall pleis his maister also befoir he entir to the said taskwork.

The dekin, maisteris, and haill craft statutis and ordains, that in all tymes comand thair be na les price tane fra intrentis in thair craft to be fremen thairin, being first maid burgessis in this citie and not burgessis sones fremen of thair craft, nor the sowme of ten pundis money, and that for the support of thair puir decayit brether of craft, and releiff of thair common charges belonging to thair craft.

Two years later, regulation of incomers is evidently necessary, as the following entries show :—

(13-2-1595).

It is statut and ordanit that na brother of craft give mair to ony servand he sall fie to serve him in his craft bot onlie x s. of fie, and twa part of proffeit for the work the said servand sall work, under the paine of xx s. for the first, and being convict to refus to paye the said xx s., to paye xl s. to the craft, and xvj s. to the baillies.

Item it is statut and ordanit that thair be na outtintownis prenteis ressavit in service in this toun, because that mony ignorantis cummis to the toune alledging thame mair experimentit nor thai ar, except that for farder learning to be gevin to thame in this toun, and tolerance to be grantit to thame to work, thay paye to the dekin of the craft for the weale of the said craft xx s. at thair admissioun to be servand in the said craft. And gif that ony of the brethreine of the said craft sall cloik the mater and ressave at thair plesure wnexperimentit and unvorthie servandis to work to thame in the said craft, not adverteisand to the effect foirsaid the dekin and maisteris of the said craft, thay that sal happin to do swa sall paye for thair falt xvj s. to the baillies and ane new wpset to the craft.

Item it is statut and ordanit that na servand fie him fra his maister to ane wther brother of craft without that he done in presens of the dekin of the craft, or, in his absence, twa or thre brethreine of the craft. In case he sall do in the contrair, sall paye to the craft vj s. viij d., and xx s. be the maister that sall fie him.

Here is an early entry as to the discipline necessary for idle and ill-behaved apprentices :—

Septimo die mensis Augusti 1602.

The dekin, maisteris, and haill craft convenit at thair Lammase court, statutis and ordeinis that quhatsumever servand of the craft sall abstract himself fra his work, working to his and his maisteris weale, and give himself to idilnes, vaging or drinking, to his hurt and neglecting of his work, and lose to him and his said maister, in swa doing sall paye to the dekin of the craft, for ilk daye the said servand salbe fund doing as said is, xl d., unforgevin.

Die xij Maij 1604.

The quhilk day, the deakin and haill brethrene of craft hes statute and ordanit, that na fremanis bairne of thair craft in tyme cuming, quhiddir thai be prenteis with thair father, or with onie uther man, or give thair father be deid, that they sall enter frie but onie payment, with privilege to onie freman of the craft notwithstanding that he resavis the fremanis bairn prenteis, that he sal have licens to resave ane uther prenteis quhen occasioun servis.

There is no earlier entry conferring immunity from entrance fee on sons of members, and it carries with it the right to the master taking such apprentice, that he should not thereby be debarred from taking one who was liable to pay his freedom fee.

That the need for discipline was not always on the side of the apprentice the following entries show:—

Septimo Maij anno domini 1608.

The same [day], the deikin and maisteris of [craft] ordanit Georg Schirilaw, within xx dayis nixt following the dait heirof, to put Johne Walker his prenteis to work at the lumb, uthermayes to denud himself of his prenteis, and pay him bak his prenteissie ressaveit be him fra the said John.

Decimo sexto Augusti 1613.

The quhilk day, in presens of John Clark, deikin, and maisteris of craft, compeirit John Gemmill, principall and John Patersoun younger, as cautioner for him, on the ane pairt; Johne Park, his prenteis, as principall, and William Clark elder, as cautioner for him on the uther pairt, and become actit ilk pairtie and thair cautiouner conjunctlie and severally bund and obleist in this maner, that is, that the said John Gemmill in na tyme heireftir sould bluid his said prenteis, nor yit stryk him unmercifully, undir the pain of fyve pundis, and freithing of the said John Park of his prenteischip; and that the said John Park sould in na tyme cuming, during his prenteischip, commit onie heiche offence agains his said maister, ather in going fra his service, or in dissobedience to him, under the pain of fyve pundis (*toties quoties*); quhilkis offences salbe tryit be the deikin and maisteris for bayth the pairties wranges and offences; and ar become actit, ilk pairtie and cautiouner, to pay xvj schillinges to the baillies for ilk tryit offence; and ilk principall obleissis thame to releif thair awin cautiouner of the premissis.

Octavo Augusti, 1621.

The quhilk day, Johne Allansoune, weifer is actit, bund, and obleist, of his awin consent, to teache, lerne, and instruct James Calder in thir four poyntis of his weifer craft, viz.,—the wound loome, sea bombacie loome, the playd loome, and playding, as also he bindis himselfe to remaine with the said Johne during the spaice conteinit in the former act; lykas Archibald Patersoune becomes cautioner of his awin consent for the said James Calder for implement of his pairt, conforme to the act above reherait. And for implement of the said Johne Allansoune, his pairt, William Kirkland is bund and obleist as cautionner for him; and ilk ane of the principellis pairties bindis and obleissis them to warrand thair cautiouneris of the haill premissis.

The following entry, for the earliest time in the records, lays down smaller fees for sons and sons-in-law than for outsiders, and

APPRENTICESHIP AND FREEMANSHIP.

this entry is also interesting in its effort to prevent wasteful expenditure at the entry to the Incorporation:—

Quarto Martij 1612.

The quhilk day, the deikin, maisteris and haill craft being conveinit, haveing weill weyit and considderit how thai daylie grow and incres in debt but releif thairof quhilk specially proceidis of thair cairlesnes qulia ressaifes friemen, servandis, and prenteiasis without gratitnd or payment to the box for supplie of thair commoun chairges. Thairfoir thai all in ane voice, aggrieand togedder, have concludit, statut, and ordainit, that in all tymes cuming thair banquettis and say drink, quhilk was sumptoous, sall be convertit in money to the commoune weill of the craft, and augmentatioun of thair commoun guidis, sua that everie frieman prenteis and frieman sall pay as followis:—That is to say, all burges wobsteris sones quhen thai ar prenteis, xiij s. iiij d., and all utheris prenteissis, xl s. and all burges wobsteris sones that becumis freiman sall pay four pundis of upset, and thrie pundis for his banquet and say drinck, and siclyk wobsteris that maryis ane frieman wobsteris dochter sall pay alyk, and uther burges sones and uther prenteissis within this burghe sall pay tuentie merkis of upset, and four pundis for thair banquet and say drink, and all utheris strangeris that becumis frie sall pay tuentie pundis of upset, and sax pundis for the banquet and say drink. To the quhilk act the deikin and maisteris and haill craft bindis and obleissis thame to stand and abyd but contradictioune or reclamatioun.

The entry of 8th August, 1621 (on previous page), and the following give an idea of the fabrics then made—playd being something much like a present day shepherd tartan homespun. In these days linen weaving had hardly begun in Scotland, and was a distinct craft; cotton, of course, was wholly unknown, and the spinning of wool only done by hand in the most primitive fashion:—

xv February 1615.

The quhilk day, in consideratioune of the complaint maid be Wm. Crawfurd to the craft, of Archibald Thomesoune, his maister, for conceilling fra him of diveris poyntis of his craft specially hyding fra him all playdis he weifes and sea bumbasies. Thairfoir the deikin and maisteris all in ane voice hes ordainit the said Archibald for the said William his instructionne to give him to warp and weife during his prenteiship ilk thrid pair of playdis that cumis in his hous to weife and als to acquent him and instruct him with sey bumbasie that is brocht to him to work under the pain of four pundis *toties quoties* as he failzies sua to do he being tryit culpabill thairin.

Apparently it was found necessary in these days to ordain that masters should not overpay their servants:—

Decimo octavo Augusti 1615.

The quhilk day, the deikin and maisteris consiiddering the greit abnis that is amangst thair servandis in prejudice of thair friemen craveing and exacting of thair

maisteris greit feyis and bountethis, thairfoir and for remeid thairof it is statut and
ordainit be the deikin and maisteris with advys of the haill craft conveinit that na
frieman heireftir sall give to ane servand attour ten shillinges in bountethe and na
uther fey bot the tua pairt of the pryce and bountethe of the work that thai sall
work as servandis with thair handis and na farder. And quhatevir frieman contraveinis
this act sall pay fourtie schillinges to the bailzies and four pundis to the deikin
and maisteris to the behuife of the craft.

Tertio Maij 1623.

The same day, the deikin and maisteris haifing consideratioun how the prenteissis
within this burgh, expres agains all thair commoun weill, tackis up and injoyis the
thrid pairt, or tua pairt of the proffeit of his wark; for remeid quhairof, it is actit,
statut, ordainit, and concludit be the deikin, and haill maisteris present, that na
prenteis heireftir, within the yeiris of thair prenteiship, sall inbraice or injoy anie
pairt or portioun, les or mair, of the work to be wrocht be thame during thair
prenteiship, and give anie maister suffir or permit the samin, the maister to pay fyve
pundis for ilk fault *toties quoties*, and the prenteis that undirtackis the samin, to be
denudit of his privilelge and benefeit of the craft (friemenis sones being exceptit).

For two-and-twenty years conditions remained unaltered as regards
fees for entrants, and then the fine for strangers was raised as
follows :—

xxiiij Februarij 1645.

The said day, it is statut and ordanit be the dekine, maisteris of craft and
haill bretherine thairof, who, for the most part war present, that everie stranger who
enters frieman heirefter with the craft, not being ane friemans son and prenteis or
maryand ane burges dochter sall pay of upset, or fyne, befoir he be admitit, threttie
pundis money to the weill of the craft.

In same minute there is an indication that the weavers had
kindly and sympathetic feelings to those in need :—

The said day Robert Kirlie, sone to James Kirlie, in Gowrok, is buikit heirin
prenteis with Johne Kirlie, and hes payit for his buiking xx s. onlie, for respect of
the poor boy.

Again, only five years later than that just recorded, there is a
further increase in the entry charge for strangers, and the minute
contains the first reference to the burden of the cost of education.
What form this took there is no evidence to show :—

xxv Februarij 1650.

The said day, the dekine, maisteris of craft, and haill bretherine of the calling
being convenit, who for the most pairt war present, and taking to thair consideratiouns

APPRENTICESHIP AND FREEMANSHIP.

the havie burdings layit on the calling for helping of the poore, and scool-maisteris, and wther burding imposit on the calling; it [is] inactit, statut, and ordanit be them all in ane voyce, that everie stranger entering ane frieman heireftir, sall pay of wpsett at his entrie four scoir markis, by and besyd the dewis to be payit for the say drink, mortclothe, and officerschip.

Many entries indicate the deliberateness and thoroughness with which the apprentice, or even in some respects already qualified weaver, set to learn specific branches of the trade. Here is a case where a bargain to be taught "dowble cuveringis" was considered matter for a legal deed registered in the County Commissary Clerk's books :—

At Glasgow the saxtein day of Julij j^m vj^c fiftie sex yeires:—It is aggriet betwixt John Cochrane weiver, burges of Glasgow, and Duncane Lorne, weiver thair on the ane and uther pairtis in this maner: To witt, the said Duncane Lorne, be thir presentis, bindis and obleissis him painefullie and trewlie to teatche learne and instruct the said John Cochrane in weiving of dowble cuveringis and that sufficientlie, and to make him ane craftisman thairin als good as the said Duncane himselff in all respectis, and that from this furthe to Mertimes nixt, and sall furnische to him ane sufficient loome for that effect ilk fourtein dayis about with himselff the said space, and at Mertimes nixt sall give him twa dowble coppies and thrie single coppies sufficientlie drawin concerning the weiving of the saidis coveringis for the said Johnes furthering and instructioune of the said warke thaireftir, and that under the paine of ten merkis of liquidat penaltie for ilk failzie of the said Duncane his pairt of the premissis, attour performance thairof. For the quhilkis premissis and paines sua to be takin be the said Duncane in maner forsaid, the said John Cochrane bindis and obleissis him to content and pay to the said Duncane Lorne tuentie merkis money, and that wpon the said terme of Mertimes nixt, butt delay, with four pundis of penaltie in caice of failzie attour the payment thairof. And for the mair securitie, the saidis pairties ar content thir presentis be registrat in the books of counsell, justice court bookes, schyreffis or comissaris bookes of Lanericke or towne court bookes of Glasgow, that letteres of executoreallis and horning, poynding and warding may pas heirupon on sex dayis, and thairto constutis.

Procuratouris &c. Writtin be James Man, servitour to Mathow Rowand, noter in Glasgow and subscrivit be them as followis at day yeire and place forsaid befoir thir witnessis the said Mathow Rowand, Johne Rowand as servitour, and the said James Man, wryter heirof.

    (Signed) JOHN COCHRAND, DONKANE LORNE.
      M. Rowand witness, J. Rowand, witnes, Ja: Man, witnes.

APPRENTICESHIP AND FREEMANSHIP.

Another entry relates how an abuse had crept in by masters not supplying prentices with their food:—

7 Maij 1658.

The same day, the dekine and his maisteris being convenit, and considdering ane grait corruptioun creipt in laitlie in the calling, to the grait hurt of maney of the bretherine be prenteissis working on thair awin meit. It is thairfoir heirby inactit, statut and ordanit, that it sall not be leasome to ony brother of the calling to tak ony prenteis heirefter to work on his awin meit during the first fyve yeiris of his prenteischip, bot on the maisteris allanerlie, and that wnder the pane of twentie pundis of wnlaw to be exactit af ilk brother of the calling who do's in the contrarie; and that all suche prenteissis who dois wtherwayis, and meitis himself the foirsaid fyve yeirs of his prenteischip, sall have no beneveit of the calling be right of his prenteischipe.

Soldiers were in these days reckoned as worthy of special consideration on their return to peaceful pursuits:—

Nono Augusti 1658.

The same day, Richard Lingwood, sojour, is permitit to work as ane frieman during his lyftyme, and his wyf also, during hir widowheid, allanerlie, she survivand him; for the quhilk he payit in to the box, and was lent out, sen syne, aughtein pundis.

The three entries following are interesting as showing the questions arising from time to time on which the deacon and masters had to legislate. From the last entry it is evident that the tide of Scottismen flowing southward had not yet begun, and the northward flow did not receive any encouragement from this Incorporation:—

The threttein day of February 1660.

The quhilk day the deacone and quhell calling, taking to thair consideratioune the great prejndice they sustein throw young friemen tacking prenteissis quha does not keip dewtie one to another as becomes. Thairfoir, to prevent the same in tyme cuming, it is concludit, statute and ordainet, that no frieman of the said calling sall have power priviledge and libertie to tack any prenteis for the space of fyve yeiris eftir thair friedome.

As lykwayis the said deacone and calling tacking to thair consideratioune the greit prejudice and truble they have betuix some friemen of the said calling and thair prenteissis by thair not aggrieing mutuallie with uthers; thairfoir it is lykwayis statute and ordanet that quhat minister and prenteis sall not aggrie together in tyme cuming, bot desyris to quatt uthers, that the minister sall not have power and libertie to tack ane uther prenteis for sua meikle of the fyve yeiris of prenteisschipe conteinet the former indentour as sall be than to run, and the prenteis quho removes and quattis his maister sall have no benefeit of the friedome of the said calling in all tyme thaireftir. And als it is statute and ordanet, that no maister sall tacke tuo prenteissis at once togither quhill the first prenteis his fyve yeiris be expyrit, and that under the paine of ane new upsett to be payit be the maister, and the prenteis to have no benefeit thaireftir.

The fourt day of August 1662 yeiris

The quhilk day, Johne Falconer, present deacone, with his maisters of craft, and the maist pairt of the remanent brethrein thairof being convenet, tacking to consideratioune the hurt and prejudice they have susteinet throw tacking of stallangers strangers in the north countrey and Inglischmen and men for farder instructionne to work with thame in tyme bygaine; and to avoyd the samyne in tyme cuming, they all in ane voice, inact, statute and ordaine, that they nor none of thame sall have power and libertie to tacke any stallanger as north cuntrey nor Inglischemen to work with thame at any tyme heirefer, dischairgeing thame thairfra; and quhat uther Scottismen sall come as stallangers to work with the said trade and calling, having ane sufficient testimoniall with thame, and being fund sufficient craftismen, sall pay, ilk ane of thame to the said tradis box fourtie schillings money; and everie servand sall come for farder instructioun, sall be bund for thrie yeris to thair maister, and to pay in to the said tradis box, sex pundis money, for the weill of the poore; and ilk maister quha dois in the contrar, sall pay to the said craftis box ten pundis for ilk failzie *toties quoties*.

M. ROWAND.

The officership and the desire to avoid its no doubt onerous duties are made a source of revenue for the use of the poor:—

At the crafts hospitall the 12 of August 1665.

The same day the deacone and maisters of trade, all in ane voice, inactis, statutis and ordanes that all stallangers and prenteissis quho ar admittit or sall be admittit friemen sall pay at thair admissione (except friemens sones, and quho mairies friemenes dochters) ten pundis money for thair officerschipe in caice they desyre not to serve the office; to be applyit for the us of the poore of the said trade; and this to indure unalterable in tyme cuming.

Here follows a very interesting entry showing again the kindly consideration of the needy, and not less so because the misfortune came in the service of his country:—

(12-8-1665).

The quhilk day, the said deacone and maisteris tacking [to] thair consideratioune that umquhile Anthonie Tode, hemmerman in Glasgow went out in the tounes service and was taikin prisoner at Innerkething feght, convict captive to Durhame in Ingland, and diet in prisone with famein thair; and Walter Tode, his sone, being one of the tounes poore, they, out of pitie and consideratioune have buikit the said Walter Tode prenteis and servand to Williame Miller, weifer, for fyve yeiris of prenteisschipe and tua yeris for meit and fie, conforme to the indentouris past betuix thame, daitit the 13 of Marche last 1665 yeris instant, for quhilk they ordanet the said William Miller to pay four dollouris with xl s. for his said prenteis buiking quhairof the said Williame hes instantly givin to the box tua dollouris with the buiking silver, and the uther tua dollouris is to be payit at Candilsmes nixt; and this buiking and admissione is declarit, be the said deacone and maisteris, not to be ane preparative to utheris in tyme cuming.

M. ROWAND. Clerk.

With more formality than in earlier cases, and apparently for the first time subject to the approval of the deacon-convener and his house, there are new acts passed, both as to apprentices and freemen, and these are the latest records on such subjects which precede the long blank from 1683 till 1793:—

At the crafts hospitall of the burgh of Glasgow the nynt day of February 1672.

The quhilk day, Walter Stewart, present deacone of the weaveris of the said burgh with his quartermaisteris and remanent brethrine of the said calling being conveined, who being present for the most pairt, and takine to ther serious consideratioune how that many of ther friemen are castin desolet of warke by the great numberis of straingeris who dailie resort to this toune and fies themselfes with friemen for farder instructioune and as jurnaymen quherby the haill warke is inhanced in the hands of ane pairt of the tread, and utheris sett quyt iydle, for remeid quherof, the aforsaid deacone, maisteris and breithrine of the calling, be pluralitie of votis, did inact statut and ordaine, and heirby inacts, statuts, and ordaines, that noe forrener or strainger, borne above aughtine mylnes aff this burgh, be receavit or admittit as ane servant for farder instructioune, or as ane jurnayman with any frieman of the calling in tyme comeing whill first he produce to the deacone and maisteris ane sufficient testimoniall of the place of his nativitie and birth and guid behaviour, and suchlyke as also to pay in to the collectour for the use of the poore of the calling ten punds Scotis money befoir he be admittit or receavit as said is. And this to remaine unalterable but prejudice to any borne within aughtein mylnes to this burgh to enter as formerlie, declaring heirby this act sall noewayes militat against them.

(Signed) PATRICK CLARK.

The same day, the act underwryttin is appoynted and ordained to be bookit in this book conforme to the tennour thairof and to the effect thairin specifeit,—quhairof the tennour fallowis:—At Glasgow the elevinth day of December j^m vj^c thrie scoir eleivine yearis,—The quhilk day William Wallace, ane of the baillies of the said burgh, James Fairie, deacon conviner thairof with the deacones of craftis and uther brethrine of counsell for the most pairt being convined, and takeing to thair consideratioune ane former act made be thair predicessouris quhairof the tennour fallowis:— At Glasgow the twentie day of October j^m vj^c threttine yearis.—The quhilk day, the deacone conviner deacones and remanent of his counsell being convined, all in ane voyce but variance, haveing considered quhat inconvencies and hurt fallis furth throw not booking of the haill prenteissis taken be the haill craftis and thair assistaris without the deacon conviner his warrand to the deane of gild, and he can give no warrand without they be booked as said is quho craves his warrand and serve conforme to the letter of gildrie. Thairfoir the said deacon conviner, deacones and counsell abovenamed all in ane voyce and with ane consent statut and ordained that the haill prenteissis who sall be receaved be the haill craftsmen and thair assistaris within this burgh in tyme comeing sall be first booked in the deacon convineris bookis as said is, and ane warrand of the clark thairof to the deacone of craft quho is to book the prenteis befoir he be receavod or booked in the deacone of his callings book quhatsoever to eshew the former dainger, and in caice any of the deacones quhatsoever and thair assisteris receave or suffer any prenteis to be receaved be the craftis or thair assisteris to be booked in thair awne crafts book, befoir he be first booked in the deacon convineris book as said is, in that caice, the deacone of craft, with quhom they are booked, to pay fyve punds money for ilk prenteis they receave *toties quoties* the contravine to the deacon conviner to be takin up and converted *ad pios usus;* and sicklyke that none of the deacones nor visitor nor thair assistaris receave any frieman with them befoir he be first booked in the deacon convineris, and his clarkis testificat to the deacon quhatsoever thairof under the penaltie *toties quoties* for ilk persoune happens to be receaved in all tyme comeing. And sicklyk the haill prenteissis who are not as yet booked, be booked to eshew the former dainger, and everie deacone to mak intimatioune to ther haill craftis of the samyne, utherwayes the prenteis sall have no benefeit be ther prenteischipe, conforme to the letter of gildrie, and that article thairof, as the said act of the dait forsaid beiris. Quhilk act above wryttin the said William Wallace, baillie, deacon conviner and deacones with ther brethrine of counsell have ratified and approven, and be thir presentis, ratifies and approves of the samyne, and ordaines the samyne to be keiped and observed be the haill respective deacones and craftis within the said burgh, in the haill heads, claussis, and articles thairof in tyme comeing, under the penalties abovewryttin thairin contained; and that whomsoever of the crafts hes ther prenteissis unbooked, they caus book them under the said penalties. And sicklyk ordaines that ilk deacone take out ane extract of thir presentis, and caus book the samyne in ther awne crafts book that non may pretend ignorance heirof. Sic subscribitur

G. ANDERSONE.

At Glasgow the secound of Maij 1673.

The quhilk day, John Patersone, present deacone of the weaveris of the said burgh, his maisteris and remanent brethrine of the said vocatioune being convined (who for the most pairt being present), and considering the great want of wark amongst the most pairt of ther friemen, occasioned by the multitud and number of straingeris entring friemen with them, by reasoune of the smallness of the fridome fyne payit to the tread at thair entrie, quhilk is lyk to put to ruine many of ther friemen and ther families, and render them burdinsum to the calling; for remeid quhairof, after serious consideratioune had be them thairanent, the said deacone, maisteris, and remanent brethrine of the said calling unanimuslie in ane voyce did inact, statut and ordaine, and heirby inacts, statutis and ordaines, that all straingeris entring friemen with the said tread in all tyme heirafter who comes in at the far hand and bayes ther freidome, sall pay at ther entrie the sowme of four scoir punds Scotis money of freidom fyne, without any demonitionne or modificatioune be the deacone and maisteris of the said tread or thair successouris in office, and that by and attour the uther causwallities and service formerly in use to be done and payed be them at thair entrie; and recomends thir presentis to the deacon conviner and deacones and thair brethrine of counsell for thair approbatioune and ratificatioune thairof.

(Signed)   PATRICK CLARK.

At Glasgow the twentie sex day of Maij 1673

The quhilk day, being convined in Hutchisones hospitall, the deacon conviner and deacones of crafts, with thes who war deacones the last year, and ane great number of ther brethrin of counsell, anent ane supplicatioune presented to them be the present deacone of the weaveris within the said burgh, maisteris of craft, and wholl corporatioune thairof, craveand ane act to be ratified and approven by them, quhairof the tennour is as [the foregoing]. Quhilk being taken to the said deacon conviner deacones and remanent persones forsaid ther consideratioune, they all in ane voyce have ratified and approven, and be thir presentis ratifies and approves of the forsaid act in the haill poynts and articles thairof, and ordaines the samyne to be observed be the said vocatioune of weaveris in all tyme comeing; and ordaines thir presentis to be insert and registrat in the deacon convineris book, and his clark to give out ane extract thairof to the said calling, and the same to be read to them once everie year that non pretend ignorance. Sic subscribitur

G. ANDERSONE.

Decimo sexto Februarij 1674

The quhilk day, it is unianimuslie concludit and inactit be the said tread that no frimane sall have libertie to take ane jurnayman or any for farder instructione in tyme comeing quhill first the servant sulliccentlie instruct and prove that he hes served thric yearis space compleit at the weaver craft in the cuntrie and that under the paine of ane new upset.

The same day, the said calling did unanimuslie inact, statut, and ordaine that no frieman within the samyne in tyme comeing take or fie any stranger for farder instructioune any shortar space then twa yearis under the paine of four pundis Scotis for ilk contraventionne, for the use of the poor.

Tenth of August 1683.

The quhilke day, the deacon, maisters and most pairt of the calling being met and conveinit in the craftis hospitall with John Wallace, present deaconveiner, and haveing tackin to thair serious consideratiounes the caice and condition of the poor of the said calliug; they all in on voyce with consent of the said deacon conveiner hath statute and ordainit, and heirby statutes and ordanes that in all tym coming that ilke prenteis and jurnayman at his booking pay in for the use of the poor thrie pundis Scotis being straugers and not friemenis sones who ar to pay conform to all use and wont attour the clark and officers dewes; and that each person intending to mak himself friman being friemens sons and goodsones sall pay at thair admission eight pundis Scotis quhairin ther say drink is to be includit and to be frie of the deacons ten shilling the clerk and officers dewes being allwayes payit; and in caice the samyn act sall happin to be contraveinit be any succeiding deacon heirefter, that the deacon for the present that sall swa breck the same sall be heirby lyable, immediatly therefter in twentie pundis Scotis for the use of the poor *toties quoties* without forgivenes; and this act they ordain to stand in all tym heirefter.

IV.

TRADE PRIVILEGES.

The earliest entry showing co-operation with any other town is the following, and it indicates that the finances were at a low ebb when £24 Scots had to be borrowed:—

> The same day, the deikin, maisteris and haill craft present all in ane voice have concludit and ordainit that the xxiiij pundis givin to the deikin and wobsteris of Edinburgh for thair supplie in defens of the commoun weill of the wobster craft sall be borrowit for proffeit upone the commoun guidis of the craft, for the quhilk this act sal be ane guid warrand.

There is a very early indication of the fears that such a new departure as a "manufactorie" was a menace to the individual worker:—

Apud Glasgow quinto Maij anno domini millesimo sexcentesimo trigesimo octavo.

> The quhilk day the provest, bailzies and counsall of the said burghe being convenit, forsameikle as Richart Allane, deacon conveiner reportit in counsall that the wivers friemen within this burghe feired that the erecting of the manufactorie within the samein sould prove hurtfull and prejudiciall to them. Thairfor Patrick Bell ane of the wndertakers of the said manufactorie, for himself and in name of his partners, was content that it sould be inactit and ordanit that during the tyme of the tak sett to them be the toun of that hous in Drygait, and the use of the buithe wnder the tolbuithe for the use of the said manufactorie, that thair sould be nae wobis wovin of touns folkis thairin be thair servandis in hurt and prejudice of the said friemen, bot by thais onlie wha ar frie with the said calling; and swa the saidis provest, bailzies and counsall ordanit the samein to stand in force during thair tak of the said manufactorie. Extractum per me
> W. YAIR.

No record has survived of the origin of the casualty referred to in the following, and it is evident that, even in these early days, with the small population and limited area concerned, the collection of such tribute was impracticable. There is no further reference to the subject, so Allan Andersone does not seem to have had any greater success as an individual than the corporate body had in collecting the impost. The arrangements between the Glasgow weavers and those of the "Gorballis" are dealt with in another chapter:—

xj Maij 1646.

The said day, the dekine and maisteris of craft taking to thair consideratioun that the craft hes ane causualitie belonging thairto viz. — twa penneis of ilk peice of lyning clothe broght to the mercat of this burghe be ane weifer to be sold and als ane wther causualitie of xxxiij s. iiij d. to be takin of ilk weifer in the cuntrey that takis out wark out of the towne to be wovine, quhairof the craft hes bein in use lang of befoir, be vertew of thair right thairof, and now hes gon out of use throw neglect or wtherwayis (except thes in Gorballis), and becaus the saidis causualiteis hes, and may, prove profitable to the craft for releif of thair poore decayit bretherine, the dekine and maisteris of craft hes gevin and be thir presentis grantis full power and commissioun to Allane Andersone, ane of thair bretherine to intromet with and collect the saidis twa causunalites (except that whilk is payit yeirlie to the craft be the weiferis in the Gorballis); and that for the space of twa yeiris, viz., to Witsonday 1648; and to appropriat the same to himself for his pains; to the effect the same may be broght in use agane for the weill of the craft; and then the craft is to enter thairto, and to mak the best use thairof they can.

While there were undoubted privileges granted by the town to tradesmen, there was, on the other hand, an onerous obligation undertaken by the Burgesses, as the following copy of a Burgess ticket will show:—

BURGESS TICKET in favor of John Boyd, tailor.
—dated 8 August 1678.

Heir I protest befor God that I confes and allow with my heart the trew religione presently profest within this kingdome and authorized be the laus theirof. I sall abyd theirat, menteine and defend the samyne to my lyfes end, renuncand the romane religione callit papastrie. I sall be leill and trew to our dread soveragne the Kings Majestie, and to the proveist and baillies of this burgh. I sall obey the officeris theirof, fortiefie, menteine and defend them in the executione of their office with my body and guids. I sall not cullor unfriemens guids under [cullor of my own]. I sall do nothing hurtfull [to] the privilidges and comoune weill of this burgh. In all taxationes, watchings, and wardings to be laid upon this burgh, I sall willingly beir my pairt theirof as I am commandit be the magestrates of the samyne, and sall not purcheis nor use exemptiones to be frie thairof, renuncand the benifiet of the samyne for ever. I sall not brew nor cause brew any malt but such as is grund att the toune mylnes, and sall grind noe other cornes except wheat, ry, peis, and beines, allenerly; and so oft as I break any poynt of this my aith I obleis me to pay to the comoune affaires of this burgh the sume of ane hundreth punds Scotis money and sall remayne in ward quhill the samyne to payit, so healpe me God. I sall give the best counsell I can, and conceill the counsell shawine to me. I sall not consent to dispone the comoune guidis of this burgh but for ane comoune cause and ane comoune profeit. I sall make concord quhair discord is to the utermost of my power. In all linicationes and nighbourheids I sall [give] my leill and trew judgment but pryce, prayer, or reward, so healp me God:——Apud Glasgow octavo die mensis Augusti millesimo sexcentesimo septuagesimo octavo:—The quhilk day, Ninian Andersone, present dean of gild of the burgh of Glasgow, and brethrine of his counsell, sittand in judgment, John Boyd, tayleor, is made burges and gild brother of the said burgh as eldest and lanfull sone to umquhill John Boyd younger, maltman, burges and gild brother theirof, who hes payit his fynes and given his oath as use is.—Extractum.

(Signed) G. ANDERSONE.

That the privileges were recognised and upheld by the Royal Authorities the following Act will show:—

> ACT OF THE LORDS OF THE EXCHEQUER in favor of the Trades of Glasgow as to privileges given to the masters of the "East Suggarie" of Glasgow, dated 5 July 1687.

At Glasgow the fyfth day of July i^m vi^c and eightie sevin years,—Anent the supplication given in be the proveist, toune counsell, deacon convecner of the trades of Glasgow for themselves and in name and behalfe of the freemen of the said burgh, to the lords commissioneris of his Majesties thesaurie and exchequer,—Bearing that notwithstanding of the fundamentall lawes and constitutions of the burgh and by severall acts granted by his sacreed Majesties royall predicessouris and seallis of causes granted to the incorporationes of severall trades within the said burgh, and quhich are all ratified and confirmed by severall acts of parliament; and particularlie the 8th act of the 19th parliament of King James the sexth all unfreemen especiallie couparis, are expreslie prohibited and discharged to work or exercise their trade within the priviledges and liberties of the said burgh; and the deacon and freemen of the Couparis are both imponred and appointed to censure and punish all unfree persones who shall be apprehended working any such work within the burgh, conforme quhairunto the petitioneris have bein in possession of their priviledges contained in the foresaids rights by apprehending and punishing all unfreemen working within the said burgh and that past all memorie; notwithstanding quhairof upon ane petition presented to the saids lords by the maisteris of the East Suggarie of Glasgow upon the first day of Apryle last, there is ane act past quhairin among severall other priviledges and concessiones granted be the saids lords to the maisteris of the said suggarie, the saids lords have allowed them the benefite of ane coupar for their work of their oune choiseing; and be vertew of the said act the maisteris of the suggarie have accordinglie brought in and doeth yet keep and make use of ane unfreeman for working of their pretended coupar work in manifest contempt of the magistrats and fundamentall lawes of that burgh and the prejudice of the deacon and freemen couparis and their rights and priviledges granted to them in maner foresaid; and as the said act was privatlie impetrat without aither calling or hearing of the petitioneris, and that in caice the petitiouneris had bein heard at the passing thereof, the humblie conceave no such act could have past against them for the reasones following, viz.—Primo, the petitiouneris haveing their rights and priviledges abovewrittin so clearlie granted and established to them according to the fundamentall lawes of this kingdom; and the same being cled with immemoriall possession, it is humblie conceaved their saids priviledges can neither be taken from them nor incroached upon except by ane legall process of reduction and declarator before the judge ordinar; and no man ever pretended such solemne rights and constitutiones, cled with immemoriall possession as said is, can be evacuat by ane delyverance clandestinlie impetrat upon ane privat bill. Bot Secundo, as the act of parliament made anent manufactories doeth allow them no such priviledges as to mantaine any unfree coupar for working of their pretended coupar work for manufactories within this kingdome did ever pretend to the same, bot on the contrare they are all expreslie precluded and debarred therefrom, as is clear by the manufactories both of the Suggaries and Soaparies at Leith and other free burghes within this kingdom, wherein none bot freemen are allowed to work any wright work or coupar work within the burgh in any of the manufactories that are set up within the same. Tertio, It is weill knowne that all the coupar work the manufactorie will stand in need of the space of ane whole year, could be wrought by ane man in the space of two or three moneths at furthest, so that they could keep no constant coupar if it were not, that, under cullour of working to the manufactorie, they doe privatlie work to severall other of the inhabitants and otheris of the countrey, to the great prejudice of the deacon and freemen of that trade. Quarto;—In caice such ane encroachment upon the burgh of Glasgow and priviledges thereof should be allowed, the maisteris of the manufactories might likewayes pretend to bring in and mantaine ane wright, shoemaker, tailzeour &c., all unfreemen, and thereby ruine and prejudge the haill trades of the burgh, and quhich the saids maisteris are actually threatning to doe albeit the same be humblie conceaved to be ane encroachment altogether unheard of and inconsistent with law. Quinto, if such encroachments should be allowed, (as in law they cannot) the haill trades would undoubtedlie be ruined, the burgh thereby rendered uncapable to pay the taxationes and impositiones due to his Majestie and the burgh should be ruined and his Majesties revenew diminished and prejudged; and seing the petitioneris are willing to furnishe the manufactorie with able and skilfull workmen both at ane ordinary and cheap rate.—Therefore humbly craveing that the saids lords in consideration of the premissis would be pleased to recall the foresaid delyverance and act extracted therupon in favoures of the saids maisteris of the Suggarie, or otherwayes remitt the same with their rights and priviledges to the lords of session to be determined be them according to law; and in the meantyme allow the petitioneris the exercise and possession of their rights and priviledges until the finall decision thereof and act extracted therupon; as the said petition in itselfe at full lenth is contained; Which petition being read and considered be the saids lords, they ordained the maisteris of the said Suggarie to see and answer the same, who gave in the answeris made be them therto in maner underwrittin viz.—that the maisteris of the said suggar work conceave that they have good and undoubted right to the said priviledge by the acts of parliament and acts of exchequer, declaring this priviledge to them of haveing ane coupar of their oune choiseing, and that likewayes for the reasones then presented, and quhich were found to be verie relevant and sufficient, bot the saids maisteris being now charged with horning at the instance of the couparis of Glasgow, and there being ane bill of suspension given in by the maisteris, the same is ordained by ane warrand in presentia produced by themselves, to be discust upon the bill, and the saids lords being the judges ordinary for discussing points in jure such as this is, it is humblie conceaved that they could not trouble their lordships with it, it being ane undoubted princepell in law, that ane process depending before ane judicatorie could not be transferred to ane other by the same pairtie who intended the process; and if it were otherwayes the maisteris would be verie glad to debate before their lordships who had alreadie decided in their favoures, bot since the couparis are not content to submitt to the saids lords decision, bot thinks they are wronged in point of law, the maisteris are verie content that the lords of the session may hear likewise their reasones to the end they may second the saids lords act and find that they have done what was suitable to the law of the Nation, and the acts of parliament in favoures of manufactories, and which they hope will at leist put ane end to all proces; by which the maisteris of the suggar works, manufactories and privat estates are ruined. Which petition abovewrittin ansueris made thereto, with the acts of parliament and acts of exchequer founded on by both parties, the lords remitted the consideration thereof to the lords president of the session, lord Tarbat and lord Castlehill, three of their oune number, to doe therein as they fand cause or to report. The lords of the committee appointed for considering of the withinwrittin petition and answeris made therto, conceaves that notwithstanding of the act of exchequer in favoures of the maisteris of the Easter Suggar Work of Glasgow for allowing them the freedom of ane coupar of their oune choiseing for working of their coupar work, yet that the saids maisteris ought not to enjoy the foresaid priviledge unlesse the coupar swa to be made use of be them be ane freeman coupar, and that the saids maisteris ought not to make use of no other tradesman of the said burgh of Glasgow without being freemen as aforesaid the petitioneris allwayes furnishing the manufactorie with skilfull workmen at ane ordinarie and cheap rate. The lords of his Majesties exchequer haveing considered the foresaid report, approves of the samen. Sic subscribitur, Perth, cancell. I.P.D. Extractum de libris scaccarij per me. Sic subscribitur Tarbat.

Avoiding needless repetition, the one record following is given as an example of how the privileges of the craft were maintained at law.

TRADE PRIVILEGES.

The process ends abruptly, so presumably an amicable settlement, which it was not thought necessary to record, was arrived at:—

Unto the deacon and masters of the Incorporation of Weavers in Glasgow.

The representation and complaint of Robert Provane, Collector to the said Incorporation.

SHEWETH

That by several acts of the said incorporation its statute and enacted that it shall not be leesom or laufull to any freeman of the said incorporation to employ or give work to unfreemen or countrey weavers not freemen of the said trade, and that the contraveeners are to be lyable to, or incurr certain fynes to be payed to the Collector for the use and behove of the poor of the said trade, and particularly by act of the said incorporation of the 23d of May 1735 years, it was agreed by the said whole trade, *nemine contradicente*, with advyce and consent of the deacon conveener, that in all time thereafter no freeman of the said incorporation shall employ any unfreeman to work any piece of thair craft under the pain of nine poundis Scots money of fine *toties quoties* to be paid by the contraveener to the collector for the behove of the poor of the said incorporation, and three poundis Scots to the informer, and that the deacon and masters shall not have power to remitt any part of the said fynes. Notwithstanding wheirof William Gemmill, late deacon and James Sym (blank) both freemen of the said incorporation have each of them contraveened the said acts, as informed by James Stewart, freeman, against the said William Gemmill, and Thomas Muir, late deacon against the said James Sym in so far as the said William Gemmill has employed James Fleming, weaver in Anderston and given him a webb of doullas one or more to work for the said William Gemmill within these six monethis past, and the said James Sym within the said time has imployed Andrew Fyfe, weaver in Westthorn and givin him a piece or pieces of check linnen to work for the said James Sym, and none of the saids James Fleming nor Andrew Fyfe are freemen of the said incorporation:—Wherefor the saids William Gemmill and James Sym should each of them be decerned, amerciat, and fyned in the forsaid sum of nine poundis Scotis of fyne to me the said Robert Provan, collector, for the behove of the poor of the said incorporation, and in the forsaid three poundis Scots to the said several informers viz.—the said William Gemmill in three poundis Scotis to the said James Stewart, and the said James Sym in three poundis Scotis to the said Thomas Muir.

(Signed) ROBERT PROVAN.

Glasgow 21 January 1747, sederunt Patrick Stevenson, deacon with the masters, William Gemmill and James Sym, cited by Mungo Muir, officer, called, appeared, craved a copy of the forsaid lybill, and a competent tyme to answer, which was agreed to, and they received a copy of the lybill, and are assigned to answer on Tuesday nixt at six of the clock, in the house of Andrew Armour, late bailie, to which time and place the court adjourned, and to which the saids William Gemmill and James Sym were warned *apud acta :—*

1747—27th January between 6 and 7 afternoon, the deacon and most of the masters convened. } called, compeared not.

Glasgow 11th February 1747, Mungo Muir, officer, verified a warning against William Gemmill and James Sym, defenders only James Sym compeared and acknouledged that he had givin work to Andrew Fyfe, ane unfreeman as lybilled. It was reported that William Gemmill was confined to his room by indisposition :—

The deacon and masters make avisandum of this process to the Incorporation of Weavers in Glasgow at their nixt meeting, which is appointed to be on Friday nixt at three afternoon in the Inner High Church of Glasgow, to which the said James Sym was warned *apud acta*, and the officer is appointed to warne the said William Gemmill, each of them under the pain of four pounds Scots of unlaw.

(Signed) PATRICK STEVENSON.

V.

RELATION TO TRADES' HOUSE AND CARE OF THE POOR OF THE CRAFT.

While the Incorporation originated not later than 1514 (as stated in Chap. I.), the combination of the Fourteen Trades, now known as the Trades' House, did not take place till 1605, and it is extremely probable that the cause of that combination was the joint ownership of the Almshouse or Hospital. The earliest reference to this subject is the following minute :—

Die xiiij Decembris 1604.

The quhilk day, Richart Kirkland, deakin being convenit within the Hie Kirk of Glasgow, accompaneit with his maisteris and haill bretherene of craft, quha all with ane consent aggreis that in all tym coming ilk freman of thair craft sall pay, ilk quarter of the yeir, tua schillingis for his quarteris wageis, quhilk salbe delyverit to the deakin for the tyme to be bestowit and applyit to the use of the puir decayit craftismen quhilkis sall happin to be imput in the hospitall in Stabilgrene, newlie erectit be the craftismen of this burgh of Glasgow, salang as puir craftismen remanis in the said hospitall, utherwyis the said quarter wageis, in cais of the decay of the said hospitall, to returne agane and apertene to thair awin craft.

J. CRAIG sst.

There is extant and in possession of this Incorporation an elegantly written copy of the Letter of Guildry under which the Merchants and the Trades' House originated. The ink has somewhat faded, but the lettering is perfect and easily read. This document is given verbatim as No. IX. in the Appendix of Crawfurd's *Trades' House*, and in Chapter XXIII. of the same volume it is stated that these same Letters of Guildry, though acted upon, were not confirmed by Parliament until 1672. The first deacon-convener was nominated in the Letters of Guildry, and his duties generally were to "judge betwixt them, and any of them, in matters pertaining to the crafts and callings, and shall make acts and statutes for good order among them, with the advice of the rest of the deacons, and their assistants."

It is evident that the weavers had not equal rights of admission to the Hospital from 1605, as the following minute shows:—

At Glasgow the eight day of December j^m vj^c and scaventie sex yearis.

The quhilk day, Robert Flaikfeild, present deacone of the weaveris of the said burgh, his maisteris of tread and most pairt of the said calling being convined, with James Farrie, present deacon conviner therof, and taking to ther serious consideratioune the loss and dommadge they sustaine by paying in no more nor fyftine punds Scotis money yearlie to the deacon convineris hous, it being soe small, and that by augmenting therof they may have ane kye of the deacon convineris box or hous, and get als many men of ther tread wpon the said hous as any uther tread hes or may have for the futur. Therfor, for remeid therof, the said deacone, maisteris of craft, and most pairt of the said calling be thir presentis have, be plurallitie of votis, statut and bund and obleist them and ther successouris in office to pay in yearlie to the said deacon convineris hous in tyme comeing the sowme of threttie punds Scotis money, the said deacon convineris hous giveing and granting ane act in ther favouris that the said weaveris sall have ane act wherin they are to have ane key of the deacon convineris box, and to have als many men wpon the hous as any uther tread hes at the first alteratioune of the hous, and to be preferred thairto befor any uther tread wha payes not als much, and they to be preferable to any uther tread wha comes in for that effect quhairwpon they have granted the premissis and nae utherwayes; and ordaines extractis heirof to be given furth for that effect wnder ther clarkis hand.

The representation on the deacon-convener's council was also less than four other Incorporations, and in 1771 an effort was made to secure equality as follows:—

At the Trades' Hospital the twenty-third day of May seventeen hundred and seventy one years—Convened, William Bell present Deacon John Robertson late Deacon with the whole of the masters except one and a considerable number of the other freemen of the Incorporation of Weavers in Glasgow the whole being warned as was verified by the Trade's officer present in Court—when the said William Bell, Deacon represented to the Incorporation that at meeting of the Convener and Deacons of the Incorporations of the City on the 18th May currt. there was presented a Petition to them signed by the said John Robertson and some of the other old Deacons of the Ten Incorporated Trades last in the order of the Roll of the Trades House, setting forth that the said Ten Trades had a fewer number of members in the Convener's council than the first four Trades in the said roll had, without any reason for it appearing in the Books of the said Trades' house or that any just reason can be assigned for it, and praying for remeid, a copy of which Petition was produced and read over in presence of the said Incorporation and the Deacon having also represented that at the said meeting it had been objected that the said Petition was given in without authority from the said Ten Incorporations for the removing of which objection the said Incorporation of weavers unanimously did and hereby do approve of the said Petition presented as aforesaid, and empowered and by this their Act of Trade empower the said William Bell, present Deacon and his successors in office for and in name of this Incorporation humbly to apply to the said Trades House to grant the desire of said Petition—That the whole Incorporated Trades of the City shall have equal numbers of Members in the Deacon Convener's Council, and to adhere to the said Petition, and to subscribe the same or any other Petition or writ necessary for that purpose, and the said Deacon and his Brethern of Trade who are members of the foresaid Trades House to do all in their power to get the desire of the foresaid Petition granted, and to insist, consult and determine as members of the house in the said matter until the final issue thereof, and the said Incorporation hereby agree and become obliged to contribute their part of what sum may be requisite for support of the dignity of the Trades House and support of the poor thereof, and empower the Deacon and Collector and their successors in office out of the Trades funds to defray the whole charges that have already been incurred or may hereafter be incurred in the said matter, and ordain Extracts of this Act signed by the Trades Clerk to be given out to the said Deacon to be by him presented to the foresaid Trades House, and for and in their name to sign this act in the Trades Book

(Signed) WILLIAM BELL

The result was an action of declarator in the Court of Session decided in 1777, which gave to the weavers the representation now acted upon, viz., the deacon and three assistants.

While the Letters of Guildry were confirmed by Parliament in 1672, there arose further need of confirmation in 1689, referred to in Chapter XXIV. of Crawfurd's book, and the following minute shows that action was required on the part of the Incorporation:—

16 of November 1689.

The whilk day, the deacon and haill maisteris haveing mett and conveinned in the hospitall with William Boill, laitt deacon annent the hundreth ponndis Scottis receaved be him for defrayeing of his and other six of the friemen ther charges both for man and horse the space of eight dayes in goeing from this to Edinburgh, being summoned to compear befor the secroit counsell annent the election of the deacon conveinner and payeing for horse hyres; and after compt and reckoning made be the said William Boill to them of the forsaid soume, they fand that the said William had deburst out the samen and more, and therfor exonered and discharged him therof be thir presents for ever. And ordainned me undersubscriver ther clerk to subscrive thir presents for them and in ther names for the said William Boill his exoneration in the premissis.

(Signed) R. FYNNISONE. clerk.

RELATION TO TRADES' HOUSE.

This action resulted in formal sanction of "the several erections of incorporations and deaconries of that burgh" (Glasgow).—*Statute 1690, Chap. 18—William and Mary.*

The members of this Incorporation who have held the office of deacon-convener are :—

In 1658,	-	Patrick Bryce.
1659,	-	John Buchanan.
1799-1800,	-	Archd. Newbigging.
1829-1830,	-	John Alston.
1838-1839,	-	John Neil.

There were at the foundation of the Trades' House 30 burgesses of the weaver craft out of 363 trades rank burgesses, and there were 213 merchant rank burgesses, making 576 as the first roll of citizens of Glasgow.

As will be seen from the various Seals of Cause, the responsibility of caring for the poor of the craft has always been upon the Incorporation, and there is evidence that many times in its history the burden was felt to be most onerous. At an early date in the history of the Incorporation all fines were laid aside for the use of the poor, and indeed, throughout, that has been the legitimate outlet for all money received by the Incorporation from every source:—

Quinto Novembris 1655.

The said day, it is inactit that all sort of wnlawis that sall be gott in tyme cuming sall cum in to the use of the poore.

Such entries as the following occur frequently during the eighteenth and the early part of the nineteenth century:—

At the Trades Hospital the second day of May seventeen hundred and one years

The said day Simeon Tennent present Deacon Convener of Glasgow William Haddin present Deacon of the Weavers thereof Masters of Trade being met with the rest of their trade when convened having considered the great burden of debt that the trade lies under whereby it is almost ruined and the great number of their poor who are like to starve for want of bread Do hereby for disburdening themselves and supply their poor by plurality of votes Statute and Ordain that the quarter accounts shall be double and that is to say that every freeman of the said trade within this city shall pay quarterly for the use of the poor four shillings commencing from this day and so to continue quarterly for the space of seven years and no longer and the refusants to be liable in the double and ordains the same to be punctually observed and paid to their Collector present and to come during the years above mentioned as also ordains the forty shillings Scots payable by each of the new Masters to be only in time coming applied for the use of the poor As witness subscribed by the Deacon Convener Deacon and Thomas Falconer Clerk to the said trade and lastly it is statute and ordained that for the space of seven years to come Ilk journeyman and prentice that receives the twa part of his winning to pay one shilling Scots quarterly

(Signed) SIMEON TENNENT
THOS FALCONER Clk   WILLIAM HADDIN

The reason for increased entry money is several times stated as being to meet the outlay for excessive poor. About the middle of the eighteenth century, and again at the closing years, there are entries arranging to purchase meal and other food to be distributed among the poor of the craft. On 29th November, 1799, a sum of £500 sterling was voted for this purpose. Happily no such calls have come on the Incorporation since that time, and its later history in its relation to the poor of the craft, owing to augmented funds, shows increasing ability to give more substantial help where it is required. An interesting statement as to the growth of the funds in modern years is given in Appendix III.

VI.

SUPERVISION OF TRADESMANSHIP.

From very early days an important duty of the deacon and his court has been the responsibility of maintaining a reputable workmanship; and it is always clearly recognised that defective work done by any member injures the whole craft:—

Quinto Maij 1593.

Quhilk day, the dekin and maisteris of the haill craft understanding that throw diversitie of price for wirking of herdein in this citie, and insufficiencie of work thairof, thair dois fall furth ane greit hinder to the craft. Thairfor thai have statut and ordanit, that in all tymes coming, that workeris of herdin work sall tak for ilk elne weving vj d. and mak the work in this citie thai tak in hand sufficient. In case the said work sall not be fund sufficient, the worker sall get na payment for his work. In case the worker sall tak les nor vj d. for ilk elne of herdin wirking, salbe under the paine following.—to wit, pay to the dekin and maisteris of craft viij s. unforgeving.

Siclyk statutis, that for ilk elne weving of gam herdin sall tak viij d. and mak the work sufficient. In case the work be not sufficient wrocht, the worker sall get na payment. In case the worker sall tak les for the elne weving nor viij d. of the said gam herdin, sall paye also to the dekin of the craft and maisteris thairof viij s.

Decimo tertio Februarij 1595.

The dekin, maisteris, and haill craft statutis and ordains, that quhosumevir of thair nombir beis tried fund and provit to have wrocht ony herdin better schape nor vj d. the elne this xij moneths bygane, sall pay to dekin for the weale of the craft xx s.

In the following excerpt a limitation is made, the reason for which is obscure:—

(13-2-1595)

Item it is statut and ordanit for the weale of the haill craft that thair be onlie ane wollen lwme haldin in tymes comming, yeirlie, in everie freman of the said craftis hous, and na ma wollen lwmes, and gif that ony freman sall contravein this ordinance in tymes comming, sall pay to the baillies of this citie xvj s., and ane new wpset to the craft, wnforgevin.

SUPERVISION OF TRADESMANSHIP.

Seemingly it was desired to confine the work strictly to the individual, and restrictions were enacted which compelled this:—

(13-2-1595)

Item it is statut and ordanit, that na craftisman tak ony persones work to work quhill he can not work. In case he sall do in the contrair, sall pay to the baillies xvj s., and ane new wpset to the craft.

Item it is statut and ordanit that nane tak work and warp the same, and eftir the saming be warppit give furth the same to wtheris to be wollfing. In case he sall do in the contrair, to paye xvj s. to the baillies, and fourtie s. to the weale of the craft; and gif the work salbe send furth of the toun to be woffin, sall paye xvj s to the baillies and ane new wpset to the craft.

Poynding seems to have been quite a usual occurrence, and is frequently referred to:—

Decimo quarto Augusti 1596

The dekin, maisteris, and haill craft statutis and ordeins that quhosoever poynd in the craft salbe tane justlie, and he fra quhome the saming salbe tane sall not louse and redeme the poynd within xv dayes nixt eftir the taking thairof, nether sall aggrie thairanent that the poynd be not disponit wpone, that the said poynd thaireftir be appraisit and wsit at the pleasure of the dekin and maisteris of craft without ony ryght thaireftir to be clamit to the said poynd be him fra quhome it was tane.

Decimo octavo die Septembris 1596

Quhilk daye, it is fund that James Blair promeisit to paye xiij s. iiij d. quhilk, he being present, was spendit in the effairis of the craft, as also it is fund that the said James stoppit the officiar of the craft for poynding for the said xiij s. iiij d., quhill the said James grantit that he did, and thairthrow hes incurrit disobedience. Thairfore the dekin and brether of craft decernis the said James to paye to the craft foure lib., and xvj s. to the baillies wnforgeven according to thair actis maid agains disobedientis to ane gud ordour, and that incontinent but ferder delaye.

It is now hardly possible to determine what the fabrics referred to from time to time in the records really were. In the times with which we are at present dealing—end of the sixteenth and early in the seventeenth century—the references are to lining and plaiding (the latter under varied spellings, such as *pleyds*, *pladdis*, and *pleydin*). These were respectively striped and checked fabrics of homespun wool. Ray in 1661 describes pladding as a "party coloured blanket," while in 1727 Defoe describes it as "a stuff cross-striped with Yellow, Red, and other mixtures for the plaids or veils worn by the women of Scotland." The two following extracts refer to such work :—

Duodecimo Augusti 1598.

Quhilk daye, the dekin maisteris and haill craft perceaveand that sum of thair craft workis wollen cleyth to ane meane price, and sum to ane equall price for thair work, to the hurt and hinder of utheris, and selandeir of thair craft. Thairfoir thai statut that nane of thair craft work ane elne of pladdein better chap nor aucht penneis the roundest elne, and that wnder the pane of xx s.

Vigesimo quarto die mensis Februarij 1599

The quhilk daye, the dekin, maisteris and haill craft, convenit in thair Candilmes court for the intreating of the effairis of thair craft, and for the weale of the saming, hes statut and ordenit, and be thir presentis statutis and ordenis, that na persone, maister, servand, or wyfe of thair craft tak wpone hand to sut or persewe ony persone to cum or resort to thame ather with lining or wollen or ony kynd of work, bot everie calane to pas quhen thay sall pleis best; and gif ony persone of the craft sall contraveine this ordinance, sall paye xl s. to the craft and xvj s. to the baillies.

It was apparently desired to prevent a practice of advancing payment before the work was done, though the following looks like a contradiction in terms :—

(24-2-1599)

Item the dekin, maisteris and haill craft hes statut and ordanit, as be thir presentis statutis and ordenis, that nane of thair craft tak fra ony calane of quhome thai have work ony kynd of silveir before the hand, except the work be wrochtand the tyme thai tak the said silveir for to help to work the same, wnder the pane of xl s. to the craft, and xvj s. to the baillies.

The weavers of 1599 seem to have had human failings in seeking to secure for themselves ample supply of work, and possibly doing so by specious promises, which it was recognised did a general injury to the trade, so the Master Court had to legislate as follows :—

ANENT OVERMEKILL WORK (24-2-1599)

Item the dekin, maisteris and haill craft hes statut and ordanit, as be thir presentis statutis and ordeins, for the weale of the craft, that quhen it sall fall furthe that work be tane in be ony brother of craft superabundantlie, that is, mair nor he is abill to work and outred in dewe seasoun, that the dekin for the tyme suffer not the said work ly in the takeris in hand thairof to the hinder of the owneris and greiff of the craft, bot that the said dekin intromitt with the said work and distribut ane pairt thairof, that the dekin and maisteris of his craft sall think the taker in may not work in dewe tyme to the said owneris thairof, amang the rest of the brethrene of the craft being honest men, and the havear of the overmekill work not to ganstand the dekin and maisteris of the craft for the tyme purposing to deale amang the rest the said overmekill work tane in be him as said is, quhill gif ony brother of craft sall ganstand, the ganstandar sall paye to the craft xl s. and xvj s. to the baillies.

(20-8-1603)

Als it is statute that nane of the brethrene tak onie man or womanis wark to work, quhill the brethrene that hes wrocht to thame of befoir be satisfeit quhat thai have to lay to thair charge.

The first reference to "linchie-winchie" follows:—

Die xxviij Novembris 1604.

The quhilk day, the deakin and haill bretherene of craft statutis and settis doun, that nane of thame sall work onie linchie winchie of the roundest sort bettir chaip nor xxx d. ilk ell, and fourtie pennyis the smallest sort ilk ell, and quha workis the same better chaip sall pay xx s. ilk falt to the box, provyding give the said wark sall not be sufficientlie and weill wroght, he that workis the samyn sall have na pryce thairfoir. And this act to stand in all tyme coming.

This was a fabric of linen warp with woollen weft, and appears later as "linsey-woolsey," and presumably was the prototype of the article wincey which in the middle of last century was a large item in Glasgow's textile trade.

The penalties of broken promises were severe in these days:—

(28-11-1604)

The quhilk day, it is statute and ordanit that gif onie brother of the craft in tym coming mak promeis befoir the deakin to outred ony work that he hes to work of onie persounes betnix and sic ane day as the deakin appoyntis him, and give he outred it not, and quha evir brekis promeis sall pay xx s. ilk falt, and be dischargit of labour quhill it be payit.

It looks as if a way of evading the enactment against taking more work than could be quickly overtaken had been found by having

SUPERVISION OF TRADESMANSHIP.

work for one weaver in more than one loom; so further legislation is required:—

(8-2-1606)

The quhilk day, the deakin and bretherene statutis that na brother of the craft in tym coming have ony ma loomis in thair hous to work in nor thai have workeris to work thairin, and quha salbe fund to do in the contrair, sall pay xl s. *toties quoties.*

Sexto Augusti 1614.

The quhilk day, John Allansoune is decernit in ane wrang of his awin confessioun for haveing of ma full lumis in his hous nor he had workeris against the actis of the craft and thairfoir is decernit to pay xl s. thairfoir conforme to the said act and thairefter has satisfiet the deikin and maesteris for his offence and is dischargeit theirof.

Banishment for bad workmanship, thus doing injury to the craft, seems to have been of frequent occurrence:—

(14-2-1607)

The dekin, maisteris and brether of craft findis Marioun Scot and James Rankeyne, workeris in thair craft, to have done wrang to the craft, for reparing of the wrang, decernis thame, and everie ane of thame, to paye thre lib. to the craft at the will of the dekin and maisteris thairof but farder delaye. And for keiping of gud ordour heireftir in times to come that gif thai salbe fund tryit and convict to do auchtand wrang to the craft be thair work or wtherwayes that thai incontinent efter triall and convicting salbe put away furt of this toun, and not to be ressavit thairin againe, and quhaever sall ressave thame eftir thai, for thair wnvorthines, beis put furt thairof, sall paye ane new wpset to the dekin of the craft for the tyme, and the saidis Marioun and James hes subscryvit heirto judicialie.—

(P.S.) J. Allanson, notarius de mandatis dictorum Mariote et Jacobi

Septimo die mensis Augusti 1607

Quhilk day, Bartie Muir, wobster, of his awin proper confessioun, bundis and obleissis him willinglie to remove him furth of the burght and toun of Glasgow, gif that evir heireftir he salbe fund tryit and convict to mak ony insufficient work in his craft and that incontinent efter his convictoun before the dekin and maisteris of his craft, and never to enter thairin agane, or to be recavit ane brother of the said craft, bot to be bonneisit and expellit furt of the samming, and requeistis the baillies of this burght for the tyme to interpone thair authoritie to this band past wpone the said Bartie Muir.

SUPERVISION OF TRADESMANSHIP.

The next two extracts deal with irregularities. "Coveringis" was probably a fabric of the blanket order:—

Vigesimo primo die mensis Novembris 1607.

Quhilk daye, the dekin, maisteris, and haill craft hes statut and ordenit, and be thir presentis statutis and ordenis, that nane of thair brether of craft that workis coveringis or pladdis sall furneis ony kynd of yarne to ony of the persones that gavis thame coveringis or plaiddis to work in ony tyme to cum, wnder the pane of fyve lib. money for the first falt heirfore that eveir ony of thair craft salbe convict heiroff.

Quhilk daye, the dekin, maisteris, and haill craft hes statut and ordenit, and be thir presentis statutis and ordanis, that na brother of the said craft sall in ony tyme to com intromitt with or ressave with ony kynd of unsufficient work fra ony outtintownis-man of craft or uther unfreman within the toun, of a craft or wthervayis, wnder the paine of ane new upset, and that nane of thame sall buy or sell of the said unsufficient work wnder the said paine.

Although Edinburgh and Glasgow were in these days separated by the slowness of the inter-communication, there seems to have been a good understanding with the brethren of the craft there, to prevent dishonest workmen passing from employment in the one town to the other:—

Decimo Decembris anno 1608.

The quhilk day, the deikin and maisteris present understanding that Thomas Ranking, wobster had feyit himself with Abrahame Ramsay, wobster in Edinburgh, and refuisit to serve him;—Thairfoir thai all in ane [voice] concludit and inhibeit all friemen of thair craft to give him service or work untill the tyme he satisfie the said Abrahame for his service, and for sik sowmis of money as he is justlie awand him, under the pane of ane new upset.

Gamheckling is a fabric whose nature it is not possible to trace, other than that it most likely was of linen, as "heckling" was not a process applied to any other material. Again it is to the desire of preserving a good reputation for workmanship that we are indebted for the entry:—

Ultimo Decembris 1608.

The quhilk day, the deikin and maisteris haifing tryit and dewlie considderit that Andro Witherspoone hes wrocht unsufficient wark to Christian Ros in weifing ane gamhekling wob to hir, quhairby scho is damnifie. Thairfoir the deikin and maisteris decernis him in ane wrang thairfoir, and to pay to the said Christiane for

SUPERVISION OF TRADESMANSHIP.

hir los and skayth, and in satisfactioune of all bountethe and payment ressavet xx s., and to weif the wob frie, and to pay to the box xvj s. money with als meikle to the baillies give he failzies thairin.

Boycotting was not an original invention when applied in Ireland last century. What Thomas Bryce's offence actually was is not stated, but there is no doubt that if the resolution was carried out it was equivalent to banishment from the town:—

Decimo primo Februarij anno 1609.

The quhilk day, the deikin and maisteris, with consent of the haill craft, undirstanding the greit truble that Thomas Bryce, wobster hes brocht this toun into, and the greit contempt and abuis done be him to the deikin and maisteris in respect quhairof he is not wurdie of followschip amangst thame; hes thairfoir all in ane voice concludit that he have na friedom of craft amangst thame heireftir, and that he be scoreit furth of thair buik and roll, and nevir to be acknawledgit amangst thame untill the tyme he be reconceillit with the craft, and pay ane new upset. And als hes all concludit, statut, and ordanit, that na frieman of the said craft by, blok, or sell with him na kynd of merchandeis, sick as yearne, woll, hair, coveringis, or uther quhatsumevir, under the pane of ane new upset.

Those of the present generation who can go back to hand-loom weaving days in last century will recognise the following as a condition of things they had frequently to deal with:—

Decimo secundo Augusti anno 1609.

The quhilk day, the deikin and maisteris, upone consideratioune of the greit hurt and prejudice done to our soverane lordis leiges be friemen of the wobstercraft in selling and laying in wed honest folkis work that is givin thame to work, quhairby be thair knaiferie the craft is sclanderit. Thairfoir, and for remeid thairof hes all in ane voice concludit and ordanit that all manir of friemen of the wobstercraft that in onie tyme heireftir sellis, disponis, or layis in wed onie manis work givin to thame to work sall los and amit thair fredome in the said craft, and nevir be permitit nor sufferit to work as ane frieman in the said craft, bot secludit thairfra as persounes infamous and unwordie. Requeisting the baillies of this burght to interpone thair authorite heirto.

Bad work is severely dealt with, as the two extracts following show:—

Quinto Februarij 1614.

The quhilk day, Richert Kirkland become in the deikinis will for the spilt work wrang evill wrocht be John Byris, within the said Richert his hous, undir his commandiment.

SUPERVISION OF TRADESMANSHIP.

The quhilk day, the deikin declairand will agains Ritchert Kirkland, be himself, and the maisteris aggrieand togidder, decerins the said Ritchert for his wrang and offence foirsaid to pay four pundis to the commoun weill of the craft, and xvi s. to the bailzeis; and requeistis the proveist and bailzeis to interpone thair authoritie heirto.

xxiiij Aprilis 1616.

The quhilk day, anent the complaint and wrang persewit be Alexander Blair, and his spous, agains James Gray, wobster, for spilling and wrang working of ane small linning wob, in casting in round hardin yearine in the midis thairof, exceiding four ellis lang, quhilk spillis the pryce of the wob. Quhilk complaint hard, and the wob dewlie sichtit in presens of the deikin and maisteris, thai all in ane voice, upone thair conscience, declairit the samin to be unsufficient work, and that the same will hurt the pryce of the wob. Thairfor thai all in ane voice decerne the said James, for the unsufficient work, to pay to the box fourtie schillinges, with xvj s. to the bailzies, and to keip the wob to himself, and pay to the said Alexander and his spous fiftein schillinges vj d. for ilk ell thairof, being tuell in numbir, quhilk thai, upone thair conscience, declair ilk ell of the samin wald be worthe give it had bein sufficientlie wrocht, requeisting the proveist and bailzies to interpone thair authoritie heirto for the weill of the leiges.

They, however, did not always punish for an offence, which may have been the first, and was probably somewhat alleviated by his "awin confessioune":—

Sexto Septembris 1623

The quhilk day, John Blair, weifer, of his awin confessioune, is tryit and convict for unsufficient work, for the quhilk he becomes in the deikin and maisteris willis; and if evir he commit the lyk in tyme cuming, to los and amit his fredome of craft, and nevir to work within this burght again as ane frieman.

W. FLEIMING, clericus. sst

What the offence was that is dealt with in the next two extracts is not quite clear. Warping had evidently to do with it. That had not yet become a separate trade, and the weaver who warped probably had, when a difficulty was experienced, the responsibility of weaving what he had warped:—

xxvij Junij 1627.

The quhilk day, William Reid is decernit to tack back Agnes Bargillie hir wob, warpit be him, and to weif the samin against Loucksmes nixt, the said Agnes

SUPERVISION OF TRADESMANSHIP.

payand to him befoir recept of the wob, xiij s. vi d. of auld debt, and the deikin and maisteris to modifie quhat pryce salbe givin for weifing thairof.

Decimo Augusti 1627.

The quhilk day, the deikin and maisteris all in ane voice decerins and ordainis Robert Andirsoun elder to imput presentlie Jonet Dowglas, spons to James Fleming, hir wob of lining, as he quha warpit the wob, and promeisit to put the samin in at Lambes last, wes and weif the samin with all diligence, and dischairges him onie uther work quhill the samin be wovin eftir his lumb beis tumb, undir the pain of ane new upset, and that, becaus, it is cleirlie provin his promeis and conditioun.

The boycott is again in evidence, though what the offence was we are not told:—

The nynetein day of August 1629.

The quhilk day, it is statut and ordanit be consent of the deacon and maisteris of craft that quhasoever resavis Thomas Stodart and gifis him service heireftir sall pay tuentie pund to the craft, and fyve pund to the baillies, and to that effect the baill honestmen to be wairnit be the officer.

Mr. G. STIRLING.

The xiiij day of August 1630 yeiris.

The quhilk day, it is statut and ordanit be consent of the haill craft, that, quhasoever he beis of the craft that sall wurk any wark to Robert Smyth, merchand burges of Glasgow sall pay four lit. for well of the craft and xxxij s. to the baillzeis.

The arm of the law was sometimes called in to deal with refractory craftsmen, but even here dire penalties are only laid down for a recurrence of the offence:—

The 22 day of Julij 1631.

The quhilk day, Robert Dalrimpill being convenit befoir the deacon John Falconer and the maisteris of craft within the hospitall for spilling of ane linyng wob pertenyng to Thomas Grower; and being convick for spilling thairof, he maist schamfullie abusit the deacon and maisteris of craft be his language not wordie to be hard; and being convenit befoir the [blank] George Barklay and Walter Stirling baillzeis, the said Robert was content and with his awin consent that if ever he commit the lyk heireftir, he be thir presentis bindis himsellf to pay fourtie pundis money to craft, and faillyeing payment, to be banissit the towne.

ROBERT DALRUMPIL. With my hand.

SUPERVISION OF TRADESMANSHIP.

We find, however, the same Robert Dalrymple dealt with for another offence and his freedom withdrawn:—

Decemo Februarij 1632.

The quhilk day, the deacon and maisteris of craft be the leist the maist pairt thairof, being convenit togedder within the craftis hospitall, anent the ordour taking with Robert Dalrymple, ane of the friemen of thair craft for laying of warpit wobs in pledge, and for selling of severall persouns wobs and work, to the great scandall of thair craft and calling. Thairfoir they, in ane voice, for eschewing of the lyck in tym cuming, dischairges the said Robert Dalrymple as frieman with them, and of all libertie he had thairof in all tym cuming ay and quhill the said Robert find sufficient cautioun to the said craft that he sall not comit the lyck heireftir, and that he mak satisfaction to the craft for the scandell, and als mak satisfaction to Robert Ros and his spous, and Jonet Hogisyaird, pairties damnifeit be him, and discharges him of his libertie quhill then.

A less penalty is enacted against the next offender:—

xliij Novembris 1634.

The quhilk [day], the deacon, maisteris of craft, and memberis thairof, being all convenit togidder in the croftis hospitall, for taking ordour with John Kirlie, ane of thair bretherin, anent the wrangs, injuries and great scandall comittit be him and his servandis, oft and divers tymes, in wranging of the Kingis leiges, pairtlie throw not delyvering back of thair work, and pairtlie in spilling thairof, with uther great wrangs comittit be him and his servandis, in the said croft and calling; have, all in ane voice, for remeid of the scandall and wrong comittit oftymes of befoir, notour and qualifeit to the said croft, dischirgit, and, be thir presentis, discharges the said John Kirlie that he, at na tyme heireftir tak nor resseiv nather servant nor prenteis to serve or work with him within this burgh; and they, all in ane voice, understanding his insufficiencie, declair, that it sall not be leasum to him to haiv ony prenteis or servant heireftir notwithstanding of quhatsumevir power or libertie had be him to that effect of befoir.

In a later chapter the agreement with weavers of Gorbals and Bridgend is noticed, but here they have combined with Glasgow in an effort to enforce better workmanship and to restrict the entrance of untrained workmen to the craft:—

At the craftis hospitall of the Burgh of Glasgow the
3 day of Maij 1689.

The whilk day, Robert Jamison, present deacon of the weavers of the said burgh, William Boil, James Alexander elder, John Fleckfeild youngest, John Armour

SUPERVISION OF TRADESMANSHIP.

Robert Spye, John Benford, M'Ilchrest, James Alexander younger, William Watson younger, John Petecrew, John Winning, William Hadway, John Stephen, lait deacon, all maisteris of the said calling, and John Wilson ther present collectour, and haill remanent bretheren of the said weaver trade being all met and conveinned in the said hospitall annent ane supplication given in to them be the poor of the said calling makeing mention how great in number they are and daillie increasing, and the said trade not able to sustain them, sua that many of the said poor is like to sterve in regaird of the callingis povertie, and the reason and cause why the samen is, is by takeing, admitting, and receaving of sua many personis in to be friemen in the said corporation, both of strangers that comes in by force and otheris of friemenis sonis, friemenis sonis in law, and prenteisses without makeing the least shaddow of ane saij, sua that by reason therof the said calling is become innumerouse, and after ther admissioune, is fund noewayes able to perform what they professed, which makes them to turn burdensome to the said calling, and to its ruing, and to the rueing of the forsaidis supplicantis, and they noewayes are found qualified to serve the liges without first they had been joyned to ane saij befor ther admissioune, by omitting wherof hes undone the said calling and poor therof as said is, and clean contrare to the laudable lawes and liberties of all burgh royallis and neighbour callings therin, speciallie the liberties and friedome, actis and statutis of all corporationis within this kingdome who are bond to serve the liges therin by sufficient work, conform to severall actis of parliament made therannent, as the said supplication at more lenth proportis. Whilk supplication above wrytten the said Robert Jamison, deacon and his saidis maisteris and collectour with the haill bodie of the said calling then conveinned haveing taken to ther seriouse considerationis the haill groundis and reasonis therof, and for avoiding of all other incumberances therannent that may araise against the said calling and poor therof in all tyme comeing, they all in one voice (nemine contradicente) with consent and by ordour of John Waddrop, present deacon conveinner as also with consent of the present oversman his assessouris and the most pairt of his bretheren of the weaveris within the regalitie of Gorbellis, who hes the like supplication and act fallowing theron for preservation of ther poor and rights and liberties concerning ther said trade dulie inacted in ther tradis book, the said deacon, maisteris, and collectour and remanent bretheren of the said weaveris of Glasgow, with consent and ordor forsaid, hath statut and ordainned and hereby statutis and ordainis from henceforth and in all tyme comeing, that noe person of whatsomever rank or degree, either of strangeris, friemenis sonis, friemen sonis in law or prenteisses shall be admitted nor receaved friemen within the said corporation without first they be injoyned to ane saij to be prescrived be the deacon for the tyme and some of his maisteris, and saij maisteris appoynted to see him perform the forsaid saij sufficientlie done wpon ther oath of weritie, and the saijs that are to be prescrived are whatever the person craveing to be admitted shall profess, and he is to consign of saij money thrie poundis; and if the saij soo prescrived be sufficientlie don be him who desyres to be frie, he is to be receaved in as ane frieman be payceing his dewes conform to use and wont; and if the saij be not sufficientlie performed, he is not to be receaved nor admitted. And what deacon and maisteris hereafter shall happen to breck or contradick any pairt of this present act shall be lyable with consent of the said haill calling in the soume of tuentie poundis Scottis money proportionalie to be payed to the deacon and maisteris for the tyme sua aft and how aft it shall happen them to transgrese any pairt of this present act in all tyme comeing; and the samen fyn to be payed in to the collectour for the tyme for the use and behoufe of poor of the said calling, attour that the transgressaris hereof shall be holden and reput as breckeris of the laudable custome rights and liberties of the forsaid corporation and all other corporationis within this kingdome. And this they ordaine to stand as ane perpetuall act unalterable in all tyme comeing. And ordainned me undersubscryver ther clerk for that effect to subscrive thir presents for them and in ther names.

(Signed) R. FYNNISONE, clerk.

VII.
MEETINGS AND PLACES OF MEETING.

There are no separate records of meetings of the Incorporation, other than those of the Master Court, until last century. The earliest accessible minute book commences in 1591, and a second book brings us continuously to 1683. An account book covers the later part of that period, and continues about forty years beyond it, with, occasionally, resolutions of the Master Court appearing among the accounts, and there is also a book containing headings and extracts from the minute books of the years now amissing. This book has entries as late as 1820, but the part referred to above was probably copied in from the original minute book fifty years earlier. These earlier minute books have afforded the matter of which this book is mainly composed, and their preservation is the principal purpose of its publication. Considering the times, the ideas of those conducting the meetings are exceedingly business-like. Were it possible that such lively proceedings as are referred to in the previous and succeeding chapters could now take place, it is hardly likely that the recorder would set down the details. They were, in these days, not afraid to call a spade a spade, and the natural man spoke out what he thought, giving a reality and picturesqueness even to so prosaic an affair as the records of a trades court meeting.

From 1793 onwards there is more routine and uninteresting matters recorded. Towards the end of the eighteenth and during the first thirty years of the nineteenth century the weaver has become a politician, and there will be found in Chapters X. and XVI. much more reference to the later minuted history of the Incorporation.

The earliest minutes bearing any indication of the locality in which meetings recorded took place name the Hie Kirk or the Session House, but soon after the formation of the Trades' House many are headed Crafts' or Croftis Hospital or Alms House, Stabil Green, and in 1665 one minute bears that the meeting was held in the "foir towre of the Castel of Glasgow." The minute first quoted in Chapter V., dated 1704, gives evidence that the Hospital was built then, and there is great probability that the conjoining of the trades in owning an Almshouse was coincident with their forming themselves into the Trades' House. There is an entry in the burgh records as follows:—

FLITTING OF THE SUBDEAN—15 July 1589.—The quhilk day Mr Patrick Walkinschaw, subdeue of Glasgow, is decernit and ordanit to flitt and remoue himselfe, servandis, and guidis, incontinent, furth and fra ane south mid chalmer, occupiet be him of the tenement of the Almous hous, besyde the Castell.

M'Ure describes the buildings around the Castle of Glasgow as they stood in 1747, evidently to the west of the Cathedral, and the Trades' Hospital referred to is known to have occupied part of the site of the Townhead Gasworks. His description is as follows:—

"Adjoining [the Castle] is St Nicholas' Chapel and Hospital, removed in 1808 to permit of the formation of St Nicholas' Street, now St. Nicholas' Place. To the left, is the *Alms House* or *Old Trades' Hospital*, with its Gable and Belfry fronting the street and projecting over the Footway. It was erected during the 17th Century as a Retreat for a certain number of reduced Members of the 14 Incorporated Crafts, and stood upon the site occupied in earlier times by the Prebendal Manse of Morebattle. Probably an older Building of the same nature preceded this."

"The Trades' House lodged and boarded in it first 5, and afterwards 13 poor Freemen of the *Trades' rank* i.e. *Mechanics* who were styled *The Poor Men of the House.* They were clothed in an ample Coat, Waist Coat, and Knee-Breeks of blue serge, with blue Hose having lappets over the latchets and heels of the Brogue-Shoes, which were stuffed with straw. Attached to the House was a small hall where the Members of the Trades' House used to meet prior to the erection of the Trades' Hall in Glassford Street, in 1791, decorated by 14 Paintings, emblematic of the several Trades, by 6 Portraits of Benefactors to the Charity, and by Inscriptions recording the gifts of others. In Oct., 1806, a Committee reported that the whole ground, including the Alms House, should be sold by public Roup, at 7s 6d a square yard. On the 21st March, 1807, the ground, with the Building, was sold at 12s. 1d. a square yard, to the Incorporation of Cordiners, the price being converted at 5 per cent. into a Ground Rent of £131 14s 2d. The Cordiners sold the ground to the first Gas Company, and it now forms a part of the site of their present Works."

Many of the minutes do not mention any place of meeting, but the probability is that, generally, until 1683 the meetings were held in

MEETINGS AND PLACES OF MEETING.

the Crafts' Hospital, but on special occasions the adjacent buildings in the Castle and Cathedral were made use of.

In the eighteenth century there are entries of meetings in the Laigh Church and the Tron Church as well as the places named above.

The records from 1793 till the present time generally name the new Trades' Hall as place of meeting, but frequently public-houses are mentioned, especially in the early part of last century. For the last sixty years the Trades' House, Glassford Street, has been the usual place of meeting for the Master Court and the Incorporation.

VIII.
DISCIPLINE.

The position of deacon, as we saw in Chapter II., was eagerly sought after and considered desirable, but, as will be seen from what follows, the rose was not without its thorn. He seems to have had more than his share of the rough tongue of those who differed from him. In many cases the language was considered too flagrant for verbatim record, and, by deduction from what is set down, it must have been "painful and free." The gentler sex are the first offenders in the records :—

Secundo Novembris 1594

The dekin and haill craft ordaius that nane of them work work to Elspay Mitchell and Marion Watirson heireftir under the pane of ane new upset, and that becaus the said. twa wemen ar vast slanderaris of Robert Dobbie and Allane Uinzet, twa honest men of thair craft.

Duodecimo Maij 1597

The dekin and maisteris of craft discharges and inhibitis Malie Brysoun, David Gemmill, and Williame Gemmill, in ony sort, to trubill, be word or deid, Agnes Bargillie, spous to Alexander Gemmill in ony tymes to cum wnder the pane of ane new wpset to the craft, and thre lib. to the sessioun of Glasgow. As also dischargis the said Williame being trublesum to the said Agnes of ony ferder working with the said Alexander. As also inhibitis the said Agnes to be trublesum be word or deid to ather of the saidis Malie, David or Williame heireftir, wnder the pane of ane new upset and thrie lib. to the kirk.

But even the men are not able to keep their counsel, and an enactment of secrecy is necessary :—

ANENT REVILARIS.   Decimo tertio Novembris 1602.

The dekin, maisteris, and haill craft statutis and ordenis that quhaever of the craft being dekin and maisteris presentlie or sall happin to be heireftir, and for the weale of thair craft, sall convein and advise amang thameselfis for the weale of thair craft in thair privie conference and counsile, and ony of thame that salbe on counsile sall revile the woittis and jugementis of the said dekin and maisteris to ony of quhome thai salbe in conference, salbe reconit wnvorthie to be in counsile, and salbe put out of his office, and another placed in the same.

DISCIPLINE. 63

The two extracts following show that the offended in the earlier, has become the offender in the later entry, the case being altered evidently altering the case:—

Die xx Augusti 1603.

The quhilk day, William Wood is decernit to cum in the deakynis will of xvj s. unlaw for invading and geving evill wordis to Robert Stewart in his awin hous, he being ane maister of craft.

The quhilk day, the deakin and haill brethrene of craft condicendis that William Baird sall not be resavit in service with na freman of the craft unto the tyme he mak satisfactioun to Richard Kirkland, deakin of the wrang done to him.

Die xij July 1604

The quhilk day, Archibald Patersoun, deakin, accompaneit with his maisteris and haill bretherene of craft, hes statute and ordanit all in ane voce that give onie brother of craft in tym coming sall misuse his deikin ather in word or deid, or yit mak onie tumult in presens of the deikin to onie brother ather be word or deid, quhat brother contravenis sall pay ane new upsett, and xvj s. to the baillies, and mak amendis at the deakin and bretherenis willis. And in the meintyme Richard Kirkland is becum in the deakynis will for the offence done be him to the deakin, and the said Richard hes satisfeit for the wrang.

J. CRAIG. sst

Here the penalty of banishment is threatened for "misreport":—

Die viij Februarij 1606.

The quhilk day, Cudbert Miller of his awin consent and content, that give it be fund that he mak misreport quhat langage betuix ony fremen of the craft in tym to cum, that he can not qualifie; the first tyme he beis convict thairof to be baneist the toun, nor yit blaspheme ony maister he is with in service.

The next extract shows what measures were taken to enforce the payment of fines imposed by the Master Court:—

Decimo quarto Februarij 1607.

Quhilk day, the dekin, maisteris and haill craft understanding that Williame Kirkland, ane of thair brether of craft, with his awin hand, for obedience of the decreit of the said maisteris decerning him to paye sex lib. for his wrang to the dekin, delyverit ane hagbut and ane pan of his, quhilk hes lyin lang wnloosit, and he, chargit to rodeme the same be paying of the said sex lib., refusit. Thairfore the said dekin, maisteris and haill craft ordenis the saming to be tane to the mercat croce of this burght incontinent, and thair to be roppit be thre sworne men of the craft, and silveir maid thairof for paying of the said sex lib. swa far as the saming will extend to.

DISCIPLINE.

The unruly member causes many of the enactments, and at this period seems to have been a fruitful source of trouble to the deacon and his masters:—

Decimo quarto Novembris 1607

Quhilk daye, the dekin, maisteris, and haill craft hes statut and ordanit, and be thir presentis statutis and ordanis according to equitie and ressoun, that nane of thair craft sall blaspheme the blessit name of God heireftir, sclander or traduce ane of thame wtheris in ony tyme to cum wnder the pane of xiij s. iiij d. money to be payit be the contravenar heirof to the dekin of the craft, and making repentance to the persone sclanderit or traduced by the unlaw of the kirk, and making publict repentatioune as the kirk and sessioun sall prescryve.

Sexto Februarij anno 1608.

The quhilk day, the deikin and maisteris of craft haifing weill considerit the misbehaviour of Daniell Bryce, prenteis to Thomas Bryce, to the said Thomas his maister, and of the schamefull and blasphemeous language givin to his said maister, hes thairfoir all in ane voice, for the said contempt and dissobedience, and for the said Daniellis depairting frome his said maister, dischargeit and refuisit him as ane prenteis in the craft, and to have na priveledge thairin as ane burges sone, unto sick tyme as he give in his supplicatioun to the deikin and maisteris offering him be thair sicht to mak ane condigne amendis thairfoir to the said Thomas, and that he repair his said wrang.

The authority of even the "baillie" is not sufficient to compel the attendance of the next offender, and his words as recorded hardly warrant the severe sentence imposed. Debarring him from work would not facilitate the payment of the fine:—

Vigesimo quarto mensis Octobris anno 1612.

The quhilk day, Johne Clark, deikin of wobsteris and haill maisteris thairof being conveinit for ordour taking with Michall Wilsoune for his misbehaviour to the deikin in thir wordis following: The said Michall being personallie warnit be the craftis officer to compeir this day compeirit not, the haill maisteris, he dew tryell and examinatioun of witnessis, findis the said Michall to have injurit the said Johne, his deikin, in thir wordis, saying to him quhen he was commandit be the baillies authoritie and deikins command to deliver ane wob, that he wald not deliver the same for him and all the wobsteris of Glasgow, and for saying to the deikin, I cair not ye man, yow hes done ma wranges to the wobsteris, I sall tell ane wors taill of ye, with monie ma injurious wordis. Thairfoir, for his contempt to the deikin and dissobedience in not compeirance, the haill maisteris in ane voice decerins the said Michall to pay ane new upset to the craft, and five pundis to the baillies, and ordainis him to be dischairgit of labour quhill the upset and baillies unlaw be payit, at leist during the baillies and deikinis will, and requeistis the bailzeis of this burgh to interpone thair authoritie heirto.

DISCIPLINE.

The readers of the present day will be, like the delinquent mentioned in the following extract, unable to understand how his offence could be hurtful to the craft. "Sicht" was, no doubt, to inspect, and "graythe" was the material with which the weaver wrought, but the present writer has been unable to discover the meaning of "wissie":—

Vigesimo primo Aprilis anno 1613.

The quhilk day, Wm Kirkland, present, being accuisit for going to Govane, without leif of the deikin and maisteris, to sicht and wissie wobsteris work and graythe, the said William confessit his offence, with protestatioune solemlie maid, that he understuid not the samin to be hurtfull to the commoun weill of the craft, and thairfoir become in the deikin and maisteris willis for his offence, promeising nevir to do the lyk in na tymes cuming.

Thaireftir, the deikin and maisteris declairing thair willis, decerins the said William Kirkland to pay to the commoun weill four pundis of penultie, and all in ane voice decerins and declair him, and all uther frieman of the craft quhatsmevir that comittis the lyk offence in tyme cuming, to be simpliciter secludit fra beiring of office in the craft, and fra all voit in electioune for evir.

The two extracts following deal with the same case; the method enjoined for making amends we should have thought would have commended itself to Alexander Gemmill. He may have been, if such a person was known in these days, a teetotaler:—

ix Martij 1614.

The quhilk day, Allexander Gemmill being accuisit befoir the bretherein of craft for blaspheming of his deikin, Georg Schirilaw, in calling him dyvour loun, not wordie to be deikin, with utheris sclanderous wordis conteinit in the bill of complaint, the said Allexander, present of his awin frie will, uncoactit or compellit, come in the maisteris and remanent bretherein present thair willis for his offence, subjecting himself to thair decrie thairanent. The haill maisteris present with sundrie utheris of the craft, in ane voice, decerins the said Allexander, in all humilitie, to drinck to the said Georg, and confes his fault faythfullie, promeising nevir to commit the lyk, and to pay of unlaw four pundis, to be usit be the deikin and maisteris advys, with xvi s. to the baillies requeisting the proveist and baillies to interpone thair anthoritie to this decreit.

Sexto Maij 1614.

The quhilk day, the maisteris and haill craft in ane voice concludis, that Allexander Gemmill, wobster, sall nevir heireftir beir office in the craft, nather deikin nor maister of craft, and that for his injuring of Georg Schirilaw, his deikin, in calling him ane knaifveische knave, sen his last offence commitit agains the said Georg, untill sick tyme as the said Allexander mak satisfactioune to the deikin and maisteris thairof.

Apparently the next delinquent complied with the sentence imposed, as his case does not recur:—

Primo Maij 1616.

The same day, James Gray, of his awin consent, frelie became in the deikin, maisteris, and haill craftis will, for his offence done to Georg Schirilaw, deikin, in his office, saying that he had done him wrang to move Alexander Blair his wyfe to persew. Thairefter the haill bretherin in ane voice decernit the said James Gray, for his offence, to pay fourtie schillinges to the craft, and xvi s. to the bailzies, and to drink to his deikin and ask him forgiveines thairfoir in all humilitie.

Again the perils of deaconship are in evidence. One threatens the Deacon's life, and another breathes a terrible defiance against him. We may be grateful that the office is now free of such terrors:—

(1-5-1616)

The same day, the maisteris all in ane voice, decernis Robert Findlay in ane wrang, be probatioun of famous witnessis, for injuring of John Baird, his deikin, in saying to him, away furt of my sicht, I sall put ane knyfe to thi heart; and thairfoir is decernit to pay ane new upset, and ordanit to be dischargit of labour, ai and quhill he satisfie the deikin in homage, be the maisteris sicht.

xix Maij 1619.

The quhilk day, anent the bill and complaint, givin in be Archibald Patersoun, deikin, agains Thomas Aiking, for injuring of him,—saying, he defyit him, he sould nevir get ane amendis of him, and he war hangit and all that wald tack his pairt; the said Thomas, present, denyit the bill. Thaireftir the haill maisteris, haifing dewlie tryit the complaint, and examinat diveris and sundrie famous witnessis thairupone, all in ane voice decernis the said Thomas in ane wrang for injuring of his deikin in the wordis foirsaid; dewlie provin, and, thairfoir, decernis the said Thomas to pay ane new upset to the box, for the commoun effairs of the craft, with xl. s. to the bailzies, and als to be dischargeit of labour quhill he first satisfie the upset, and ask the deikin forgiveines upone his kneis, and the haill craft publictlie, and be reconceillit to thame again befoir he be ressaveit frie, and declairis the new upset to be tuentie pundis; requeisting the proveist and bailzies to interpone thair authoritie heirto.

7 February 1621.

The same day, Archibald Thomesoun become in the deikin and maisteris will for his offence in speiking injuriouslie agains the deikin, being laufulie prohibeit to give work to prenteis or servand, quhill thai war buikit in the craftis buik.

Many similar incidents appear about this period, and they are

DISCIPLINE. 67

given here as records of what constituted offences as well as how the Master Court dealt with such offenders:—

xv Maij 1621.

The same day, Harie Davidsoune heirby bindis, actis, and obleissis himself of his awin consent, to pay to the deikin and maisteris tuenty pundis money, and fyve pundis to the bailzies, in caice he be tryit heireftir to injure be word John Patersoun, weifer.

Vigesimo octavo June 1621.

The quhilk day, anent the complaint givin in be John Clark, deikin, agains Williame Allansoune, for injuring him in his office, becaus he commandit him to weife James Hallis wob, saying to him he durst not luik in ane bailzies faice, thrawing his faice and girning contemptibilly upone him as deikin. The maisteris and haill craft present, haifing dewlie tryit the complaint, findis that the said William, contrar to the actis of craft, hes injurit his deikin in his office, speiking to him contemptibilly, without reverence, the wordis foirsaidis, thrawing his faice and grinning dispytfullie upone his deikin, and als persisting thairin, contemptibilly, this day, the tyme of his censour. And thairfoir is decernit and ordainit to pay ane new upset to the box, and threttie tua s. to the bailzies, and to be dischairgit of labour quhill the same be payit, and nevir to be reput ane frieman again. Requeisting the bailzies to interpone thair anthoritie heirto.

Quarto Julij 1621

The quhilk day, William Kirkland, weifer, is become actit, bund, and obleist, of his awin consent, as cationner for William Allansoun, weifer, that he sall concent and pay to the craft and box, the sowme of twentie pundis money, for ane new upset, and that at sick terme, and tyme, as thai sall appoynt and designe for his offence committit agains the deikin.

(Signed) WILLIAM KIRKLAND.

The same day, the said William Allansoun is become actit and obleist of his awin consent, to warrand, releife, and skaytles keip the said William Kirkland of his becomeing cationn for him for the upset abovewrittin, and of all danger he can incure thairthrow.

W. FLEMING. sst

Then there follow about the spiciest in the whole records. John Patersoune seems to have fallen foul of two deacons in succession, and to have had a remarkable gift of invective. The picturesqueness of his language shows that the weavers of the seventeenth century had an earlier form of these imaginative qualities which gave us the weaver poets of a later period:—

Septimo November 1621.

The quhilk day, John Patersoune, present, confessit that he reckleslie, and in his angir had offendit his deikin, John Baird, in thir wordis, saying to him the divill tir the skin af him, for the quhilk he become in the deikin and maisteris will, subvirting himself to thair sentence and decreit, quha all in ane voice decernit the said Johne Patersoune to pay four pundis penultie, and to ask the said John Baird forgiveines upone his kneis in all humilitie, and in the meantyme the maisteris referis the four pundis in the deikinis will.

Septimo August 1622

The quhilk day, Michaell Scot is decernit to deliver to John Clark, weifer, ane beim, grantit and confessit be him to be borrowit fra the said John ane yeir syne, or thairby, or ellis fourtie schillinges thairfoir; and that, becaus, the said Michaell allegit he deliverit the same to John Patersoune at his command, and failzeit to prove the same, diveris termis being assignit to him for that effect.

Vigesimo primo Decembris 1622.

The quhilk day, in presens of the maisteris of the weiferis of the brughe of Glesgow, William Kirkland, Johne Patersoune, and George Patersoune, his brother, weiferis, all personnalie present, ar fund and tryet, be probatioune of famous witnessis, led and ressavet against them, to hawe injured and contemned John Clark, thair present deikin, in thir wordis fallowing:—That is, the said Williame Kirkland, for saying, within the tolbuithe, about ten dayes since or thairby, quhen, as the said Johne Clarke was pleiding befoir the bailzeis with the said George—"fye, fye," ife I had beine thair, I sowld have raschet ane quhinger in him, and maid the craft quyt of black Jocke. And the said Johne Patersoun for saying, that, the said Johne Clarke was thryse mensworne the day of his electioun, and at the Hallow court last, for saying to him, in his faice, contemptabillie, that, he and his bund slaves rewlet all the craft. And the said George Patersoune for saying to him,—I sall skinne thy chaftes, and tack ane buckie afe thy cheike, and als for vanting of his injures and wranges done to the said Johne Clarke sen syne, saying, that, he had gart him play clatter on the cassie lyk ane awld pige, and that he and his brother had woundit him wpon the heid with ane beime stalfe heid. Thairfoir thei and everie ane of them ar decernet in ane wrang thairfoir; and ilk ane of them decernet to pay ane new upsett to the craft, with threttie twa schillinges, ilk ane of them, to the bailzeis of Glesgow, for thair injure and contempt of thair deiking; and ar ordaint to be discharget of labour quhill the samin be payet; and ilk ane of them decernit and ordainet to aske the said Johne Clark, thair deikin, forgivenes publictlie wpon thair kneis.

DISCIPLINE. 69

These worthies do not seem to have had any greater respect for places than they had for persons, and there is a Gilbertian "fitting of the punishment to the crime" in the sentence pronounced in the Andirsoun case given below:—

Quinto Maij 1624.

The quhilk day, Thomas Aiking, weifer, is fund and tryit be probatioun of famous witnessis, led and ressaveit and examinat, to have sclanderit and injurit Thomas Andersoun, deikin, in John Lockis hous, nyne nightis bygain, in calling him ane ruger and river, and ane oppressour, and thairfoir is decernit to pay ane new upset to the box, and threttie tua schillinges to the bailzies, and is dischairgit of labour quhill he pay ane new upset, and ask the deikin forgivnes upone his kneis, requesting the proveist and bailzies to interpone thair authoritie heirto.

Undecimo die mensis Augusti 1627.

The quhilk day, Robert Andersoune, weifer, is fund and tryit, be probatioun of famous witnessis, to have injurit and wrongit James Grahame, his present deikin, within the Hie Kirk, upone the aucht day of August, instant, saying to him, dispytfullie, that he spack untreuth and the *divill rug out the leyeris saull*, with monie ma injurious wordis, without respect or regaird of his office. And thairfoir the maisteris of craft, present, all in ane voice, decernis and ordainis the said Robert Andersoun, personallie present, to pay tuentie merkis of upset *ad pios usus* for the commoun us of the craft, with fourtie schillinges to the bailzies, and als to *sit doun upone his kneis* within the bodie of the Hie Kirk, and thair ask the deikin forgivenes, and be reconceallit to him again.

The penult. day of August 1628.

The quhilk day, the deacon and maisteris of craft being convenit in the hospitall for taking ordour with William Cuthbert for abusing of the deacon and being fund that he had sua donne; thairfoir the said deacon and maisteris of craft decernit and ordanit that nane of the craft gave him wark wndir the pane of ane upset to be put in the box be the deacon and maisteris of craft; and that ay and quhill he satisfie the deacon and craft.

The offences become less flagrant for a time. One wonders why it was always the deacon who got the benefit, but, from the record immediately following, others, unnamed, were sometimes included. They seem also to have sometimes fallen foul of each other, and the second record below gives an instance where two are bound over to keep

DISCIPLINE.

the peace. William Pollok evidently believed that a Glasgow weaver's house was his castle, and his extract runs closely in force of language some of those recorded above:—

The xiij day of November 1630.

The quhilk day, the deacon and maisteris of craft being convenit in the hospitall it [is] fund be them that Robert Boik had slanderit his [deacon] and certain honest men of the craft and thairfoir it was statut and ordanit be thame that the said Robert sould hauf na wark quhill he satisfeit the deacon for the said slandir; as lyk, befoir the said Robert be admittit frieman with craft, he to pay the utermaist as any hes payit of befoir.

The 7 day of August 1631.

The quhilk day, it is statut and [ordanit] be the deacon and maisteris of craft, that if it sall happin John Kirlie to slandir Petir Finnesoune or any uther of the craft be his schamefull language, or the said Petir to slandir the said Kirlie or any utheris of the craft and being convick, to pay twentie pund to the well of the craft or be beneissit the toune. Quhairwith, the saidis persounes being present was content, and commandit me, notary, undirsubscryvand, to subscryve for thame, layand thair hand to the pen.

Mr G. STIRLING

Quinto Maij 1632 yeirs.

The quhilk day, William Pollok, weifer, burges of Glasgow, being present, and accusit be the deacon befoir the craft for injuring and wranging of the deacon, and violentlie putting of him furthe of his hous, the deacon being present thair, with sum of his brethern, for taking furthe of the said Thomas his lume, certan work, and for inputting thairintill ane pair plaids, perteining to Thomas Andersoun; the said William Pollok, not onlie violentlie output the said deacon and theis present with him furthe of the said hous schoiring to strek them, bot als avowit and utterit thir words, that in despyte of the deacon and all the craft, he sould not work the foirsaids plaids, nor that na work sould be tane furt of his lumes be the deacon nor his maisteris in despyt of thair hartis. Quhilk being all verifeit and cleirlie provin be famous witnessis ressevit sworne and admittit in presens of the said William befoir the said craft, the present maisteris thairof ordanes the said William for the foirsaid wrang comittit be him to the deacon to pay ane new fyne and upset to the craft, and to satisfie the baillzies of Glasgow conforme to the ordour; and the said William Pollok being present as said is becom in the craftis will, quha gave furthe thair will and declaratioun in maner foirsaid.

The deacon and his court seem to have had some powers of

imprisonment, which surely were rarely exercised, as this is the only occasion on which they are referred to:—

19 Augusti 1644.

Findis Charles Snyp to [have] dissobeyed and wrangit the dekine and thairfoir ordains him to go to ward and thair to remyane xlviij houris or langer at the dekins will.

There is a lengthy spell of orderly conduct, which makes the records uninteresting reading, and it is evidently felt that when two cases do occur, there is no need for summary procedure, so a word of caution is sufficient:—

Sexto Maij 1670.

The same day, Walter Dobbie, weaver, is heirby become actit that he sall carrie himselfe soberlie and discreitlie towards his deacone of tred present and to come, and sall not upbraid them ather be word or deid under the paine of ane new upsett and to be farder punished at the will of the deacon and maisteris of craft.

12 November 1670.

The same day, John Jamisounne elder, and John Glen, weaveris, are bothe of them heirby become actit of ther awne consentis to carrie them selfes bothe civeallie and discreitlie towards otheris, and sall not flyt, backbyt or miscall on another as they have done heirtofoir, and that in no tyme comeing they sall truble or mollest otheris nither be word or deid utherwayes then be ordour of law and justice and that under the paine of twentie punds Scotis to be payit in be ilk them to the deacone and his successouris for the use of the poore be this act subscrivit befoir thir witnessis John Maxwell and John Findlay, weaveris.

(Signed) JOHNE JAMISOWNE
(Signed) PATRICIUS CLARK, notarius, pro Glen, subscribo.

The last recorded case is mainly of interest for the undetailed "punishment of his persone" referred to. We are left to imagine the form that was to take:—

At Glasgow the twentie twa day of March 1672.

The quhilk day, compeired Robert Maxwell, weaver, burges of the said burgh, and forswamikle as he hes bine fund giltie heirtofoir of scandelizing and reproching of his deacones name and utheris, quhilk fault is now past and remittit to him and forgivine upon his promeis of amendiament in tyme comeing. Therfor the said Robert Maxwell heirby inacts and obleissis him of his awne confessioune that he sall carray himselfe civellie in tyme comeing towards his present deacone and maisteris of the said weavers tread, and sall not scandelize reproche or miscall them or ther successouris in office deacones and maisteris thairof, bot behave himselfe civillie in all things as becometh, and that under the paine of fyftie pundis money, by and attour punishment of his persone at the will of the baillies for the tyme be this act subscrivit befoir thir witnessis William Crightoune, ane of the ordinar officeris of the said burgh and Patrick Clark, wrytter thair and heirof.

(Signed) ROBERT MAXWELL,—

William Crichtoun, witnes; Patrick Clark, witnes.

Whether such cases occurred in the hundred years or so following 1672 we have no records to show, but towards the end of the eighteenth century and onwards they are completely absent.

IX.

MONEY MATTERS.

It is now difficult for us to realise the primitiveness of accounting and dealing with money matters over three hundred years ago. A bank was started in England in Cromwell's time, and the second in the kingdom was the Bank of Scotland, started in 1695. Education, to a degree which qualified to keep accounts, was somewhat exceptional; consequently when money had to be collected from members the usual voucher was the fact of the transaction being done in presence of members, and likewise the only security of its actual deposit was the same publicity and a box locked with several keys. These old boxes remain, and an illustration is given of the boxes used for safe keeping of the Incorporation's funds by the deacon and collector, until the day of banks. This explanation makes the following early entries comprehensible:—

Quarto Novembris 1592.

The dekin and maisters of craft and remanent brethren thairof heif statut and ordanit that none of thair commoun guidis be ressavit be the dekin except that the maisteris of craft be present at the ressat thairof, and that the saming be input in thair box, to be furthcumand to the weal of thair haill craft.

Quarto Novembris 1592.

The dekin, maisteris, and haill craft for bringing of thair quarter wages to ane gud end hes statut and ordanit that thair haill quarter wages extending to foure s. to ilk ane of thair craft be brocht in ane haill sowme at the election of thair dekin and befor his choosin be delyverit to the dekin, and quhilk of the craftismen hes not thair quarter wages in readines than salbe poyndit incontinent thairefter for payment ilk ane of thame for vj s. viij d.

Irregularities in payment were bound to occur, and one means of bringing pressure to bear on defaulters was "No payment, no vote":—

Decimo sexto Novembris 1608.

The same day, the deikin, maisteris and haill craft understanding that thair is unthankfull payment maid of thair commoun guidis, and specially thair quarter waiges,—Thairfoir thai have all in ane voice statut, ordanit, and concludit, that thair sall na frieman in tyme cuming have voit in electioune of thair deikin and quartermaisteris untill sick tyme as thai have compleitlie payit to the auld deikin thair quarter waigis, unlawis, and upsetis quhatsnmevir thai salbe put into.

The irregularities are, however, not all outside the deacon and his "maisters," and an ordinance is made that the deacon is to make all outlays from his own pocket, during the whole of his term of office, and only to be recouped on presenting his account of outlays on demitting office:—

Octavo Augisti anno 1610.

The quhilk day, the deikin, maisteris and remanent memberis of the wobstercraft being convenit haifing weill considerit the greit hurt and los that hes befallin thame be the decay of thair commoun guidis, pairtlie be thair deikinis intromissioune thairwith, and pairtlie be the ressaveing of friemen, prenteissis and servandis for meane pryces beyond the tennour of the lettere of deikinheid, sua that except remeid be provydit thairto thair haill commoun guidis will decay. Thairfoir, and for remeid thairof, the deikin maisteris and haill craft all in ane voice with ane willing mynd and consent, have statut, ordanit, and concludit, that in all tymes cuming thair salbe nather frieman prenteis nor servand admitit, ressaveit, and buikit, bot at quarter courtis, and upone sick pryces and sownes as is appointit and designit in thair lettere of deikinheid and the samin sownes nawayes to be intromettit with be thair deikin, conforme to the auld us, bot sall be immediatlie at payment be put in the box, and nane sall be buikit quhill thair upset, prenteis, and entres silver be laid doun on the box, and na feist to be thairof; and that the deikinis in all tyme cuming sall deburs of thair awin money in the commoun chairges and effairis of the craft quhill the end of his office, and sall mell with nane of the commoun guidis bot allanirly the quarter comptis. And quhatevir beis restand awand to the deikin at the fut of his compt salbe than payit to him at the end and fut of his compt, and quhill payment to him thairof, he sall detein and keip in his possessioune the box, ben chartour, and uther wreitis of the craft that ar givin the deikinis in keiping. To the observing of the quhilk act and statut as being set doun to the weill of the craft, the haill memberis of craft bindis and obleissis thame and to stand and abyd thairat but contradictioune, undir the pane of perjurie.

There are no accounts extant until a much later date, but apparently at no time in the early history of the craft was there any capital fund. The Incorporation lived hand to mouth, and its dependents received directly in help whatever was collected. There are frequent entries showing that a debt had been incurred, and that consequent efforts were required to meet it. The entry immediately following shows that money matters have been put into the collector's hands:—

(23-3-1611)

The same day, the haill persounes of craft, be thir presentis, ar becum actit and obleist, ilk ane of thame, of thair awin consentis, to contribut and pay xiij s. 4 d. to the box for releif of thair debt of ane hunderethe merkis money, awand to John Clark, dekin, to be payit compleitly to Johne Patersoune younger, collectour, appointit befoir the first day of Maij nixtocome, and quha evir beis unpayit thairat sall pay xx s. but contradictioune.

W. FLEMYNG sst

Ultimo Decembris 1613.

The same day, payit be John Clark to Georg Schirilaw four pundis for the owtintownes payment, with fourtie schillinges spent in expenssis, in respect quhairof, the said John aucht to be exonorit.

Septimo Octobris 1615.

The quhilk day, the haill craft have condiscendit of thair awin consentis to pay amangst thame, conforme to thair awin offeris, in row, xl li. for releif of thair commoun debt, compleitlie, befoir Hallow day nixt, and quhaevir beis unpayit upone the secund day of November nixt, sall pay the doubill thairof of thair awin consentis.

Decimo quarto Novembris 1615.

The quhilk day, in presens of the haill maisteris, Georg Schirilaw and John Clark have tane upone thame the payment of the commoun debtis, awand be the craft to Thomas Gray, and to the said John, for payment quhairof, the maisteris grantis and assignis to thame the haill stent silvir in William Flemingis handis, and that is to come in with Allane Andirsoun and Johne Muire thair fynis for thair upset, and als to be payit in payment to the said John Clark of all that is awand to him at the fut of his compt. Quhilk thai have acceptit, and obleissis thame presentlie to releif and disburdein the craft of the fiftie pundis awand to Thomas Gray, and of John Clarkis debt.

Signed {GEORGE SCHIRILAW.—with my hand.
{JOHNE CLARK.—with my hand.

An explanation of the strong feelings shown against the Deacon (referred to in Chapter VIII.) may be found in such entries as these:—

xxvii Septembris 1616.

The same day, the deikin and maisteris, all in ane voice, but variance, in consideratioun of the abuis bygain of thair commoun guidis spendit be thair deikinis, with tua or thrie of the maisteris, without ane commoun consent, hes, thairfoir, and for remeid thairof, statut and fullie concludit, that the deikin, heireftir, sall nevir have liberty to spend anie of the commoun guidis exceiding xiij s. iiij d. at ane tyme, without the maist pairt of the maisteris consent thairto; and give he do in the contrar, sall have na allowance thairof in his comptis.

Quinto Octobris 1625.

Nota, that the band registrat in the toun court buikis of fiftie pundis be ane greit number of the craft, is fullie satisfiet and payit be all men except Georg Schirilaw.

Quinto August 1626.

The quhilk day, in presens of William Neilsoun, deikinconveiner, the deikin, maisteris, and haill bretherein of the craft for the maist. It is concludit, statut and ordainit with consent and advys of the haill craft present, that it sall nevir be leasum to the deikin and maisteris of craft to spend in drinking onie of the commoun guidis of the craft, les or mair, for na pretence quhatsumevir, nather sall it be leasum to the deikin or maisteris, be privat or particular consent, to spend or deburs anie of the commoun guidis, in anie caus or occasioun that sall occur heireftir, albeit the bussines be nevir so urgent, without the same be done be advys of the deikin and maist pairt of the maisteris for the tyme, and if thai do in the contrar, the deikin and maisteris doaris, and consentars, sall pay ten merkis *toties quoties* to the box, and sicklyk sall los thair office, and nevir beir office, ather deikin or maister of craft heireftir; nather sall the sowmes debursit without full consent be admitit or allowit in the deikinis compt undir the pain of perjurie to the allowers thairof.

W FLEMING, St.

An outside control of the deacon and his spendings had become necessary, and a practice is enacted which continued for at least a hundred years, the books between 1670 and 1740 being extant, and bearing that the audit of the collector's accounts took place each November, after the election of the new deacon, and always in the presence of the deacon-convener and a bailie:—

xv Decembris 1630.

The said day, the deacone and maisteris of craft be advys of the deacon convenar, deanes, and remanent bretherin of his counsill convenit in the craftis hospitall hes, all in ane voce concludit and ordanit that, in the act of the admissioun of ilk frieman and prenteis, thair ordinar fynis sall be put in the act of thair admissioun according to the guid auld and lawdable custoum to the effect the deacone may be chargit with his intromissoun contre to the buik, and that they mak their compt yeirlie heireftir befoir thair deacon convenare deaconis and bretherine of thair counsill; and farder that they giv doun na fyns nor na pairt thairof to any persone admitit friemen or prenteis without consent of the deacone and haill bretherine of craft; and the contravenar heirof the present deacone and contravenar sall pay to the hall deacons tuentie pundis money.

MONEY MATTERS.

It was a common practice to lend the funds to members, and the following entry shows a transaction and the security given:—

I Robert Haistie, weifer, burges of Glasgow, grant me to hawe borrowit and actuallie ressevit fra Johnne Falconner younger, present deacon of the weiferis of Glasgow, as ane pairt of the money and guidis belonging to the said craft, the sowme of twelf punds money of Scotland with full exoneratioun thairof for evir. Sek sowme of twelf punds money foirsaid I bind and obleis me my airis, executouris and intromettouris with my guds and geir quhatsomevir, to content and pay to the said John Falconner and to his successouris in office, deacones of the said craft betwix and the last day of August nixtocom, with fowre pund of penaltie in caice of failzie; and for his better securitie I hawe presentlie impignorat to him ane muskat with bandileiris and rest to be keipit be him thairfor quhill the said day, so that it be I failzie in payment of the foirsaid sowme betwix and the said day I remese and discharge the said muskat bandileiris and rest to the said John and his foirsaids, and sall nevir claime or pretend ony ryght or kyndnes thairof in ony time heireftir; consenting thir presentis be registrat in the buikis of counsel and sessioun or commisseris buikis of Glasgow, or burght court buikis thairof that executoriallis of horning poynding and warding may pas heirupoun on ane simple charge of sex dayis, and constitutis.———Procuratouris conjunctlie and severallie wrettin be l'atrik Baird, notar in Glasgow subscrivit be him for me and at my command becaus I can not wrett at Glasgow the aucht day of July j^m vj^c threttie ane yeiris befoir thir witnessis William Falconner, weifer burges thair and James Winzet, weifer thair,

Ita est Patricus Baird, notarius publicus in premissis de mandato dicti Roberti Haistie scribere nescien.

    JAMES WINZET, witnes. WILLIAME FACONER, witnes.

Stripped of its wordiness, the following entry looks uncommonly like implying that the deacon's hand was in the box for other than the purposes of the Incorporation:—

Decimo May 1634.

The quhilk day, the deacon, maisteris of craft, and haill bodie thairof, being all conveinit togidder, and having weill considerit the great lose of thair guids the tyme of the deacones electioun, and pairtlie utherwayes be the deacones intromit and uplifting of thair guids in tyme bypast and evill governament of the samen throw not boxing of thair moneyis, have all in ane voce appointit aggriet and ordanit, that it sall not be lawfull nor allowabill be the craft at na tyme heireftir to ony deacon quhatsumevir that sall happin to be electit and chosin the tyme of thair election, viz. the verie day thairof quhatsumevir he sall be happin to bestow or wair to get ony allowance thairof of the craft, bot the samen sall be upon his awin chairges and expenssis; als it is statut, aggriet and ordaint be the deacon, maisteris of craft and memberis thairof, that the haill guidis and geir belonging to the craft will, and in all tyme cuming sall nevir be upliftit nor intromettit with be ony deacon heireftir, nor he na uther persoune nor persounes, bot the samen sall be imboxit for the weill of the craft, thair to remaine quhill the samen be lende furthe; and the deacones haill depursmentis that it sall happin him to be depurs during the haill tyme of thair office, sall be payit and ramburst to them the tyme quhen thair office expyres, conforme to thair compt to be givin in to thair successour and maisteris of craft. And quhasoever of the said craft, at ony time heireftir, sall consent and vote in the contrar of this act above specifeit, sall nevir beir office in the said calling thairof bot haldin and reput as perjurit and infamous people, not worthie to be respectit as memberis of the said craft.

Pressure is evidently required to bring in the quarterly payments, and power to apply that pressure is renewed to the deacon:—

6 November 1643.

The said day, the dekine and maisteris of craft, all in ane voyce, ratefis and approvis the haill former actis sett doun of befoir anent thes who absentis themselfs fra burriellis, and quha cums not to pay thair quarter comptis being warnit in the haill ordinancis thairof; and ordains the dekine to exact the wnlaws af ilk persone contraveineris of the saidis actis without any mitigatioun, and speciallie af all thes who ar now absent fra thair quarter comptis in regaird thair number ar so grait.

The beginning of what has been a large source of revenue to the Trades' House and the crafts is to be traced in the following minutes. This matter is more fully gone into in Chapter XIV.:—

Decimo quinto Aprilis 1650.

Thair is delyverit to the dekine ane hundrethe pundis viz ane hundrethe markis, as ane pairt of the money that was awin to Mr. Johne Herbertsone, and 1. markis out of the box to help to mak up the money quhilk the craft is to pay to the Gorball money.

The said day, the bandis following ar takin out of the box and gevin to the dekine and collectour to tak up the money, or to put to executioun, viz., viz., William Algees, of 200 markis, James Sympsone of 100 mark, Archibald Leis of 100 markis, Johne Falconer 50 markis, Robert Merschell 100 markis.

24 Julij 1650.

The said day, Robert Merschell and Johne Falconeris bandis ar agane put in the box, and the 400 markis contenit in the wther three band above writtin, with the hundrethe pundis that was in the dekines hand, conforme to the former memorandum, and fyftie markis now delyverit to the dekin out of the box, with 100 markis he receavit fra Robert Hall, compleitis to him the sevine hundrethe markis was payit out be the dekine to the dekine convener in pairt payment of the 1000 markis promiest be the craft for performing the Gorballis bargane.

MONEY MATTERS.

There are frequent records of entry monies received under the agreement with Gorbals and Bridgend weavers referred to in Chapter XI. One is given here:—

3 November 1651.

The said day, Patrik Bryce producit twentie markis quhilk he had fra the Gorball men, quhilk is put in the box.

The Trades' House makes an annual distribution of the respective shares from Gorbal lands, the purchase of which is referred to above:—

At the craftis hospitall.
The tuentie fourt day of August 1663 yeiris

The same day, ther is putt in the box tuenty fyve pundis money receavit of the Gorball rent for the crope and yeir of God 1662.

From about 1670 there are extant complete accounts of all intromissions, and one of these is reproduced here; the account is in Scots money—*i.e.*, a shilling Scots = a penny sterling:—

At the Craftis hospitall of the Burgh of Glasgow wpon the elevinth day of October j^m vj^c and seavintie twa yearis being convined Patrick Bryce present deacon-conviner and Simone Tennent ane of the brethrine of his counsell, John Patersone, present deacone of weaveris with his quartermaisteris and bodie of the calling who for the most pairt war present for the affgiving of John Cochrane, present collector to the said calling his compt of his intromissionne with the craftis guids and geir the year preceiding and his debursmentis thairof as fallowis in charge and discharge.

CHARGE.

In the first the compter charges himselfe with the sowme fallowing receavit fra John Maxwell lait collector at the giving off of his compt.—	13	13	0
Item receavit at Hallow court of quarter comptis—	6	2	0
Item receavit att Hallow court for booking of Jonet Stevins man	0	13	4
Item receavit of quarter comptis at the deacones ellectione quhilk was in the box.—	8	14	0
Item receavit of yeard maill fra John M'Kie	26	13	4
Item receaved fra John Woodrow, maltman for ane yearis annuelrent of 200 markis.—	8	0	0

MONEY MATTERS.

Item receavit fra Patrick Lang the Mertimes and Whitsonday termes maill of his hous.—	20	0	0
Item for the said twa termes maill fra John Findlay for his hous—	16	0	0
Item fra John Walker, cuik for the maills of his hous the said twa termes.—	9	0	0
Item fra John M'Nair for his friedome fyne.—	5	0	0
Item fra John Young for his Mertimes and Whitsonday maills of his hous.—	20	0	0
Item fra John Lang for his Mertimes maill	10	0	0
Item fra Jonet Gibsone for her Mertimes and Whitsonday maill.—	8	0	0
Item fra William Reid of freidome fyne	5	0	0
Item for booking of James Gallis man	4	0	0
Item for William Snyps fridome fyne	5	0	0
Item for booking of Patrick M'Morrie	2	0	0
Item for booking of Robert Patersones man	2	0	0
Item for booking of James Alexanderis man	2	0	0
Item for booking of Robert Flaikfeildis men	4	15	4
Item fra Allane Marchell for a yearis maill	10	13	4
Item for William Watsone for his freidome fyne	5	0	0
Item for John Jamfrayes fridom fyne	5	0	0
Item fra James Foyer for his fridom fyne	5	0	0
Item from David Hoge	5	0	0
Item for booking of John M'Murries man	2	0	0
Item for John Flaikfeilds man	2	0	0
Item of quarter comptis at Lambes court	3	0	0

RECEAVED AT BRIDGEND.

In the first of quarter comptis at Hallow court	6	0	0
Item at Candelmes court	12	0	0
Item at the same court of fridome fyne fra Alexr. Hamiltone	3	0	0
Item of friedome fyne fra John Young	15	0	0
Item of friedome fyne fra John Andersone	2	13	4
Item of fridome fyne fra Patrick M'Illew in Gorbellis	12	0	0
Item fra John Stapert of fridome fyne	15	0	0
Item for quarter comptis at Beltane	7	0	0
Item fra William Milleris guidsone in Gorbellis	3	10	0
Item fra Andrew Hamiltone of quarter comptis		10	0
Item of quarter comptis at Lambes court	8	0	0
Item of quarter comptis at the finishing of the old roll	4	13	4

MORTCLOATHES.

Item receavit for the thrie mortecloathes	53	3	8

MONEY MATTERS.

FALLOWIS THE DISCHARGE.

In the first deburst to Robert Anderson the deacon convineris officer.—	1	16	0
Item for beiring donne the mortcloth kist to the collectouris kist.—		4	0
Item to John Muires man and to the foolk in the hospitall.—		18	0
Item for carring up a lether to the treads land and a distrest strainger.—		6	0
Item to the clark for his liall	8	0	0
Item to helpe to burrie John Muiris man	1	16	0
Item to a distrest brother of tread.—	3	0	0
Item for dressing of the mortcloth and to a poor brother of tread.		15	0
Item of charges in intaking of ane frieman in Gorbellis		12	0
Item to thrie distrest straingeris	1	10	0
Item for aggreing to dress ane lumheid of the treads		2	0
Item to the deacon convineris hous the four severall termes.—	15	0	0
Item for carieing of twa stones to the treads land to be threshellis.—	0	8	0
Item to Robert Smyth for laycing of thrie threshwellis		19	0
Item to Patrick Lang for ten daillis	4	0	0
Item of charges in the clarkis at the aggreing with a frieman in Gorbellis		10	0
Item for dressing of John Findlayes glass window and Robert Smith for dressing of the yeard yett and stone and lyme thairto.—	2	2	0
Item for mending the treads purs in the box		3	0
Item to James Muir a poore member for supplie		18	0
Item to John Bartoune for laying of the cassay.—	8	1	6
Item to John Trumble for stones thairto.—	9	9	4
Item to William Crightoune, officer.—	1	16	0
Item to John Bartoune for laying a strand at the hous end.—		13	4
Item for carieing of certane irone to the treads land quhilk was in David Pitcairnes		4	0
Item of supplie to Dougall M'Androw a poore brother—	5	18	0
Item of supplie to Robert Dalrumples relict being a frieman.—	1	4	0
Item to the convineris officer att the receaving of the act anent the booking of prenteissis.—		12	0
Item for a brood to Robert Douglas hous and at the intaking a frieman in Bridgend.—		7	0
Item for supplie to John Tods wyfe.—		12	0
Item to ane distrest brother of tread.—	1	4	0
Item to James Craufuird, officer to the calling.—	1	16	0
Item for mending of a band to John Findlayes chamber doore and for naillis to mend the treads dyks.—		8	0

L

MONEY MATTERS.

Item to pay Robert Dalrumples relictis mortchist	2	8	0
Item of charges in the baillies hous anent William Milleris man	1	16	0
Item of charges at a students burriell in the Colledge		10	0
Item at ane uther occasioune in the deacon convineris hous of charges.—	1	4	0
Item for receaving of John Youngs fridome fyne in Gorbellis.—		4	0
Item to John Rae for a book to the tread.—	3	12	0
Item of supplie to William Dobbies relict.—	1	4	0
Item to helpe to burrie John Allansones bairne.—		18	0
Item of supplie to Allane Andersones wyfe.—		18	0
Item to John Paullis wyfe for supplie.—		12	0
Item of charges at the receaving of James Andersones entrie frieman in Gorbellis.—		6	0
Item to Androw Zeimock, thicker for mending the hollis in Balwastie land.—		6	8
Item for thrie stouks of bear strae thairto.—		14	0
Item to James Craufuird, officer to the tread for serving the thicker.—		3	4
Item for ther morning drink and four houris.—		2	0
Item to Gilbert Hendersoune a poor man of the tread.—		12	0
Item at receaving of Patrick M'Ilewis fridome fyne in Gorbellis.—		6	0
Item in the Clarkis at ane occasione with the deacone and maisteris.—		6	0
Item to a distrest brother.—	3	0	0
Item to a distrest strainger that was robed in Ireland.—		18	0
Item in the deacon convineris hous anent Jonet Stevinis dornick web.—	3	0	0
Item at the receaving of William Stapertis friedome fyne in Gorbellis.—		6	0
Item to a poor woman quhich come from the countrie.—		8	0
Item to Alexander Gilcreist, messenger for grund anwell of Balwastie.—	5	8	4
Item to Robert Kirklands wyfe of supplie.—		12	0
Item to Robert Watsone quhen his wyfe was gripped of the gravell.—	1	16	0
Item to Robert Kirklands wyfe when she was lying on death-bed.—		18	0
Item to ane poore woomau at the deacon convineris directioune.—		12	0
Item at a meiting in the clarkis with the deacone and maisteris.—		8	0
Item at the laird of Balvies burriell.—		6	0
Item for Robert Kirklands wyfes deid-kist	2	8	0
Item for aquanting the baillie anent Jonet Stevines web and paying the officer thairanent:—		14	0
Item at sighting of plyds be the deacone and maisteris.—		8	0
Item of procuratour fie to Robert Fynisone anent the dornick web.—	1	10	0

MONEY MATTERS.

Item for ryding of the laird of Pollokis sones burriell	3	6	0
Item for 3 stones for thrashwallis.—	2	0	0
Item for the bookit poore of the tread at Hallow court.—	12	0	0
Item for the bookit poore att Candlmes court.—	12	0	0
Item for the bookit poore at Beltane court.—	13	4	0
Item to John Young for casting the stank and stobing the treds dyck.—		16	0
Item to a poor man at ordor of the deacone and deacon conviner.—		18	0
Item to James Craufurd, the treads officer for a pair of shoone at Lambes court.—	1	10	0
Item to a distrest brother of tread	3	0	0
Item to Walter Stewart for a yearis annuelrent of 400 merkis.—	16	0	0
Item at Lambes court to the bookit poore of the tread.—	12	12	0
Item to David Pitcairne for the annuelrent of 2000 merkis for a year.—	80	0	0
Item to John Androwis sone for sarkis cloath to be cloathes and buttons thairto.—	2	19	0
Item to a north cuntrie man that the Hieland doctor cuttit of the gravell.—	1	10	0
Item to Robert Smallie, officer at the ellectione of the deacone for his attendance.—		12	0
Item to William Crightoune, officer for his attendance the said tyme		6	0
Item of hors hayer to John Flakfeild quhen he went to Raploch.	1	0	0
Item to Robert Falkoneris wyfe at the comeing in of the comissiouner.—		15	0
Item to James Craufuird, officer that was restand of his fiall.—	2	16	0
Item for making of John Androwis sones cloathes		10	0
Item in the clarkis with the deacon and maisteris		12	0

Quhilk compt above wryttin being particularlie read both charge and discharge laid and calculated the forsaid charge was fund to extend to the sowme of thrie hundreth fyftie sex punds aughtine shilling twa pennies Scotis money, and his discharge and debursmentis to the sowme of twa hundreth aughtie ane punds fourtine shilling sex pennies money quhilk being calculated and compaired ther was fund restand in the hands of the said John Cochrane collectour the sowme of thrie scoir fyftine punds thrie shilling sex pennies Scotis money quhilk he instantlie payit in to John Ritchie, present collectour and he to be chargit therfoir. Quhilk compt befoir wryttin being read and allowed, the said tread deacone, maisteris and communitie heirby exoneris and discharges the said John Cochrane his aires and executouris of his haill intromissioune with the said trends geir as collectour the year above wryttin be thir presentis for now and ever.

(Signed) PATRICK CLARK.

MONEY MATTERS.

There was still difficulty in guiding a proper expenditure on the part of the deacon and collector, and there had to be a re-enactment of controlling arrangements which have already been recorded:—

At the crafts hospitall of the burgh of Glasgow the elevinth day of October, 1672 yearis.

The quhilk day, being convined Patrick Bryce, present deacon conviner, Simone Tennent, ane of his brethrine of counsell, John Patersone, present deacone of the weaveris, his quartermaisteris, and most pairt of the brethrine of the said weaver craft—In farder corroboratioune of ane former act made anent the collectouris intromissioune with the haill geir belonging to the tread, to witt:—in uplyfting and receaveing the samyne, and debursing thairof; it is againe statuted and ordained, that in all tyme comeing, the collectour of the said tread, present and to come, intromett with and receave the haill commoune goods and causwallities belonging to the said calling, and to deburs the samyne accordinglie as he sall be ordoured; as also that the collectour nor deacone distribuit to no poor in the calling for supplie above aughtine shilling Scotis, and that the samyne sall [be] at sight, and be the consent of some of the maisteris; as also that ther be none of the treads geir spent at any meitting in tyme comeing bot out of thair awne proper money, except at ane extraordinar occasioune with certificatioune the samyne sall not be allowit, and the contraviner to be punished farder at the optioune of the deacon conviner and his successeris.

(Signed) PATRICK CLARK.

In Chapter V. a reference has been made to a movement on the part of the ten trades which had smaller representation in the Trades' House for equality with the four which had larger representation. Funds were required for this purpose, and provision to raise the needful is made in the following minute:—

At Glasgow the twentie day of Maij 1676.

The quhilk day, the deacone, maisteris, and most of the tread being convined, the said haill tread, be plurallitie of votis, they appoynted the deacone and maisteris to borrow such sowmes as sall be fund neidfull for purchasing ane inleargment of ther liberties, conforme to the votis marked in the treads rowllis.

It is difficult to trace the beginning of accumulation of a capital stock. In the earlier days, that took the form of investment in land and house property, which is dealt with in Chapter XIV. There is one book extant recording that in 1743 the Incorporation had a capital of £1479 sterling, which stock had in 1780 increased to £1908 sterling. The large increase of funds, which gives the yearly income now available for the relief of poorer members, has taken place in the latter part of last century, and a tabulated statement showing their growth will be found in Appendix III.

A frequent preliminary to the docquet on accounts is the phrase, "Salve justo calculo," presumably an earlier form of the E. & O. E. (errors and omissions excepted), which itself has now been dispensed with.

The four terms appear in the books of the seventeenth century as Candlemas, Beltan (for Whitsunday), Lambmass, and Hallowday (for Martinmas), and in the earlier part of the century rents were paid at Candlemas (February), and Lambmass (August), not as at present in May and November.

Some interesting items appear from time to time, such as:—

About 1676 items of outlay in attendance at "Leadie Montrose buriell" and also at "Leadie Eglintounne's buriell"—"To a poore man that had his hous burnt in Ireland"—"To ane gentlewoman that was robed by the way." In 1695 there appears "deburst of expensiss anent the trouble with the souldioures."

In 1717.—Item to 3 horse hyres and defenses at convoying his grace the Duke of Montrose.
Item to expense of pursuing 3 Gorbals masters for disobedience £5 Scots.
Item to morning drink four hours.
1718.—Item to James Dawson, a man that was broke at the Sheriff Muir.
Item to John Campbell, an broken seaman.
Item to another who was slave with the Turks.

Towards the end of the eighteenth century there are entries of borrowing from the Antiquity Society and the St. Mungo Society.

X.

LEGISLATION AND LITIGATION.

Among the charters and deeds, several of which are reproduced in this volume, there have been preserved a series of documents bearing on a restriction upon the export of linen yarn. This question has been mixed up with limitations as to the breadth of certain linen goods. The exceptions to these limitations were within the power of an individual and to be procured by a payment to him. The series of papers is incomplete, as the decision of the case is not recorded, but the restriction was removed, and there is no record that the damages claimed were ever paid. The main interest for us is, that in both cases it was found that interference by legislation was harmful to the trade. As some of these papers have not hitherto been in print, they are given here in full:—

COPY ACT OF PRIVY COUNCIL. discharging the exportation of linen yarn, dated 13 January 1603.

At Halyrind House the threttene day of Januair, the yeir of God j^m vj^c and thrie yeiris:—Anent the supplicatioun presentit and gevin in before the Kingis Majestie and lordis of secrite counsile be the wobstiris, weavaris, and claithmakeris within this realme; Makand mentioun that quhair albeit his Majestie, for the bettir setting fordwart of that good worke and interpryse of the making of claith, fustianis, stemmyngis, grewgranis and all uther kynd of stuffis, hes expreslie prohibit and dischairgit the transporting and carying furth of this realme of woll and sic uthir necessairis as are meete for furtherance of the said wark, and that it wes his Majesteis guid mynd and meaning the tyme foirsaid to mak a restreaint of all thingis quhilkis onywyse micht hindir or impeid the course of the said warke and namelie of the lynning yairne quhich is so necesserlie to be had and requisite to the making of the saidis stuffis, and without the quhilk the same can not tak effect; yit the merchandis, passingeris, and trafficqueris, alswele his Majesteis awne subjectis, as straingearis within this realme, quha evir prefeiring thair awne particulair gayne to his Heynes honnour and commoun wele, hes begun of long tyme syne to buy and transporte grite quantiteis of lynning yairne fra divers of his Majesteis leigeis, and daylie caryis the same beyond sey, be the quhilk unlauchfull treade thay have reasit the price of the said yarne to sic ane exhorbitant and feirfull derth, that within thir tua yeiris the same, the commoun price thairof is quadrupillit to the grite hinderance of the said wark and uttir wrak of his Majesteis subjectis, laboraris, and workeris of the saidis stuffis. So that except his Majestie according to his Heynes guid meaning as said is give and grant ane particulair act of restreaint of the said lynning yairne, the same werk quhilk hes had so guid a progres and florischeing within this realme salbe left af be thame throw meir povirtie and the haill estaite of the commonnis salbe all utterlie wraikit. Maist humelie desyreing thairfore the Kings Majestie and the saidis lordis to pas and expeid in thair favouris ane act of restreaint of the said yairne in maner and to the effect following, lykis as at mair lenth is contenit in the said supplicatioun. Quhilk being red, hard, and considderit be his Majestie and the saidis lordis, and thay thairwith being ryplie [advisit], and finding the desyre [thair] of verie reasonnable: The Kings Majestie and the saidis lordis thairfore have statute and ordanit, and be thir presentis statutes and ordains that na manir of merchandis, passingeris nor trafficquaris within this realme alswele his Majesteis awne subjectis as strangearis quhatsumevir presome nor tak upoun hand at ony tyme aftir the dait heirof to cary and transporte furth of this realme ony of the said lynning yairne abovewrittin undir quhatsumevir cullour or pretens, dischairgeing and inhibiteing thame thairof undir the pane of confiscatioun of the same to his Heynes use; with certificatioun to the contravenaris heirof the same pane salbe execute upoun thame without favour; and ordains letteres of publicatioun to be direct heirupoun gif neid beis to all and sundrie his Majesteis leigeis that nane of thame pretend ignorance of the same, in forme as effeiris. Extractum de libris actorum secreti consilij S.D.N. regis per me Jacobum Prymrois, clericum ejusdem sub meis signo et subscriptione manualibus.

JACOBUS PRYMROIS.

LETTERS by King James VI against the transportation of linen yarn. 12 March 1612

James be the grace of God King of Grite Bryttayne, France and Ireland defender of the faith. To oure lovittis, messingeris oure schireffis in that pairt conjunctlie and severalie specialie constitute greting. Forsamekle as it is humelie meanit and schawin to ws be oure lovittis the wobstaris, weavaris and claithmakeris within this oure kingdome that quhair we and the lordis of our prevey counsale be ane speciall act of restreant maid upoun the threttene day of Januair lastbypast hes expreslie statute and ordanit that na manir of merchantis, passingeris nor trafficquaris within this our realme alswele our awne subjectis as straingearis quhatsumevir presome nor tak upoun hand at ony tyme aftir the dait foirsaid of the said act to cary or transporte furth of this our realme ony lynning yarne undir quhatsumevir cullor and pretens, dischairgeing and inhibiting thame thairof undir the pane of confiscatioun of the same with certificatioun, to the contravenaris thairof the same pane salbe execute upoun thame without favour, as the act foirsaid at mair lenth beiris, quhich is dewlie publeist with all solempnities and cerimonyis requisite to all and sundrie oure leigeis and subjectis to the effect thay pretend no ignorance of the same in tyme cuming, notwithstanding quhairof divers of the saidis merchantis and trafficquaris alswell oure awne subjectis as straingearis yit continewis in the unlauchfull trade of transporting of lynning yairne forbiddin to be transportit as said is, and nicht and day privelie convoyis the same yairne in grite quantyteis both be sea and land furth of oure countrey, makand small accompt of the effect and force of the said act, to the heich contempt of ws and to the hurte and prejudice of the saidis complenairis and mony utheris our guidis subjectis of this oure realme. Oure will is heirfore and we chairge you straitlie and commandis that incontinent thir oure letteres sene ye pas and in oure name and auctoritie fens and arreist all and quhatsumevir lynning yairne whilk is to be caryed and transportit furth of this oure realme in whatsumevir barkis, boitis, crearis, and veschellis be sea, or packis be land; and to that effect that ye mak oppin duris and utheris lokfast lowmes and use oure keyis thairto, to remane undir arreistment ay and quhill sufficient cautioun and souirtie be foundin that the same salbe furthcumand to oure thesaurer in oure name and to oure use and utheris oure leigeis as accordis of the law; the quhilk to do we commit to you conjunctlie and severalie oure full pouers be thir oure letteres delivering thame be you dewlie execute and indorsat agane to the [lordis]. Gevin undir oure signet at Edinburgh the twelft day of Marche, and of oure reigne the nynt and fourty fyve yeiris 1612.

Ex deliberatione dominorum secreti consilij etc.

JA. PRYMROIS.

SHEWETH

To the lords of his Majesties most honourabill privie counsell. The humble petition of all the Weavers of Scotland, dated 21 November 1666.

That by ane old act of parliament linen cloath was ordained to be 3 quarters and a halfe broade which was convenient for the use as weill of the cuntrie as strangers, but upon representation of some merchants who were not interessed in linneng cloath, ther was ane act of parliament past in anno 1661 wherby all linnen cloath above ten shilling the elne was appoynted to be ane elne and tuo inches broad and conforme therto a gift being granted to David Weemes he hes summarly chairged all the weavers of Scotland for bygaine penalties and contraventiouns. And albeit suspensiones were raised by great multitudes of the saids weavers, yet the said David without discusseing the said suspensione, have still of new charged the first suspenders every moneth, resolveing therby to put the suspenders to the expens of new suspensiones and of so continwall and uninterrupted attendance as will serve thousands of families and will occasioue the leidges forbeare absolutly to weave for fear of confiscation and breakes all the mercats quhairof linnen cloath used to be a great commoditie, and therby publict traffiq for the advantage quhairof this act was introduced will be by this act absolutly ruined. My it therfor please your lordships to call for the first suspension, and to ordaine the said David Weemes to insist therin, and to command the said David Weemes not to raise aney new letteres, nor to chairge upon the old letteres untill the first suspension be discusit, for it clearly appeares by the not discusseing of the old suspensione that the said David is conscious to himselfe that the same will discus in favoures of the weavers; and before the lordis of session, the old suspension most receave a decision before aney new charge be given, whereas, if the old suspension were to be discussit, it wold appeire that the weavers were opprest from thes following reasones:—

First that it is unjust and against the interest of the leidges that they sould be forced to weave quhat is for their owne privat use at aney uther measure nor quhat they think fitt and convenient for their owne exigencies; and trew it is, that for hand towells, childrins skirts and for maney uther domestick uses linnen cloath of les breadeth then quhat is prescryved be the act of parliament is absolute necesser; and forraine seall being only designet be the act of parliament as the motive for quhich that breadeth is introduced, it were against all reasone and publict advantage, that quhat is made for privat use should be lemited by reulles of forraine traide in quhich the same is nowayes concerned (Second) The said David Weemes does naewayes manadge the trust or publict imployment quhich is the designe of the act for aney publict advantage seing he grants licence upon compositione to aney of the weavers in Scotland to weave cloath of quhat breadeth they pleas he being satisfied by the said transactione as his privat interest. (Third) The weavers are naewayes lyable in contraventione of the said act, for they serve the leidges in the way prescryved to them, bot the cloath should only be confiscated quhich so woven at the desyre of the leidges, for it is in the power of the leidges to present them the yearne commensurable to the act of parliament, bot they most either work as the act of parliament prescryves or sterve themselfes and their famillie (Fourth) The penalties and exactiones are by the act of parliament only applicable to the use of magistrats of burghes, lords of regalities, barrons and shyreffes before quhom the weavers may be persewed and fyned or confyned quhich were introduced be the said act in favores not only of thes bot of the weavers, it being supposed that ther were magistrats or maisters wold be more favorable to them then aney strangers, and to prevent the petitioners being drawen to the utter destruction of their traide and poore families; and it is confidently expected that the saids lords of regalitie, shyreffes, barrons and utheres as to this particular will look to their owne interest especially being most of the gentlemen in Scotland wold by this preparative be ruined in their rents and privat fortounes (Fourth) [*sic*] The said chairge is most summar and unwarrantable seing it requyres no preceeding decreet as the ground therof quherby maney innocent people are daly charged who were never guyltie of aney breach of this act; and it is against a principall in law that execution sould preceed sentence quherof it is the effect and should not be the cause. (Fifth) The letteres ought to be simpliciter suspendit as bygaines in respect the leidges could nather get scall for their cloath abroad nor could the weavers be accomodat in materials such as reeds and utheres fitt for working cloath of the breadeth prescryved be act of parliament, and that in respect of the warre and the interruption of commerce.

In respect of all quhich it is humbly creaved, that seing this act is of the natoure of penall statutes, and seing this act was never in observance, in consideration quherof the exchequer, at the passeing of the gift, doeth reserve a power to themselfes to limite or recall the same as they thought fitt, that therfor your lordshipis finding the maney inconveniences that wold arrise to the nation would therfore be pleased to call before you such of the said traide and of other disinteressed magistrats and gentillmen who understand the same, and after mature deliberation regulat the execution of the said act as ye shall see convenient, and that in the interim your lordships wold discharge aney execution untill the reasones of the first suspensione be discussit as said is.

xliij Act dischargeing the exportation of Linnen yearne and regulating the bredth of Linnen cloath &c. 1641.

Our Soveraine Lord conceiving it necesar for the good and wellbeing of his Majesties subjectis to project and indevore the improvement of all the native commodities of his Majesties antient kingdom and to mak lawes and ordinances for eviting and preventing of all fraud and deceit used heirtofore in making seall of the saidis commodities and considering that it wold tend more to the advantage of his Majesties subjectis and promoteing of manufacturies to restraine the libertie that merchandis have taken to export linnen yearne then suffer them to carrie the samen unto uther places and kingdomes. Therfor his Majestie with advyse and consent of his esteatis of parliament discharges any merchant or utheris whatsomever to transport out of this kingdome any linnen yearne under the pain of confiscation of the samen the on half to his Majesties use and the uther half to the use of the attacher and apprehender of the said yearne, and statutis and ordainis that all yearne be sold be weight and that noe reell be maid use of within this kingdome under the measour and length of ten quarteris and that under the paine of confiscation of any yearne brought to the mercat of a shorter reell, the one half to his Majesties use and the uther halfe to the use of the delateris and apprehenderis of the said yearne; [as] also his Majestie considering that linnen cloath is on of the most usefull commodities of the product of this kingdom [w]herby much money in ancient tymes was brought in and that now to the great prejudice of the said commoditie the samen is [become] in contempt abroad and become hardlie vendable through the deceitfull making evill bleetching and unequall bredth [thereof. Ther]for his Majestie with advyse and consent of the saidis estatis doth discharge and prohibit all weaveris to mak any linnen [cloath] of the pryce of ten shilling Scotis the ell or above under the bredth of ane ell and tuo inches efter the first day of [N]ovember nixt to come under the paine to be imprisoned for the sp[ace] of fourtein dayes and of tuentie poundis Scotis to be payed for each fault to magistratis of burghes, shirefis of shires, lordis of regalities and barronis within ther respective boundis and of the confiscation of the samen to the use of the attacheris and discovereris therof; and statutis that all linnen cloath be taken up by selvage and not by the rigg and so to be presented to the mercat, and that all linnen cloath be bleatched without lime under the paine of tuentie poundis for each fault to be payed to the magistratis forsaid within ther respective boundis; and lastly it is heirby decleared that all flax and linnen yearne imported, and all linnen cloath exported by such as shall enter in to the companies and manufacturies for making of linnen cloath shall be fre of custome and all uther imposition for the space of fyftein yeiris efter the saidis manufacturies shall be esteablished in the personis of such as shall enter themselves in the saidis compainis betwixt and the first of Januarie next, conforme to ane nther ordainance of parliament for esteablishing of the saidis compainies.

At the craftis hospitall the 22 of Junij 1663.

The quhilk day, Johne Falconer, deacone, and the maist pairt of the calling being conveinet, have, be pluralitie of voatis, nominat and appoyntit Micheall Watsone and John Clerk, tuo of thair number, to pas to the heigh court of parliament for supplicating thame to gett redres or mitigationne of the 43 act of parliament of King Charles the first of blessed memorie, maid anent the dischairgeing and prohibiting all weifers to make any lining cloathe of the pryce of ten schilling the elne or above wnder the breadthe of ane elne and tuo inches under the paines thairin conteinet, conforme to the commissionne grantit be the said deacone and calling for that effect of the dait thairof thairanent; and for that effect, the said deacone, collectour and maisters ar to borrow four hundrethe merkis money, and if the same be superexpendit in the bussines, that thei get farder is to be furnischit be them to thair saidis commissioners, quhilk is to be allowit and furthcuming for thair releiff af the said craftis guidis accordinglie.

M. ROWAND, clericus.

Informatioune for the weaveris of Glasgow Brigend and Rutherglen against David Weynies.

The saids weaveris are chargit at the instance of the said David for making payment to him of twentie pund for each contraventione in workeing and weaveing or caussing to worke and weave lining cloath at the pryce of ten shilling Scots ilk ellne and upward wnder the brend of ane ellne and two inshes, and that since the terme of Lambes 1666 conforme to the 33 act of the I sessioune of parliament in August 1661 &c.

This charge is founded upon ane gift granted under the privie seall the 8 of Junij 1666 yearis, and is given by the clerk and under the signet to the privie counsell. This charge is lykwayes suspendit by the weaveris in Glasgow, Brigend, and Rutherglen wpon thir reasons :—

(1) The said suspenderis could not be sumerlie chargit, bot should have beine persewit befor ther awine magistrats uther if they had bein callit they wauld alledge that they could not be layable for contravention of the said act in respect they only wrought woolne stuffe.

(2) The magistrats of each burgh have the uplifting of the said penalties and non els.

It would be fitt to reforme the reasones thus (1) By the constant law of this natioune, all sumar charges such as horneings aught to be warranted be ane express act of parliament appoynteing per expressum, for horning being executioune it does of its awine nature requyre a preceiding sentance, and therfor, ather a sentance should proceed or this necessatie should be expreslie remitted by ane express act of parliament, for nothing les cane remitt what is naturallie and essentiallie requisit; lykas be the express acaptioune of severall acts, it is expreslie seine that they beir warrand for letteris of horning when the parliament thought fitt to indulge the samyne and all other penall statuts such as his is, as usurie &c. are putt to executione not sumerlie but by preceiding decreits.

(3) To repeitt the second reasone in the suspensione without reformeing to ad this thrid reasone viz.—that the counsell or exchequer have reservit power to themselfes to recall the act when they sall think fitt, but soe it is that lining cloath being only appoynted by former lawes and express acts to be of thrie quarteris and ane half broad, and the lining cloath being only appoynted to be of ane elne and twa inche for the use of straingeris, ther cane no executione be craved upon this gift but in swa far as concerns lining cloath maid for the use of straingeris, and soe confiscatioune should be onlie wsed for quhat is transported, and not for quhat privat persones cause make for ther awne use and weireing &c.

Since this act is only intentit for commerce it cane only receave executioune at quhat tyme commerce is allowed and oppine, bot now quhen his Majestie who hath granted the gift is in oppen sea ware, wherby comerce is locked up, and seing the materiallis for weiveing as reds and otheris ar to be brought from abroad, that therfor this act cane receave no executione wntill the seas be oppen that such materiallis may be brought homb; lykeas when this act wes first hard of, the saids weaveris did absolutlie sitt idle for the nixt enschewing half year.

To remember that the former actis of parliament appoynting thrie quarter and ane halfe are not expreslie advocat by this act, is uswall in such caices, and therfor to contend that this act should regulate the measure of home bread cloath, and this act to be according to the narative restricted to the cloath made for commerce, it being a principall in law that no act excepted be expreslie abrogat is presumed to be soe bot most stand in vigore if it cane receave ane interpretatioune, and that this interpretatioune is most sutable bath to the natture of the subject matter and to the previledge of the leiges who cannot be in law obleidged to use what is maide for ther awne privat use wtherwayes then themselves intendit for otherwayes what was desyned as ane advantage to the kingdome in generall would much prejudge and damnifie at the privat leidges and to gratifie straingeris the natives should be then extream great loseris and much retrinsched in ther privat liberties.

To remember to gett the agent of the borrowes to concure for the entres of the burghs to whom the collecting belonges, and to contend that it is in ther power to remitt or regulate the saids fynes as they sall sie the samyne fitt for commerce;

Wota that this would be lykwayes aledgit be the noblemen and gentillmen within burghes regalities, shyreffs of scheiris, and stewartis of stewartries and regalities to remember the King is to receave litle advantadge, becaus the said David compeiris and gives licence for a considderable tyme, &c. &c. &c.

At Glasgow the aucht day of October j^m vj^c thrie scoir seavin yeires.

The quhilk day in presens of me notar publicke undersubscryvand and witnesses efternamit compeirit personaly Johne Clerke, present deacone of the weivers of the burgh of Glasgow for himself and in name and behalf of the remanent britherein of the said trade and vocatioune of the samyne burgh, and als compeirit John Cumyng, present oversman of the weivers of Gorballis for himself and in name and behalf of the remanent britherein of the said trade and vocatioune within the said village of Gorballis; Quho past to the personall presence of James Bryce, messenger in Glasgow as he who hes chairgit certane persones of the saids weivers of Glasgow and Gorballis at the instance of David Weimes, merchand in Dundie as alledgit having right be his Majesties gift wnder the privie seall daitit the aucht day of Junij 1666 yeiris to the multes and fynes dew and lyable be the transgressouris of the 43 act of the first sessione of parlament in anno 1661 to mak payment to him or any havand his warant of tuentie punds Scotes money of fyne imposit be the said act for ilke transgressioune in working weiving or causing worke and weive lining cloath at the pryce of ten shilling Scotes ilke ellne and wpwards wnder the bodie of ane ellne and two inche since the terme of Lambes 1666; and thair the saids John Clerke and John Cumying for themselves and in name and behalf forsaid producit befoir the said James Bryce, messenger ane atestit double wnder the subscriptiounes of Mathow Rowand and Quintein Finday, notaris publicke of the letteres of suspensiouno purchesit and raisit be the saids weivers of Glasgow and Gorballis agenst the said David Weimes befoir the lords of secreit counsell daitit the tuentie twa day of May last bypast, quherby they have suspendit the letteres and chairges raisit be the said David Weimes aganst them in the said mater and made laufull intimatioune to the said James Bryce, messenger therof, and of ane former instrument takin be the saids weivers against James Mudie, messenger who had chairgit them thairanent or befoir protesting against the said James Bryce, messenger in the meintyme that he give out no executioune against them nor he nor no uther messenger chairge them nather proceid any further against them in the said mater be vertue of the letteres and chairgis raisit or to be raisit be the said David Weimes against them in tho said mater—ay and quhill the saids letteres of suspensioune raisit be the saids weivers against him in the said mater be discusit quhilke is lying in proces befoir the saids lords; and for remeid of law thairof if the said James Bryce doe anything in the contrar. Quhairupone and upone all and sundrie the premisses, the saids John Clerke and John Cumying for themselves and in name and behalf forsaid, askit and tuike instrumentis ane and mae in the hands of me notar publicke underscryvand; thes things wer done within the duelling hous of the said James Bryce messenger, lying on the south syde of the Gallowgait of the said burgh of Glasgow betwixt ten and allevin houres in the foirnoone day moneth and yeir of God respective abovewrittin, being ther present John Weir, messenger in Glasgow, William Stewart, workman ther and William Stewart his sone, with divers utheris witnesses reqnyred and desyred to the premisses.

Ita est Matheus Rowand, notarius publicus in fidem robur et testimonium veritatis omnium et singulorum premissorum rogatus et requisitus testan his meis signo et subscriptione manualibus.

The weavers were fond of litigation, and had frequently to appeal to the strong arm of the law. Some reference has already been made to this subject in Chapter IV. In addition to disputes settled by the magistrates or sheriffs, they had several actions in the Court of Session. In the middle period of their history, late in the eighteenth and early in the nineteenth century, they frequently petitioned Parliament on such subjects as the repeal of the laws against Popery, the Corn Laws, the Slave Trade, and Parliamentary Reform; while on every movement in Parliament, and of the Magistrates and Town Council, they freely expressed their feelings, which frequently were in opposition to those of the representatives of the city.

XI.

RELATIONS WITH GORBALS AND BRIDGEND WEAVERS.

We have no record whether previous to the 1605 seal of cause (given in Chapter I.) the earlier powers under the 1523 charter had been exercised against weavers residing on the south side of the river, but it is evident that as soon as the second charter had been granted (1605) it became necessary that there should be a working arrangement with such near neighbours. The reasons given are quaint —*for the special love, favour, and kindness of the Deacon and Glasgow weavers to the provost and weavers of Bridgend.* The text of the agreement has not previously been printed, and is given here in full:—

AGREEMENT between the Weavers of Glasgow and the Weavers of Gorbals dated 8 May 1605.

At Glasgow the aucht day of Maij the yeir of God j^m vj^c and fyve yeirs. It is appointit, aggreit and finallie endit betwix the persouns pairties wnderwrittin; Thay ar to say Ritchert Kirkland, deikin of wobsteris, Archibald Patersoune, Findlay Schakschaw, William Kirkland, Georg Herbisoun, Robert Lang, maisteris of the said craft for thameselfis and takand the burdeine upone thame for the haill wobsters friemen of this burght on the ane pairt, Georg Bryss, John Walker, John Pollock, Nicoll Gemmill, John Man, James Baxter, Waltir Mair, James Thomesoune, Williame Brysse, Andro and James Bryssis, wobsteris, induellaris at Brigend, upone the landis of Gorballis on the uther pairt in maner following :—Forsameikle as the wobsteris of this burght haveing granted unto thame be proveist baillies and counsall certane liberties and priviledgis conteinit in thair lettere of deikinheid for the weill of thair craft, quhairby thai may hinder the foirsaidis persounis in using ony of thair liberties and priviledges within this burght be wertew of the quhilkis priviledgis and liberties granted wnto thame be proveist, baillies and counsall thai may pwnische and wnlaw the saidis wobsteris of Brigend and all wtheris wnfriemen hantand or usand thair liberties within the fredom and libertie of this burght, and speciallie to caus thame pay custome of ilk wob thai present to the markat of this burght, and for all wrocht wobis thai be apprehendit bringand in within this burght; and siclyk to wnlaw thame for all work that thai or ony of thame can be chaulengit taking furth of this burght; and generallie to stay and stop and hinder thame and all utheris wnfriemen to hant or use the priviledgis of thair craft within this burght. Thairfoir for the speciall luife favour and kyndnes quhilk the said Ritchert Kirkland maisteris and remanent wobsteris of this burght hes and beiris towardis the ryght honourabill Sir Georg Elphinstonne of Blyswood, knicht, proveist of this burglit, and maister to the saidis wobsteris of Brigend; and for the yeirlie payment be ilk ane of the foirnametis wobsteris of Brigend to the said deikin and maisteris of craft of the sowme of aucht schillingis money to be payit at four termis in the yeir, the said Richert Kirkland deikin and maisteris foirsaidis for thameselfis and in name of the remanent wobsteris of this burght hes givin and grantit lykas be thir presentis givis and grantis full libertie priviledge and owersicht in hanting using and ocupying of the wobster craft to the snidis wobsteris of Brigend, and to ilk ane of thame and to thair bairnis beand wobsteris and haveand thair speciall residence and duelling within the landis of Gorballis or ony utheris landis perteining heritabilly to the said Sir Georg without this burght and libertie of the samin (prowyding alwayis thair bairnis beand wobsteris pay the custome wnderwrittin); and generallie givis and grantis wnto thame full libertie and powar to hant us or exerceis ony nther fredome of the said craft within the libertie of this burght quhairof thai micht have hinderit thame be wertew of thair lettere of deikinheid. For the quhilk libertie priviledge and owersicht grantit wnto thame be the said Ritchert Kirkland maisteris foirsaidis for thameselfis and remanent wobsteris of this burght. The saidis Georg Brysse, John Walker, John Pollock, Nicoll Gemmill, John Man, James Baxter, Waltir Mair, James Thomesoune, Williame Brysse, James and Andro Bryssis bindis and obleissis thame and ilk ane of thame yeirlie to content and pay to the said Ritchert Kirkland and maisteris of craft foirsaid or to ony uthir deikin or maisteris of the said craft of this burght for the tyme, the sowme of aucht schillingis money [ilk an]e of thame at four termis in the yeir, viz.—Beltane, Lambes, Hallowmes, and Candillmes [making] the first quarteris payment presentlie for the terme of Beltane last bipast, and sua furth [termely and] quarterlie during thair lyftymis. And in cais it sall happen ony of the foirsaidis personnis wobs[teris of] Brigend to remove thameselfis furth of the said Sir Georg landis and not to remaine his tennentis nor pay him maill and dewtie, that than and in that caice, the said libertie priviledge and owirsicht na farder nor langer to be extendit towardis the foirsaidis persounis or ony of thame that remaine not the said Sir Georg tennentis. And for the mair securitie all the saidis persounis pairties abovewrittin ar content and consentis that thir presentis be insert and registrat in the buikis of counsall, commissaris buikis of Glasgow or burrow cowrt buikis thairof, that ane decreit of the lordis, commissaris foirsaid or proveist and baillies of the said burgh may be interponit heirto that executoriallis of horning poynding and warding may pas and be direct heirupone the ane prejudeice of the uther, and the horning to pas upone ane single charge of sax dayis allanirly and to this effect makis and constitutis   thair procuratouris and ilk ane of thame conjunctly and sewerallie *in uberiore forma*, etc. *promitten. de rato*, etc., withe powar, etc.; In witnes quhairof thir presentis wreitin be William Fleming, nottar, we have subscrivit with our handis as followis

RELATIONS WITH GORBALS AND BRIDGEND WEAVERS.

befoir thir witnessis Andro Car, Waltir Schirilaw, Georg Schirilaw, John Clerk, wobster, and Mathew Fischer, nottar.

> We, Ritchert Kirkland, deikin, Archibald Patersoune, Findlay Schakschaw, Robert Lang, Georg Herbisoune, Georg Brysse, John Walker, John Pollock, Nicoll Gemmill, John Man, James Baxter, Waltir Mair, James Thomsoune, Williame Bryss, Andro and James Bryssis with our handis at the pen led be the connotaris wnderwrittin becaus we could not wreit ourself.
>
> ......(Paper worn)......... Notarius Publicus. De mandatis omnium predictarum personarum scribere nescien, testante manu ....(Paper worn).........
>
> Ita est Robertus Blair, notarius publicus ac conotarius in premissis requisitus manu sub^t 1605.
>
> George Schirilaw, Wittnes. Williame Kirkland with my hand, Johne Clerk, witness. Mathow Fischer, notar, witness. Wallter Schirrillaw, witnes. Androw Ker, witnes.

Whether or not a dispute had arisen there is no record, probably not, yet less than a year after the signing of the agreement it was found advisable to agree upon a means of settling disputes, as follows:—

(8-2-1606)

The quhilk day, the deakin and maisteris and haill bretherene of craft on the ane pairt, Niniane Paislay, George and Andro Bryceis, and John Pollok, on the uther pairt, takand the burdene on thame for the remanent wobsteris of Brigend and Gorballis, all in ane voce condiscendis, statutis and ordanis that quhatsumevir accident or contraversie sall happin to fall out betuix the saidis pairties concerning the privileges and liberties grantit be the wobsteris of this burgh to the saidis wobsteris of Brigend contenit in the lettir set doun thairanent betuix thame, salbe judgit, tryit, and decydit befoir the deakin of the wobsteris of this burgh and maisteris of craft for the tyme, and four of the honest men of the wobsteris of Brigend for the tyme, and be na uther judges concerning the foirsaid lettir and privileges thairin specifeit; and give ony of the pairties, wobsteris of this burgh and Brigend appeillis thame to ony uther judge anent the premissis, the persoun appeilland sall pay ten li. of unlaw *toties quoties* to be equally resavit and devydit betuix the wobsteris of this burgh and Brigend in all tym coming as the samyn sall happin to incur.

J. CRAIG. sst

98 RELATIONS WITH GORBALS AND BRIDGEND WEAVERS.

There are for several years succeeding 1641 regular entries such as this:—

xvj Octobour 1641

The quhilk day, Patrik Bryce, and Allan Andirsoun, hes instantlie payit to the croft tuentie merkis, upliftit be them fra the weiferis in Gorballis, as heaving power of the croft to uplift the same the last yeir; and thairfoir the croft exoneris and discharges them of the said yeiris intromissioun, quhilk wes upliftit be them, be thir presentis for evir.

Then as a preliminary to a new agreement occurs the following:—

17 November 1656.

The said day, it is wnamouslie concludit that the mater anent the weiferis in Gorballis be followit out to the outermost.

There had been a purchase of the lands of Gorbals and Bridgend by the Magistrates and Town Council, who later made over the same to the Trades' House and Trades. Being the successors of Sir George Elphinstone, with whom the 1605 agreement was made, the "proveist, balzies, and counsall" are instrumental in having a new agreement come to, as follows:—

CONTRACT AND AGREEMENT between the Weavers of Glasgow and the Weavers of Gorbals, dated 10 April 1657.

Att Glasgow the tenth day of Apryll j^m vj^c fyftie seven yeires It is appoynted and agried betuixt the discreit persones pairties following They are to say Johne Falconar, present deacon of the weivers of the said burghe of Glasgow, Patrick Bryce, Michaell Watsone, Johne Kessane, collectour, Archibald Glen, Ritchart Flaikfield, William Falconar, Andrew Lies, Johne Lies, Johne Clarke, Walter Stewart, James Graham, James Falconar, Robert Nisbit, and Johne M'Allester for themselfes and as takand the burding in and upone them for the haill remanent brethreine of that calling and ther successouris weivers and burgessis of the said burghe one the ane pairt, and William Boigle, John Marschell elder, David Scott, Johne Andersone, Johne Glen, David Hoggisyaird, Robert Watsone, Thomas Wast, William Allexander, William Gordoune, Johne Fleyming, Archibald Barre, Walter Livingstoune, Johne Walker, Johne Filppe, William Andersone, Thomas Andersone, Johne Montgomerie, Robert Gemmill, Patrick Ritchie, Thomas Hill, James Scheillis, Hew Duchall, William Robiesone, Johne Marschell younger, William Gilkersone, Alexander Hammiltone, Johne Cummyng, Johne Scheillis, Thomas Muir, Archibald Barre, and Johne Davidsone now weivers in Gorballis and Muir therof for themselfes and as haveing full power warrand and commissioune of the haill remanent weivers now presentlie indwellers in the saids lands of Gorballis and Muir therof foirsaid and as takand the burding in and upone them for the saids remanent weivers now presentlie dwelling in Gorballis and Muir therof foirsaid one the other pairt in maner forme and effect following That is to say forsameikle as about fyftie (blank) yeires since or therby ther was ane mutuall contract and agriement made drawne wpo and subscryved betuixt the deacon and maisters of the said burghe of Glasgow for the tyme, and the weivers of Gorballis also for the tyme Wherin for diverse and sundrie liberties grantit and conferrit be the said weivers of Glasgow upone the saids weivers of Gorballis the saids weivers of Gorballis were bund and obleist to performe diverse and sundrie obleismentis to the saids weivers of Glasgow at lenth mentionat in the said contract wherthrow ever sen syne ther hes beine ane mutuall love and correspondencie kept amongst them: And now sieing be the providence of God they doe all now leive under one heid and superiour the proveist bailzies and counsell of Glasgow now undoubtit laufull superiouris of the saids lands of Gorballis. And the saids pairties being all most willing that the foirsaid old love peace and amity that hes beine betuixt the weivers of this burghe and the weivers of the saids lands of Gorballis may be rather augmented nor diminished; and following the example of uther weill governed pairtis in the lyke, as amongst the weivers of Edinburgh, Westport and Potterraw, it is thoght good be the saids pairties following the advyse and consent of the saids proveist bailzies and counsell of Glasgow, and for eschewing the hurt and prejudice might fall out be the act of parliament sett doun in anno 1592 anent craftismen exerciseing ther crafts in suburbs to burrowes to sett doune certane heids and articles whilkis are to be keipt and observed be them heirefter for the good and commoditie of all of them; and are to be keipt observed and fulfilled to others not onely for the present bot be all of that calling dwelling in the saids bounds in tyme and adges succeeding:—In the first,—It is declared be the saids weivers of Gorballis under-subscryveand for themselfes and in name and behalfe of the haill remanent weivers inhabitantis therintill present and to come, that whatsumever freedom, tollerance, or libertie they have for exerceing ther calling in the saids bounds of Gorballis in taking furth and bringing work fra and to this burghe according to ther wont use and habeit that the samine is givin and grantit to them be the saids weivers of the foirsaid burghe of Glasgow. Secondlie—It is accordit agried and mutually condescendit upone betuixt the saids pairties that the saids weivers in Gorballis present and to come sall have libertie yeirlie heirefter to have ane oversman conforme to the warrand already grantit be the saids proveist, bailzies and counsell for that effect who sall be choysne in this maner,—To witt, the saids weivers in Gorballis shall choyse out thrie of the most qualified men amongst them and putt ther names in leit, and present that leit ilk first Fryday of Maij yeirlie heirefter to the deacon of the saids weivers of Glasgow and his maisters of craft in the crafts hospitall within the samine burghe to the effect one of them may be electit oversman for the yeir ensewing; and the said oversman being swa electit that he with the haill weivers in Gorballis sall have power to choise out twelve in number of the worthiest of ther brethreine, and out of these twelve they sall make choyse of sex to be assessouris to the said oversman; and to begin efter the dait heirof or in Maij nixt. Whilks oversman and assessouris being swa choysne sall have power to judge in all maters betuixt brother and brother relaiting to ther calling allennerlie; and for giveing satisfactioune to the pairties who sall have ther workis spilt wronged or longer keipt nor is promeist, the saids weivers in Gorballis being alwayes subject to the anthorities of the bailzies ther, according as the weivers of Glasgow are subject to the magistratis therof. And if they cannot agrie in maters amongst themselfes then the said mater sall be brought to the saids deacon of weivers of Glasgow and his maisters, who sall have power to determine theriutill. Item.—It is farder agried that the saids weivers in Gorballis and ther successouris present and to come sall not accept ressave or suffer any stranger weivers to sitt doune and setle himselfe ther in tyme cuming, or to set wpe any workhous or loome, without the speciall advyse and consent of the deacon of weivers of Glasgow and his maisters of craft and ther successouris had and obteined therto, and that he sall be first bookit in ane book to be made for that use, to be under the keiping of the weivers of Glasgow and ther clerk. And the compositioune for ther wpsetis both for the saids strangers as also for prenteissis, friemens sones and suche as maries friemens dochters ther, sall be, in quantitie, and be payit in maner following by and besyde the clerkis fies, viz.: Ilk stranger weiver intending to make his dwelling and residence in the Gorballis the sowme of fourtie merkis Scotts money les or mair as sall be thoght good be the said deacon and sex of his maisters of craft of Glasgow, and be the said oversman in Gorballis and his sex assessouris. Item.—Ilk prenteis taking wpe his tread and working at his owne hand the sowme of sextine punds money foirsaid les or mair. Item.—Ilk freemans sone or ony that maries ane freemans dochter being ane inhabitant and ane weiver intending to make his residence in Gorballis, sall pay the sowme of eight punds money les or mair as sall be thoght good in maner foirsaid, and all to be bookit as said is. Whilkis haill sowmes sall be equallie dealt and devydit betuixt the weivers of Glasgow and the weivers of Gorballis to be imployed be them for the helpe and supplie of ther poor decayed respective brethreine. Item.—It is farder accordit and agried betuixt the saids pairties, that every persone weiver in Gorballis that keips one or mae loomes, or workhous ther for the former freedome grantit as said is shall pay yeirlie to the weivers of Glasgow and ther successouris the sowme of twentie shillings Scotts money for ilk loome proportionallie at the four quarters in the yeir Candlemes, Beltan, Lambes, and Hallowmes, beginand at Beltan nixt, and whilk is to be imployed for the weill and behoufe of the poor decayed brethreine of that calling within the said burghe of Glasgow allennerlie bot prejudice to these in Gorballis to astrict themselfes to pay quarterlie some meane small thing as they can agrie amongst themselfes for the use of ther owne poor. Item,—It is condescendit and agried upone betuixt the saids pairties, that it sall be leissume to every one of the saids freemen weivers in Gorballis to take ane prenteis ilk fourth yeir, and that prenteis sall be bound fyve yeirs as ane prenteis who sall be bookit as said is, and dureing all that tyme he sall be furnished be his maister in meit, and sall not be upone his owne meit; and that prenteis swa takne and bookit, sall pay of booking silver (by the fies) twenty

RELATIONS WITH GORBALS AND BRIDGEND WEAVERS.

four shillings Scotts, whilk sall be divydit equallie as said is. And farder it is agried betuixt the saids pairties, that it sall not be leissume to the weivers in Gorballis to give or pay any mair or greater fies to ther jurneymen nor is payit to the jonrneymen in Glasgow of that tread be the freemen burgesses therof. And last the saids weivers of Gorballis binds and obleidges them and ther successouris nowayes to incrotch upone the freedome of the saids weivers of Glasgow and liberties belonging to them; and the saids weivers in Glasgow oblidges them not to wrong the saids weivers in Gorballis in ther liberties, bot sall defend them therintill to ther uttermost. And heirto baith the saids pairties binds and oblidges them to observe keip and fulfill the hail premissis ilk ane of them *hinc inde* to uthers in all tyme heirefter. And the pairties failziers bindis and oblidges them to pay to the pairties keipers and observers of the premissis or willing to keip and observe the samyne fourtie punds Scotts money for ilk failzie *toties quoties* by and attour fulfilling of the premissis. And for the mair securitie, baithe the saids pairties are content and consents thir presentis be insert and registrat in the hie court bookis of justice, towne court bookis of Glasgow, or in any other judicatourie court bookis ordinar within this natioune to have the strenth of ane act and decreit of any of the judges therof interponit heirto, that letters and executoriallis of horneing one ane simple charge of sex days only may pas heirupone in forme as effeirs; and for that effect constitutis thair procuratouris &c. In witnes wherof (writtin be Johne Young, wryter in Edinburgh) they have subscryveit thir presentis with ther hands day yeir and place foirsaids befoir thir witnessis Johne Patersone, weiver in Glasgow, Robert Maxwell, weiver ther, Donald M'Gilchreist, servitour to William Yair, towne clerk deput of Glasgow, and the said Johne Young.

Signed by David Scot, John Anderson, David Hodgisyard, Robert Watsoune, Thomas West, James Scheillis, Johne Davidsonne, Patricke Bryce, Johne Kessne, Ard. Glen, Williame Faconer, and Johne Leis.

(P.S). We John Falconer, deacon of the weivers of Glasgow, Michaell Watsoune, Richard Flaikfeild, John Clerk, James Glen, James Falconer, Robt. Nisbit, John M'Alester, and Andro Lie, weivers in Glasgow, and we William Bogle, John Merschell elder, John Glen, Wm. Gordoune, John Fleiming, Archbald Bar elder, Walter Livingstoun, John Walker, John Fillp, William Andersoune, Thomas Anderson, John Montgomry, Robt. Gemle, Patrik Ritchie, Thomas Hill, Hew Duchell, John Merschell younger, Alexander Hamilton, John Cuming, Johne Scheill, and Thomas Muir with our hands at the pen, becaus we cannot wryte ourselvis.

I Williame Yair, notar publict subscryving for thir persones abovenamed at thair command becaus they cannot wrytt as they affirmed.

I Thomas Scheirer, notar publict doe subscryve the premissis at comand of the foirsaidis persones quho cannot wryt witnessing my sign and subscription manuall.

Signed Roberte Maxwelle, witness, John Petrsoune, witnes, Jo: Young, witnes, and D. M'Gilchrist witnes.

102 RELATIONS WITH GORBALS AND BRIDGEND WEAVERS.

There are some supplementary entries closing up the whole matter satisfactorily:—

11 Maij 1657.

The said day, thair was producit the contract past betuixt the calling and the weifers of Gorballis, with ane book, quhairin is contenit the dowbill of the said contract, and all wther thingis hes bein payit betuixt them, and quhairin are to be insert all thingis relaiting to the Gorballis; and quhilkis contract and buik is put in the box.

27 Maij 1657.

The same day, the dekine with Patrik Bryce and Michaell Watsone producit ane compt of some money they had receavit pairtlie from the collectour, and pairtlie out of the box sen Candlemes last, and that for bringing to pas the agriment now maid with the weiferis in Gorballis they chairgit themselfis with the sowme of ane hundrethe twentie three pundis j s. iiij d., and be ane compt product, red, and allowit be the haill maisteris present, they have debursit thairintill twa hundrethe nyntein pundis, twelf schillingis, aught penneis; swa they ar superexpendit the sowme of four scoir sextein pundis xj s. iiij d., quhilk is appoyntit to be payit with all diligence; and the haill maisteris present gave the honest-men, the comptaris, grait thankis for thair paines in bringing that mater to so happie and wischitfor clois.

2 November 1657.

The same day, it was declairit be the dekine, be Patrik Bryce and Johne Falconer to quhoum the mater of agriment with the Gorballis was commitit declairit that they war compleitlie payit of the money was awin to them relating to that mater and is mentionat in the act of the dait the 27 of Maij last and the haill maisteris present dischargit them of the haill moneyis intromettit with be them anent that mater, declaring the haill thairof to be lawfullie debursit, conforme to the compt gevin in and now revine.

(8-2-1658)

The same day, the oversmane of the weiferis in Gorballis and his assessouris producit thair book conteaning certane actis set doun for the weill of that corporatioun. They war all fund verie fair lawfull and honest and thairfoir ratefeit and approvine be the dekin and his maisteris, ane of them being exceptit; quhairby it is ordanit that on of the bretherine thair in Gorballis of the weiferis may not instruct ane wther, and ordains ane wther act to be set doun for anulling of that act; and becaus the graitest debait and contraversie amongis them is for the act set doun anent the maner of the ingathering of thair saidis quarter comptis, findis the said act to be set doun most agriable to conscience, and could not be better set doun if it war yit to do; and thairfoir the same is approvine with the rest as said is.

At the craftis hospitall the 14 day of Februarij 1690.

The quhilk day . . . . . . John Gilchrist, present deacon conveinner and Simon Tennant, baillie of the Gorbells, and John M'Ilchrist, present deacon with his maisteris and most pairt of the bretheren of the said calling being mett in the said hospitall annent the auditing of the [collectouris] compt, and after auditing therof, haveing taken to ther serious considerationes the abuse done heretofor by the deacons and the maisteris of the said calling and other callings within this burgh ther neadless spending of the poors goods in randering of visits to the trualis baillie and deacon conveinner yeatlie and others, such as seeking concurrance of the Gorbell baillie against the weaveris ther annent ther quarter comptis yearlie, the skaith and dammage wherof greatlie redounding to the poor of the said calling. And for preventing hereafter the forsaid spending, the said deacon conveinner and baillie of Gorbells with consent of the said deacon, maisteris, and remanent bretheren of the said calling hes statut and ordainned likeas they hereby statuts and ordaines in all tyme comeing after the dait hereof, that noe deacon nor maisteris shall have libertie nor pouer to spend any of the poors means at any of the forsaidis wisits, but discharges the same, except what they shall spend of ther oun money allenderlie. And whosoever shall be found guiltie herafter in committing any of the forsaidis faultis, shall not onlie be lyable to make up what they shall happen to spend of the poors goods, but also shall be hereby obleidged by this present act to make payement for the use of the poor the soume of ten pounds attour what they shall be found in spending as said is. And this they ordaine to stand as ane perpetuall act in all tyme comeing.

Signed R. FYNNISONE., clerk

The "mutual love and correspondence" between the weavers on each side of the river had been disturbed in course of time by the southerners accepting journeymen at lower entrance fees than the agreement of 1657 bore, and it was found necessary to call in the Magistrates and Council of Glasgow as judges between the parties. Their judgment, given below, seems to have settled matters satisfactorily, as there is no record of any further differences:—

> EXTRACT ACT of the Magistrates and Council of Glasgow, dated 3 October 1692, as to certain privileges in the Contract and Agreement between the Weavers of Glasgow and the Weavers of Gorbals, dated 10 April 1657.
>
> Att Glasgow the thrid day of October j^m vj^c nyntie and two yeares,—

The whilk day the proveist, baillies and counsell of the said burgh being conveened.—Anent the petition given in to them be John Loch, late deacon of the Incorporation of the Weivers of the said burgh, for himselfe with advyce and concurrance of the masters and haill remanent members of the said Incorporation,— Mentioning that where be ane transaction between the deacon, masters, and remanent members of the Incorporation of weivers of the samen burgh on the ane part, and the weivers of the Gorballis on the other part dated the tenth day of Apryll j^m vj^c fiftie sevin yeares, the saids weivers in Gorballs in consideration and contemplation of diverse and sundrie priviledges and liberties granted to them be the said Incorporation of the weivers of Glasgow becam bound and obleidged that they should not suffer any stranger weivers to settle themselves within the said jurisdiction of the regalitie of Gorballs, or to set up any workhouse or loom without the speciall advyce and consent of the deacon and six of the masters of the Incorporation of weivers of the said burgh of Glasgow, and the oversman of the weivers of Gorballs and six of his assessors for payment of the soume of fourtie merks Scots money for his upset les or more. Item,—ilk prenteis takeing up his trade and working at his oune hand paying the soume of sixtein punds money les or more. Item, ilk freemans sone or any that maries ane freemans daughter paying the soume of eight pund Scots money les or more as should be thought good in maner foresaid; and all of them were to be booked in a book which was to be keeped be the weivers of the burgh of Glasgow, and the respective compositiones abovewrittin to be payed be the saids intrants was to be equallie divydit between the poor of the weivers of Glasgow and the poor of the weivers of Gorballs; as also be the said agreement they are lyable for twentie shilling yearlie for ilk loom, to be payed quarterlie at the four quarters of the year to be applyed to the poor of the weivers of Glasgow without prejudice to the weivers of Gorballs to asstrict themselves in some small thing to be payed to their oune poor in Gorballs. Likeas be the said agreement it was agreed upon between the saids parties, that it should be leisom and lawfull to every one of the saids freemen weivers in Gorballs to take ane prenteis ilk four yeares and should be bound for fyve yeares, provided that the saids weivers in Gorballs should not give more to their journeymen prentises then what was usewallie payed be the freemen weiveris of Glasgow to their journeymen, that nane of them might be prejudiciall to one another in the point of their servants fees; and in regaird at the tyme of the said transaction and agreement it was not customarie for the weivers in Gorballis to have or intertaine any journeymen bot what had bein their oune prentises. There was no condition nor liquidation made be the said agreement for the booking money of strangers journeymen which the saids weivers in Gorballis have introduced and made practicable sensyne and daylie receave journeymen strangers to them and take only from them twentie or threttie shilling of booking money; Whereas the saids petitioners be their Chartor are limited and restricted to the soume of three pund ten shilling eight pennies Scots money for each journeymans booking, whereby the petitioners are extreamlie prejudged by their admitting journeymen at ane easier rate then the petitioners can doe be their said Chartor, and is ane express transgression of the said Contract of Agreement, which obleidges aither partie to doe nae fact nor deed prejudiciall to one anothers priviledges. Likeas the petitioners humblie presumed that since the liberties and priviledges granted be the weivers of the burgh of Glasgow to the weivers of Gorballs was in consideration of their makeing payment to the poor of the Incorporation of the Weivers of Glasgow of the just and equall halfe of all compositiones and bookeing money, and that the custome now

RELATIONS WITH GORBALS AND BRIDGEND WEAVERS.

introduced of receaving of strangers journeymen being a supervenient priviledge which could not fall under the consideration of the parties transacteris being then impracticable.—That therefor the saids weivers of the Gorballs ought not only to be ordained not to receave any stranger journeymen bot such as payed the equivalent booking money with the petitioners journeymen for preventing a monopolie, but siclike ought and should be decerned and ordained to make payment to the petitioners of the just and equall halfe of the said booking money, and ordaine them to make payment of the said twentie shilling for each loom at the crafts hospitall of Glasgow quarterlie conforme to the said agreement, as being the undoubted ground and reason for which the weivers of the burgh of Glasgow did indulge and priviledge the weiveris of the Gorballs with the liberties contained in the said agreement.—Craveand therefor the saids proveist baillies and counsell to take the premissis to their serious consideration and prevent the petitioners priviledges from being invadit or violat and the meanes of their poor from being unsupplied or appropriat to uthers then the designed uses, as the said petition beares.—Whilk petition and contract of agreement past made and endit betuixt the saids weivers of Glasgow and weivers in Gorballs of the date abovespecifeit, with the ratification therof be the magistrats and toune counsell of the said burgh dated the ellevinth day of the said moneth of Apryll j^m vj^c fiftie sevin yeares foresaid, and the report of the proveist, baillie Tennent, John Andersone, late proveist, dean of gild, deacon convecner, and Peter Corbet, baillie of Gorballis (of the comoning that was betuixt the saids weiveris of Glasgow and the weivers in Gorballs) who were appointed to hear both parties anent the premissis, being tacken to the saids proveist, baillies, and counsell their consideration, and after mature advyce and deliberation had be them theranent, they of new againe for them and their successors in office have ratified allowed and approvine, and hereby allowes, ratifies and approves of the said Contract past betuixt the saids weivers of Glasgow and weivers in Gorballs, and declares this general ratification to be alse valide as if the samen were verbatim hereintill insert; And in respect after peruseall of the said Contract, they find it hath been entered into be the weivers of Glasgow and the weivers in Gorballs represented in that Contract by severall of their oune number as haveing full power warrand and commission from the haill remanent weivers in Gorballs, wherein there is concedit to the saids weivers in Gorballs by the weivers of Glasgow power to them to choise ane oversman and assessors who are to have the government and oversight of the weivers within their oune incorporation, who have obleidged themselves and their successors in office, that every person weiver in Gorballs that keepes ane or mae loomes, or workhouse ther sall pay in consideration of their freedome granted be the said Contract twentie shilling Scots for ilk loom to the weivers of Glasgow and their successouris in office yearlie and quarterlie in all tyme therafter as is at more lenth contained in the said Contract. As also considering that it was not to be leisom to the weiveris in Gorballis to give or pay any more or greater fies to their journeymen nor is payed to the journeymen in Glasgow of that trade by freemen and burgesses therof, by which cause, and severall other articles contained in the said Contract, it clearlie appeares that it was the designe of both parties contracters that nothing should be done that might be hurtfull or prejudiciall to the weivers of Glasgow by intiseing or drawing away servants or journeymen from the weivers of Glasgow by giveing them greater encouragement nor what is given them be the weivers of Glasgow. And seing the weivers in Gorballs receave journeymen for payment onlie of twentie or threttie shilling of booking money, which is fare les then what the weivers of Glasgow are limited and restricted to be their chartor, which is three pund ten shilling eight pennies for their bookeing, by which encouragement the weivers in Gorballis draw away and intise the greatest part of the journeymen alse effectuallie as if they did pay more or greater fies to the said journeymen, which is contrare to the designe and intent of the saids parties contracteris. And likewayes seing at the tyme of the said Contract, the weiveris in Gorballis were not in use to have any journeymen, and that what priviledges was granted to the saids weivers in Gorballis they did acknowledge it to be from the good will favour and tollerance of the saids weiveris of Glasgow, and ane dispensing with what right they had granted them be the 156 act of King James the 6th parliament 12, intituled exercise of crafts within suburbs adjacent to burrowes is forbidden. Therefore the saids proveist baillies and counsell as superiors and haveing power to determine and decyde in all contraversies that may arise betuixt the saids weivers of Glasgow and weivers in Gorballs, have inacted, and hereby inacts, statutes and ordaines the oversman and assessouris of the weivers of Gorballs to collect and inbring to the deacon and collector of the weivers of Glasgow the twentie shilling for ilk loom to be payed as aforesaid be the said Contract. And likewayes that they shall exact no less then three pund ten shilling eight pennies of bookeing money from everie journeyman admitted be them, and that the samen shall be divydit betuixt the saids weivers of Glasgow and weivers in Gorballs in the same maner and way as the other fees contained in the said Contract are to be divydit. And appoints the baillie of Gorballis and his successouris in office to cause the saids fynes to be payed to the collector of the weivers of Glasgow and his successouris for the use abovementioned, be the saids weivers in Gorballis summarlie without any persute or process of law, upon application or complaint to be made be the said collector or his foresaids against the saids weiveris in Gorballis who shall refuse and give obedience and not pay the samen. And ordaines the Clerk to give out Extracts heirof.—Extractum.

(Signed) G. ANDERSONE.

XII.
RELATIONS WITH CALTON AND BLACKFAULDS WEAVERS.

Although from its present position, in the heart of the city, one might expect that Calton was identified with Glasgow at an earlier date than Gorbals, yet it was a good century later than the date of the first agreement with Gorbals before there was a sufficiently large population in Calton to make a working arrangement necessary. The preliminary of a general agreement is found in a minute between an individual living in Blackfaulds and the Deacon and Collector, as follows:—

Att Glasgow the nyntein day of October j^m vij^c and ten yeiris, it is contracted and aggreed betwixt James Boyll and John Rankin, present deacon and collector of the weaveris in Glasgow for themselves and in name of the maisteris and memberis of the said corporatione on the ane pairt, and William Miller, weaver in Blackfaullis on the other pairt, in maner form and to the effect following:—That is to say the said deacon and collector heirby bindis and obleidges them and thair successores in office to permitt the said William Miller to outtake and intake work, and not to bring out work nor in work except for his oun workhous out of the toun of Glasgow, and that without ony trobell or mollestatione quhatsomever; for the quhilkis premises the said William Miller heirby bindis and obleidges him his aires &c. to content and pay to the saidis deacon and collector or to ther successores in office the sume of ten shilling Scottis quarterlie and ilk quarter for ilk loom during his abood in the said Blackfaulis for ilk loom as said is. And in caice it shall happen the said William Miller nott to make thankfull payment of the forsaid ten shilling Scotis quarterlie, in that caice he obleidges him to pay to the deacon and collector forsaid the sume of twentie shilling Scottis in caice of failzie for each loom, and sua furth to continow; consenting thir presentis be registrat in the bookis of counsell and sesiane or ony otheris, that letteris of horning on six dayes and otheris may heirupon pass, and constitutes   Procuratouris, writtin be Thomas Falconer younger, writter in Glasgow and subscrivit at day year and place foresaidis before thir witneses Robert Loch, weaver in Glasgow, and the said Thomas Falconer.

                                                    (Signed) JAMES BOYLL.
Robert Loch, Wittnes   JOHN RANKIN.
Thos. Falconer, Witnes.   WILLIEAM MILLEAR.

108 RELATIONS WITH CALTON AND BLACKFAULDS WEAVERS.

In the year 1725 the Magistrates and Council and the Trades' House conjointly, three-fourths interest for the Council and one-fourth for the Trades' House, bought the lands of Calton and Blackfaulds from John Walkinshaw of Barrowfield, and resold them in 1731 to John Orr, by whom they were laid out for feuing. On this purchase being made by the Council a full agreement was made with the large colony of weavers to whom the Council were now superiors. This agreement was as follows:—

> CONTRACT AND AGREEMENT between the Weavers of Glasgow and the Weavers of Calton or Blackfauld, dated 23 February 1725.
>
> Att Glasgow, the tuenty third day of February, one thousand seven hundred and tuenty five yearis It is contracted appointed agreed and finaly ended betwixt the persons partys afternamed. They are to say John Lang present deacon and William Bryson, late deacon and James Bogle, John Robertson, Thomas Cochran, John Hamilton, James Davidson, William Aiken, John Gibson, John Gray, William Watson, youngest, Robert Picken William Cninghame &c. (blank) present Masters and Robert Morthland, Collector of the Incorporation of Weaveris of Glasgow and Robert Wood, William Ritchie, John M'Gilchrist, Robert Loch and James Petegrew, late Deacons, William Watson elder, John Warden, James Lang and John Uric:—brethren of the said craft in name of and taken burden upon them for the haill other brethren and memberis of the said craft and their successoris weaveris and burgessess of the said burgh of Glasgow on the one part, and John Freeland, James Taylor, John Brooks, William Millar, Archibald Provan, William Wilson, William Parland, Walter Buchanan, William Buchanan, John Paterson, Robert Jamison, Robert Fleiming, James Dyckis, Alexander Kirkland, John Durie, William Dickson, Thomas M'Kean, James Whittan, John Allason, James Broun, William and John Drews, Andrew Scott, James M'Keehnie, John Paterson, David Selckrig, John Buchanan, Robert Adam, John Duncan, John Henderson, John Aikman, James Hamiltoun, James Dongal, Walter Arroll, Andrew Menzies, James Waker, Robert Howat, David Low, James Hogg, Robert Maxwell, Robert Clerk, Samwel M'Kenzie, George Robertson, James Clark, John M'Kean, Daniel M'Kechnie, James Paterson, Edward Graham, Gilbart Norie, James Blackburn, Walter Muir and John Whyt all weaveris, indwelleris in the Caltoun of Glasgow, adjacent to the said burgh, and one of the suburbs thereof now belonging to and holding of the magistratis, toun councill and community of the burgh of Glasgow now superioris and proprietoires of the Caltoun and the lands of Blackfauldis and otheris adjacent lands lately belonging to John Walkinshaw of Burrowfeild for themselves and in name of and takeing burden upon them for the haill remanent weaveris now indwelleris in Caltoun, and Blackfauldis on the other part, in manner, form, and to the effect following:—That is to say, Whereas by the

RELATIONS WITH CALTON AND BLACKFAULDS WEAVERS. 109

154 act of the 12th parliament of King James the 6th the exercise of craftis in suburbs adjacent to royal burrows as being hurtfull to the leiges for the insufficiency of the work and as damnifeing free craftismen resident within burrows who bear great part of the charges of the burghs and for other reasons thereinmentioned is forbidden and the Provost and Baillies of the said burrows are allowed to intromett with the work so working to whomsoever the materialis belong and to escheat; the same to be applyed to the common works of the burgh next adjacent to the said suburbs, which act is also ratified by several actis of parliament since made. And whereas the said partys are most sensible that not only many of the leiges are damnified in their work made by such as pretend to be craftismen who are neither capable nor has good workloomis fitt for the work they undertake, and not being under any particular government regulation or inspection of proper judges they make their work in such sort as has brought the manufactorys of cloath in this countery into very much discredit of late and given occasion to our neighbouris in some peices of work to outdo us which must tend to the ruine of our manufactories and impoverishing our countery unless remead be provided for preventing which evils and attaining the end and design of which laws and for mantaining mutual love and good neighbourhood betwixt the weaveris of the said burgh of Glasgow and the weaveris of Caltoun and Blackfauldis, the said partys following the example of other weel governed parts in the like case as amongest the weaveris of Edinburgh, Westport and Potteraw; and also following the advice and consent of the said Provost Baillies and councill of Glasgow, - Have agreed to the following articles and conditionis to be keep'd and observed by the said weaveris of Glasgow and their successoris freemen of the said Incorporation, and by the said weaveris now indwelleris in the said lands of Caltoun and Blackfauldis, and by the weaveris duelling in the said lands in all time and ages succeeding, vizt. In the first itis declared by the said weaveris of Caltoun and Blackfauldis subscribeing for themselves and in name of and acting and takeing burden on them for the haill remanent weaveris inhabitantis of said bounds now and in all time comeing that whatever freedom tollance and liberty they have for exerciseing their calling in the said bounds of Caltoun and Blackfauldis, and in takeing and bringing work to and from the burgh of Glasgow, is given and granted to them by and holden and to be held by them off and from the Incorporation of Weaveris in the said burgh of Glasgow. Secondly itis agreed and mutually condescended upon betwixt the saids partys, that the said weaveris in Caltoun and Blackfauldis present and to come shall have liberty to have ane oversman of their own number to be chosen yearly in this manner, vizt: The said weaveris of Caltoun and Blackfauldis shall on the first Fryday of May yearly in all time comeing, elect and present three of the worthyest and most qualified of their number on lyte to the deacon of the weaveris of Glasgow and his masteris of craft in the craftis hospital within the burgh of Glasgow, to the effect they may ellect and return one of the said lyte to be oversman of the said weaveris in Caltoun and Blackfauldis for the year insueing, who being elected shall give his oath *de fideli*, and the said oversman thereafter shall, with the remanent weaveris of Caltoun and Blackfauldis who shall be entered and inrolled have power to chose six of their number to be assessoris to the said oversman - beginning said

elections in May next; which overisman and assessoris shall have power to judge in all matteris betwixt brother and brother relating to the calling allennerly, and as to sufficiency and insufficiency of work in said craft wrought within the bounds foresaid, and of the dammages sustaind by the leiges through spoiling their work or not working the same in the time agreed upon application of the leiges injured; the said weaveris in Caltoun and Blackfauldis (being allways subject to the magistratis and councill of Glasgow, the baillis if any shall be named within the bounds, according as the weaveris of Glasgow are subject to the magistratis of Glasgow); and either party disagreeing or being dissatisfied with the sentence of the said overisman and assessoris haveing liberty to apeal to the deacon and masteris of the weaveris of Glasgow, who, in that case shall have power to deside and determin thereintill. Item, the said weaveris of Glasgow being satisfied as to the qualificationis of the weaveris before named now residentis in Caltoun and their capacitys to serve his Majestys leiges, doe allow them to exercise their trade in said bounds in time comeing subject allways to the terms and conditions of this present Contract and Agreement, and shall inroll them for the said liberty and freidom in Caltoun and Blackfauldis in a book to be keep'd by the said weaveris of Glasgow for that effect, and for the purposes aftermentioned, and in time comeing no person shall be allowed to sett up a workhouse or loomis within the bounds foresaid to work weaveris work untill first they give essay to the satisfaction of the deacon of the weaveris of Glasgow and six of his masteris and to the overisman of the said weaveris of Caltoun and Blackfauldis and his six assessoris or the plurality of them of his or their capacity in said art and craft sufficiently to serve the leigis and be inrolled in the foresaid bookis wherein also all apprentices and servantis taken within the said bounds are to be inrolled for the liberty of which upsett and inrollment and toward raising a fund for mentainance of poor and decayed brethren of the said calling and their widows and orphantis, and for defraying the common affairis of the said craftis; the following composition or fynes shall be payed (over and beside the clerk and officeris fees to be regulated according as the weaveris of Gorballis pay) by all intrant freemen jurneymen servantis and apprentices before they shall be allowed by the said weaveris of Caltoun and Blackfauldis or their successoris to work within the said bounds, vizt.,—Each stranger that has not his residence within the said bounds at this time or at least hes hired houses therein against Whittsunday next tuenty merkis Scotis money less or more as shall be thought fitt and determined by the deacon of the weaveris of Glasgow and any six of his masteris to be called by the deacon, and by the overisman of the weaveris of Caltoun and Blackfauldis and his six assessoris, or the plurality of the said fourteen persons. Item, each apprentice serveing within the said bounds and entreing freeman ten pounds Scotis less or more and each freemanis son or son in law, six pound Scotis less or more to be determined in same manner as the strangeris; and for the booking of each apprentice, tuenty four shilling Scotis; and which compositionis or fynes shall be equally divided betwixt the two Collectoris for the behalf of the poor brethren of the weaveris of Glasgow, and within the bounds foresaid of Caltoun and Blackfaulds and their widows and orphanis. Item, The said respective weaveris of Caltoun and Blackfanlds and their successoris weavers, inhabitantis within

RELATIONS WITH CALTON AND BLACKFAULDS WEAVERS.

the said bounds in all time comeing after Candlemass last shall be bound and obliged for the foresaid liberty and freedom to make payment to the weaveris of Glasgow or to their collector for the time for the behove of the poor of the Incorporation of Weaveris in Glasgow of twenty shilling Scotis yearly and so proportionally for ilk loom in their several houses and workhouses within the said bounds of Caltoun and Blackfauldis according as the said loom shall be listed by any tuo of the sworn masteris of the weaveris of Glasgow from time to time as they think fitt, and that at the termis following vizt. —Whittsunday, Lambmass, Martinemass and Candlemass by equal portions with six shilling Scotis of penalty and expences by each of them that failzie as oft as they shall suffer themselves to be charged for any of the said quarterlie paymentis; provideing allways that before giveing any such charge, the collector of the weaveris in Glasgow with tuo of the masteris of said Incorporation shall fix a diet for receiveing the said quarterly paymentis in some place or other within the said lands of Caltoun and Blackfauldis to which the overisman there being acquainted thereof the night before shall be obliged by his officer to have all the weaveris in Caltoun and Blackfauldis cited; and they being either cited thereto by the officer in Caltoun or by the officer of the weaveris of Glasgow shall be obliged to send their said several quarterly payments or to attend personally and pay them. And but prejudice to the weaveris of Glasgow to charge the said weaveris of Caltoun and Blackfauldis for any loomis they shall have more then shall be listed and to prove the same by their oathis. But prejudice allso to the said weaveris in Caltoun and Blackfauldis by their oun consent and statute to impose such a small fyne on themselves yearly or quarterly as shall by them be thought neccessary for supplying and mantaining their poor. And the saids partys do further agree that intrantis shall before admitting them to essay be obliged to consign in the hands of the deacon of the weaveris of Glasgow the following sumis of essay money, vizt.—each stranger fourty shilling Scotis, each freemans son or son-in-law or apprentice serveing within said bounds, one pound ten shillings Scotis money; and that it shall not be lessum or lawfull to the said weaveris in Caltoun or Blackfauldis to take ane apprentice for less time then five yearis, or to take any apprentices but house apprentises to be mantained in their oun familly, and that they shall not give more wages or hyre to servantis or jurneymen then the weaveris of Glasgow are or shall be allowed to do by the actis and statutes of their Incorporation. And the said weaveris of Glasgow oblige them to stand by and defend the said weaveris in Caltoun and Blackfaulds conforming and agreeing hereunto in the possession and exercise of the freedom and privilege hereby granted, to the outmost of their power. And in case of any differance arriseing betwixt the said partys hereafter, they shall hereby declare the magistratis and toun councill of Glasgow or their baillies in the saids lands of Caltoun and Blackfauldis if they are or shall be erected into a barrony to be judges thereof in the first instance and oblige them to bring the said differances first before them or their said baillies; and that they shall not intent or prosecute any process thereanent untill the same be first insisted in before the saids magistratis and councill or their said baillies. And both partys oblige them and each of them and their successoris foresaid *hinc inde* respective to fullfill and perform their respective

112 RELATIONS WITH CALTON AND BLACKFAULDS WEAVERS.

partis of the premisses to otheris under the pain of fourty poundis Scotis money of penalty to be payed by each party failzier or contraveener *toties quoties* to the observer or willing to observe attour performance; and for the more security the said partys consent to the registration hereof, with the several listings foresaid of the loomis to be made and taken from time to time, in the bookis of conncill and session or any otheris competent, that letteris and executoriallis of horning on fifteen days or otheris needful may thereon be direct, and for that end constitute.

Procuratoris In witness whereof these presentis written by Moses Buchanan, servitor to John Robertson, writer in Glasgow upon stampted paper on this and the tuo above sheetis with ane other double hereof are subscrived by the said partys at place day moneth and year foresaid before these witnesses Robert Robertson younger, maltman in Glasgow, Alexander Dunlop, Wright there, Daniel Campbell, servitor to the said Alexander Dunlop and the said Moses Buchanan, the joyning of the sheetis being signed by the said John Lang and John Fryland in name and at the disire of the haill other partys date wryter and witnesses foresaid.

(Signed) John Lang, James Whitlaw, Johan Alison, James Broun, William Drew, John Drew, John Freeland, James Taylor, John Brooks, William Miller, Arch. Provan, William Nilson, William Parland, Walter Buchanan, William Buchanan, John Paterson yor., Ro. Jemison, Robert Fleiming, James Dyckes, Alexander Kirk[land], John Darrie, William (blank), paper torn) William Bryson, James Bogle, John Robertson, Thomas Cochran, John Hamilton, James Davidson, William Aitkin, John Gibson, John Gray, Robert Machline, Robt. Wood, William Ritchie, John M'Gilchrist, Robert Loch, William Watson, Thomas Pettigr[ew] (paper torn off where remaining signatures were adhibited).

Et ego vero Joannes Robertson, notarius publicus in premissis requisitus de mandato dicti, Gulielmi Watson juvenissimi, Roberti Picken, Andree Scott, Jacobi M'Kechnie, Joannis Paterson senioris, Davidis Selkrig, Joannis Buchanan, Roberti Adam, Jacobi Hamilton, Jacobi Dougall, Walteri Arroll, Andree Menzies, Jacobi Walker, Roberti Howat, Davidis Low, Jacobi Hogg, Roberti Maxwell, Roberti Clark, Samuelis M'Kenzie, Georgij Robertson, Jacobi Clark, et Joannis M'Kean, scribere nescientium, ut asseruere calamumque tangentium pro illis subscribo.

Et ego Joannis Colquhonn, notarius publicus in premissis etiam requisitus de mandato dicti Gulielmi Watson, juvenissimi, Roberti Picken, Andree Scott, Jacobi M'Kechny, Joannis Paterson, senioris, Davidis Selkrig, Joannis Buchanan, Roberti Adam, Joannis Duncan, Joannis Henderson, Joannis Aikman, Jacobi Hamilton, Jacobi Dougall, Walteri Arroll, Andree Menzies, Jacobi Walker, Roberti Howett, Davidis

Plate VII.

Seal attached to Titles of Eddleston Manse (See Page 119).

Seal attached to Titles of Gorbal Lands (See Page 120).

RELATIONS WITH CALTON AND BLACKFAULDS WEAVERS.

Low, Jacobi Hogg, Roberti Maxwell, Roberti Clark, Samuelis M'Kenzie, Georgij Robertson, Jacobi Clark et Joannis M'Kean. Scribere nescientium ut asseruerunt calamumque tangentium pro illis similiter subscribo.

JOHN COLQUHOUN. N.P.

De mandato etiam Jacobi Paterson, Edwardi Grahame, Gilberti Norrie, Jacobi Blackburn, Scribere nescientium ut asseruere calamumque tangentium pro illis subscribo.

Robert Robertson. Witnes
Alexander Dunlop. Wittnes
Daniel Campbell. Wittnes
Moses Buchanan. Witness

JOANNES ROBERTSON. not. pub.

The only further record on this subject is the following petition which presumably solved the question in dispute, as there is no further reference to it:—

Unto the Deacon and Masters of the Weaveris of Glasgow. The petition of James Bell, Thomas Davidson, John Campbell, Walter M'Queen, James Porter, John and William Grays and William Reston, weaveris at present resideing in Caltoun or Blackfauld, adjacent to and one of the suburbs of the City of Glasgow.

HUMBLY SHEWETH

That we being most willing and desirous to sett up, use, and exercise our said craft in Caltoun under the conditions and regulations, and to enjoy the privileges agreed on by a contract betwixt the weaveris of Glasgow and weaveris of Caltoun dated the tuenty third day of February j^m vij^e and tuenty five years, in order theirto did require the present acting oversman in Caltoun to concurr with you in taking essay of our capacity to serve the leiges in our said craft, and modifying our fyne for our admission in terms of the forsaid contract, which they have refused, as appears by ane instrument thairon takin this day in the handis of John Marshall, notar publick.

May it therefor please you to admitt us to ane essay as to our sufficiency in said craft to serve the leiges and to modifie the fyne for our admission to the freedoms and libertys granted from your trade by said agreement to the weaveris resideing in Caltoun, and submitting to the termis thairof, and being found qualified and paying our fynes to admitt us to the liberty of taking out and in work from said burgh and other libertys specified in said agreement, for which we heirby promise to fullfill said agreement and haill termis thairof, and to pay the dues of tuenty shilling Scotis yearly and so quarterly and proportionelly for each loom we shall have in our houses and workhouses within the boundis forsaid of Caltoun and Blackfauld; and quhairas the weaveris in Caltoun concurr not, we hereby promise to pay the half of the fyne to them quhen they are regularly acting in termis of said agreement.

(Signed) James Bell, William Gray, Thomas (T.D). Donaldsons mark, John Cambell, Walter M'Queen, William Reston, James (J.P.) Porteris mark.

P

114 RELATIONS WITH CALTON AND BLACKFAULDS WEAVERS.

Att Glasgow the elevnth day of September j^m vij^c and thirty three years.— Conveend William Buchanan, Deacon with the Masteris and several other members of the Incorporatioun of weaveris in Glasgow.—The which day they, taking the within petition to consideration, with the Instrument thereinmentioned, and that the weavers in Caltoun did not compear to concurr as required in taking the petitioneris essay, modifying and receiving thair part of the fyne, and that of late the said weaveris in Caltoun, subscriberis of said agreement, refused altogether to conform theirto; therefor in the present vue they appointed the said petitioners their several essays and took tryal of their sufficiency to serve the leiges; and they having givin their essay to satisfaction, and each of them payed in five poundis Scotis as half of ten poundis Scotis modified for thair fyne to the Collector for the weaveris of Glasgow for the poor of said trade, and being by express condition heirof obliged each of them to pay us the other half of thair furder fyne to the Collector for the weaveris of Caltoun for thair poor so soon as the said weaveris of Caltoun have ane oversman assestoris and collector regularly chosin and acting according to the within agreement. The within petitioners in respect thairof were admitted to the privilege of taking out and in work to and from the said City of Glasgow, and to the other libertys and freedomis mentioned in said agreement on the conditionis forsaid, and gave thair oathis *de fideli* as use is.

XIII.
SOCIAL MATTERS.

The old minute books have few references to social matters, but those which do occur are extremely interesting. These were primitive times, and the "dekin and maisteris" undertook serious responsibility in looking to the conduct of the whole lives of those under their charge. Prentices, and even some journeymen, lived entirely with their employers, whose responsibility was much more parental than in later years. In Chapter VIII., on "Discipline," there were given such extracts as referred to the proper conduct of trade matters. In this chapter are grouped those which refer to matters outside of the workshop. The earliest is one of the most dignified deliverances in the books :—

Vigesimo quarto Augusti 1594.

Quhilk daye, the dekin, maisteris, and haill craft of the wobsteris hes statut and ordanit that quhosoevir of thair brethrein in ony tymes heireftir sall use scornefull langages, mockingis, jestingis, or tantingis, be word or deid, agains ony of thair brethrene, or ony wther persones not being of thair awin craft, to the dishonour of God, provocatioun of the persones tantit or mockit to angro or disdain, and of wtheris that sall heir the saidis tantingis, the said brethrene of thairis, everie ane of thame sall paye xvj s. to the dekin of the craft sa oft as that the foirsaid langag or tantingis be word or deid salbe wsit, and that unforgevin.

Although the drinking habits of the time caused frequent gatherings in hostelries, yet the deacon had his restraining hand on them, and he had the responsibility of preventing debt being incurred, thus discrediting the craft :—

(7-8-1602)

The dekin and maisteris of the craft, and haill craft convenit at thair Lammasse court, statutis and ordeins that quhatsumever persones of the craft sall pas with the dekin for the tyme in ony ostlar hous and drink, and at that tyme hes not silver to paye, sall paye the said silver that he salbe comptit in within xv dayes nixt eftir the drinking to the said ostlare. In case he pays not, the dekin for the tyme will discharge him of work quhill he paye the said silver to the said ostlare.

SOCIAL MATTERS.

Abstainers are not a modern innovation; they existed in olden days. The records do not disclose how far the vow—with its naive reservation—was kept by the "haill craft":—

Vigesimo secundo Septembris 1621.

Thaireftir the deikin and haill craft, conveinit for the tyme, haifing ane greit regaird of thair awin commoun weill, considdering that the daylie drincking of wyne in tymes bypast, hes not onlie drawin tha fra thair craftis, spent thair tyme ydillie, abuisit thair bodies, and wraikit thair haill guidis and geir, that ar become for the maist pairt indigent and puir. For remeid thairof, in tyme cuming, all with ane consent and assent concludit, that, nain of thame sall drinck anie kynd of wyne, of anie sort, within the burgh of Glasgow, furt and fra the allevint day of November nixtocome, quhill the allevint day of November, in the yeir of God i^m vi^c and tuentie tua yeiris (except it be that in seiknes for thair helthe, or ife ane stranger caus thame drinck for the quhilk thai sall not pay). And ife onie of thame contravein, they do heirby, and ilk ane of thame, act, bind and obleis thame for thair awin pairtis being tryit to pay of thair awin consentis ten pundis to the box, and fyve pund to the deikin conveiner *toties quoties.*

The next extract throws a strong light on the social habits of the time. The bottle was evidently convenient at every meeting. It might even be suggested that the entertainment sanctioned was likely to cause the offence reprobated:—

The viij day of Maij 1629.

The quhilk day, it was statut and ordanit be consent of the haill craft, that it sall not be liesume to na freiman of the said craft to haif his wyf at the tabill quhair the craft is doeing thair leisum bussines, bot if scho cam, to tak ane drink and go hir way, bot if scho skall and speek schamfull language, and hir housband put hir not out of the hous quhair they ar, the housband and the wyf sall pay xl s. to the craft, and xvi s. to the baillies *toties coties.*

Mr G. STIRLING

There seems to have been a hatless brigade even in these early days, whether for sanatory reasons or any other reason is not disclosed:—

At the craftis hospitall, the xj of February 1665.

The quhilk day, the deacone and maist of the brethrein of craft being conveinit, considering the disgrace hes bein in the maisters and collectour thair not coming out honestlie to meit thair deacone at thair quarter comptis, buriallis and uther meitinges with hattis on thair headis this long tyme bygane being contrair to actis sett doune thairanent of befoir; thairfoir to prevein the lyke in tyme cuming, it is statute and ordainet with all thair consentis, that no maister or collectour in the said trade and calling, sall come out to thair quarter comptis, buriallis and uther meitinges quhatsumever with thair deacones present and to come, being wairnit thairto, without hattis on thair heidis, and that under the paine of ten pundis money for ilk failzie *toties quoties* to be payit be the contraveiner of this present act for ilk failzie, to be applyit for the us of the poore of the said trade; and this to remayne unalterable in all tyme cnming.

The weavers could show gratitude for favours done *and to be done*:—

At the craftis hospitall, the 14 of August 1669 yeires. The quhilk day, Williame Dampster, clothier, being recommendit be Williame Andersonne, proveist of this burghe to the deacone and maisters of the saidis weivers to admitt him as frieman with thame for certane guid deidis and gratitudis done and to be done be the said Williame Andersoune, proveist to thame; and the said deacone and maisters, taiking the same to thair serous consideratioune, have, at the said proveistes earnest requeist and desyre admittit and receavit the said Williame Dampster frieman with thame fric gratis, and quho, being present, gave his aithe as use is.

M. ROWAND.

The last extract refers to the one social event which the Incorporation continues to observe until this day, and it will be observed that even in 1673 it was arranged on the independent footing still customary:—

At Glasgow the nyntine of September 1673. Convined Patrick Bryce, deacon conviner, John Patersone, deacone and his maisteris of craft, with the most pairt of the calling.

The same day, the particularis fallowing are inacted, statuted, and discharged as fallowis be comoune consent. In the first,—that the denner yearlie at the electione of the deacones in tyme comeing, if any be, shall be payed proportionallie be thos persones wha are present at the samyne with quhat sall be givine to the tounes drumeris after the same maner. As also it is statuted and inacted that the wholl maisteris of tread be yearlie putt out upon ane lyte in tyme comeing, to the effect ane thairof be ellectit deacone for the year fallowing; and als discharges the dollour formerlie in use to be givine to the new deacone, and thir presentis to remaine wnalterable in all tyme heirafter.

(Signed) PATRICK CLARK.

XIV.
PROPERTY HELD BY THE INCORPORATION.

There is now no capital of the Incorporation invested in lands or houses, but there is some interest in tracing the property which has been held from time to time. The oldest is certainly that at the corner of Weaver Street and Rottenrow, of which the nucleus was purchased about 1655, and which only passed from the ownership of the weavers last year. It is difficult to identify the property referred to, as there has been rebuilding during the holding of it by the Incorporation, but the following very early sasine record refers to a portion afterwards acquired by the weavers:—

(Original in Latin.)
INSTRUMENT OF SASINE 14 March 1537-8.—11 Ind. 4 Paul III

George Barbour, procurator and in name of a noble man George Sterveling of Gloret resigned in favour of a discreet man, Mathew Muirheid, burgess of the city of a waste tenement (vastum tenementum) lying in the city of Glasgow in the Ratounraw (vico ratonum) on the north side thereof between the manse of the rector of Edilstoun on the west and the tenement of the late Mr. John Boswald on the east. Sasine given by George Elphinstoun, bailie. Common seal of city appended [seal now wanting] Witnesses John Buntyne, Adam Knox, Alexander Wilsoun, Robert Ker, John Akinheid, Robert Herbertsoun, and John Martin, serjeant.

Nicholas Withirspoun, master of arts and preist of Glasgow diocese and notary public by apostolic and royal authority.

Michael Hucheson, master of arts of Glasgow diocese, notary by apostolic authority.

This also refers to a further purchase of adjoining land:—

At the craftis hospitall, the 7th of September 1664.

The same day, the deacone and maisters, taking to consideratioune the pryce of the landis of Bowastie bought be thame from Jonet Wardane, and the chairges and expenssis debursit for bountethes, with infeftmentis, and utheris had be thame thairintill; it is fund that the saidis landis standis ane thowsand merkes money—in this manner, viz.—nyne hundretlie and fourtie merkes money contenet in the dispositione thairof as first aggriet upon thairfoir, and fourtie pundis money of chairges besyd as afoirsaid.

M. ROWAND. Clerk.

PROPERTY HELD BY THE INCORPORATION.

The two properties referred to in the following are buildings erected on the ground referred to in the two preceding extracts, and it is evident that the land on which the parson of Edilstoun's Manse itself stood also passed into the ownership of the weavers. A very interesting old document referring to this property is produced as Plate IV. It dates from nearly four hundred years back, and bears the Royal seal on soft wax, both sides of which seal are also reproduced on Plate VII.:—

22 July 1665, In the craftis hospitall.

The quhilk day, Patrick Bryce, deacone, and maisteris of craft being conveinet, they all in ane voyce inact thameselves, that ilk maister sall attend day about upon the workmen that is bigging at the new hous in Robertsounes land as the deacone sall appoynt thame quhill the stone work be finischit, and thair to tack notice ilk day of the menes work quhat they sall be thairat, and of quhat stane and lymb and sand sall be furnischit thairto the tyme of thair attendance thairat, and give upe ane accompt thairof at ilk night to the deacone; and quha of thame failzies thairintill quhen the officer reqnyris then thairto, sall pay in to the box fourtie schillingis money for the us of the poore.

M. ROWAND. Clerk.

At the foir toure of the castell of Glasgow, the 21 of September 1665.

The quhilk day, Patrick Bryce, deacone, Mathew Davidsoune, collector, Micheall Watsoune and David Pitcairne, having maid just compt and reckoning to the wholl remanent maisters of thair haill intromissioune with the moneyis borrowit from severall persounes, and taikin out of the craftis box; it is fund that the samyne is dewlie and trewlie debursit, wairit, and bestowit upon the building of the new hous in Robertounes land, beiting and repairing of the old houssis thairof, and upon Balwastie houssis, as also in the new morteloathes and uthers concerning the said trade; and thairfoir the saidis four persounes ar cleired and dischairgit thairof for ever.

M. ROWAND. Clerk.

The building having been completed, a lease of a certain portion is recorded:—

Quarto Novembris 1670.

The same day, twa takes subscrivit, the ane in favouris of John Findlay and the uther in favouris of Patrick Lang, of the back land in Ratounraw for seavine yearis fra Witsonday nixt, quhilk the haill tread ratifies and approves.

PATRICK CLARK.

120 PROPERTY HELD BY THE INCORPORATION.

The weavers held the land between Rottenrow and Stirling Road, on which, early in the eighteenth century, Weaver Street was formed, but the greater part, lying north of the tenement at corner of Weaver Street and Rottenrow, was disposed of. The whole property at that corner was rebuilt in 1796, and some of the ornamental portions of the original building had been preserved and incorporated in the new tenement, where they can yet be seen.

There were properties held in the New Wynd and "nigh the Wynd head," which were disposed of in 1767. In addition to the Gorbals lands acquired by the Trades' House and the Trades conjointly in 1605 (referred to in Chapter XI.), there was also a building, known as "The Corner House," owned by some of the Trades for a short time previous to 1767. This building stood at the corner of Gallowgate and Saltmarket, which then met, diagonally opposite the Cross Steeple. It was sold in the year named.

In addition to the mortcloths referred to in next chapter, the Incorporation owned and both loaned and sold Reeds to the members for the purposes of their trade. These in the early part of the eighteenth century were quite a material asset of the Incorporation. They were bought in bulk in Belgium and Holland and distributed as required for the work current. The only real estate now in which the Incorporation has any holding is the Gorbals lands held by the Trades House, the income of which is distributed annually according to the relative proportions of the purchase money originally contributed. The title to this property is produced as Plate III., and the seal attached to the same document is shown on Plate VII.

In addition to the books and documents which have been largely used in the production of this book the Incorporation possesses many articles of great interest and value. The Deacon's Box which was latest in use; the Deacon's Snuff-box, which bears the inscription "Wm Buchanan to Deacon Jo^n Alston of the Incorporation of Weavers Glasgow 1811"; the Deacon's Bell, marked "Gift of Niel MacBrayne Deacon 1793"; a Fly Shuttle, marked "Joseph Adkin 1772," and a Throwing Shuttle Snuff-box, marked "Old Wynd Society," and bearing

PROPERTY HELD BY THE INCORPORATION.

the Arms of the Weavers' Incorporation, are shown in Plate V. The last-named is the property of late Preses Norrie of the Grand Antiquity Society.

The Collector's Box, which in the catalogue of the Old Glasgow Exhibition, 1894, is marked as of 1763, and which bears the inscription "The Weavers Art it is renowned so that rich nor poor without it cannot go"; the Collector's Snuff-horn—silver-mounted, with scroll bearing the names of Collectors continuously from 1834 till now—marked "Deacon Thomas Waddell to Collector David Gowdie Junior of the Incorporation of Weavers and his successors in office—Glasgow, 1834"; and the Collector's Mallet, of ivory, marked "Glasgow, 1834," are shown in Plate VI.

In addition, the Incorporation owns the Gold Medal and Chain, purchased by the Incorporation in 1861, and worn by the Deacon in Plate VIII.; an older Box than either the Deacon's or Collector's referred to above, without either date or inscription; a Silver Gong, inscribed "Presented to the Incorporation of Weavers by Deacon J. S. Mair as a memorial of his father, who was Deacon in 1868 and 1872"; a Chain for measuring warps, and some minor articles which were included with the Incorporation's exhibits in the Old Glasgow Exhibition of 1894, and are specified in its catalogue.

XV.
BURIALS AND MORTCLOTHS.

The "last sad offices" to brethren of the craft were looked on as a duty for the omission of which there was no excuse, and penalties were attached:—

13-2-1595.

It is statut and ordanit that na brother of craft absent him fra convoying of the buriall, being warnit be the officiar of the craft to that effect, without he have ane laufull cause to be admittit be the dekin and maisteris of craft, under the paine of foure s.

The present generation can hardly understand the use of a mortcloth, and as little could the past generation have realised that, so soon after their time, it would be so completely disused. The coffin was usually carried to the grave upon two poles with handles, and it was covered with a pall or mortcloth, usually of black velvet. This article was owned by the craft:—

Decimo tertio Februarij 1611

The same day, it is statut, concludit, and ordanit be the deikin and maisteris, that thair mortclayth in na tymes to cum sall not be lend to na persoune bot to friemen in the wobstercraft bot npone the conditiounes following,—That is, give the samin beis lent to ane unfrie persoune within the libertie of this burght, thai sall pay thairfoir xiij s. iiij d., and thes that borrowis the same without the burght, sall pay xx s. thairfoir (*ad pios usus*), and the samin not to be lent without the consent of the deikin and maist pairt of the maisteris for the tyme.

The following extract further shows that the attendance was regarded as a duty not only to the deceased but to the craft:—

Decimo septimo Augustij 1611

The qubilk day, it is statut and ordainit be the deikin maisteris and haill persounes of craft present, that all friemen of the said craft, in all tyme cuming, sall convein quhen thai ar warnit to all buriallis of thair awin craftes, and that thai compeir at the duelling hous quhairfra the buriall cummis, in dew tyme, and convoy the same to the kirkyeird, and quhatevir he be that cumis not, being laufulie warnit, except it be for ane lanful tryit excuis or utherwayes, quha cumis mid gait, or half gait, or be the gait, sal be as culpabill as give he war absent, and sall pay of unlaw viij s., *toties quoties*, unforgivin, to the weill of the craft.

An increasing membership increased the need for the mortcloths, and it was arranged that two should be provided for the weavers. Separate accounts were kept for these, and the general idea seems to have been that here was a necessary item of expenditure in connection with a burial, out of which some money might be made for the benefit of the poorer members of the craft:—

xxvj Februarij 1649.

The said day, it is statut and ordanit be the dekine, the maisteris of the craft, and haill bretherine, quhairof the most pairt war present, that thair be twa mortclothis mad with all diligence as uther craftis hes, and that the dekine caus provyde and by the same, and pay thairfoir, out of the first and reddiest of the craftis moneyis and guidis; and to the effect that these moneyis may be maid wp agane, and the poore receav no domage thairby; and to the effect the saidis mortclothis may be the better upholdin. It is also statut and ordanit that all stranger stallinger entering frieman heirefter sall pay to the saidis mortclothis four markis; everie prenteis, xl s. when he enters frieman, and everie friemans sone xx s. by and besyd thair ordinar fynes and wpsettis; and this to remayne in all tyme cuming.

3 Julij 1649.

The same day, the dekine declarit he had receavit fra Mr. Johne Herbertsone, for Mr. Johne Ferrieris annwalrent, twentie sex pundis, and farder he receavit fra Adame Tod for his fridome with the calling sextein pundis; and this day thair is takin out of the box sevine scoir ane markis, and swa the dekine hes in haill twa hundrethe and four markis; quhilk haill moneyis the maisteris orlains the dekine to wair and bestow upoun the bying and making of the twa new velvous mortclothis quhilk the craft ordanit to caus mak and provyd conforme to thair act of the dait the 26 of Februarij last, and quhat he debursis farder for the saidis clothis, ordains him to be payit out of the first and reddiest of the craftis moneyis.

26 Augusti 1649.

The said day, the dekine producit the twa mortclothis maid of velvous quhilk he was ordanit be the craft to caus mak and provyd conforme to the former act maid thairanent quhairwith the haill bretherine (quhairof the most pairt being present) war content, and he producit thairwith the compt and his debursmentis of the haill bying thairof, in the quhilk thair is nyne ellis of velvous, and of silk to be fassis, twa pundis and ane half; and the haill compt being red thairof and of ane steik of fustiane boght for lyning thairof and for making of the fassis and clothis extendis

BURIALS AND MORTCLOTHS.

in haill to the sowme of twa hundrethe thrie pundis fourtein schillingis iiij d., and the dekins chairgis in going to Edinburgh for bying of the said velvous and wtheris foirsaid being sextein pundis, extendis in haill to the sowme of twa hundrethe nyntein pundis xiiij s. iiij d. quhairof he hes recevit twa hundrethe and four markis conforme to the act of the dait the 3 of Julij last; sua restis awin to him four scoir four pundis; quhilk is ordanit to be payit to him out of the first and reddiest of the craftis goodis.

There is something ominously like pursuing the members of the craft beyond the grave in threatening with a fine the brother who did not use the mortcloth. A strong compulsitor for their use is found in making *that* a condition of warning the craft to attend the burial:—

(26-8-1649)

The said day, it is statut and ordanit that quhat brother of the calling sall not mak use of the craftis mortclothis that the calling sall not be wairnit to the buriell, and that ilk frieman who sall mak use of the mortclothis for thair awin use alfanerlie sall pay twelff schillingis for the mikle clothe and sex schillingis for the litle clothe, with twa schillingis at ilk tyme for ilk clothe to the officer who is to attend the saidis clothis at all tymes when they ar lent out and to be cairfull to bring them back agane and to tak the said twa schillingis ilk tyme for his panes.

There must have been disorder in the response to the calling to burials, so a re-enactment is necessary:—

4 December 1654.

The same day, the former actis set doun anent the keiping of buriallis ar ratefeit and approvine with consent of the haill craft, who for the most pairt war present, and the dekine ordanit to sie and caus put the same to execution, and the absentis wnlayit accordinglie.

There is no entry for several years, and by that time the craft appears to own four cloths, of varying size and age, the charges for the use of which are graded:—

8 Februarie 1681.

And in lyk manner the baillie and deacon conveiner, deacone, maisteris, and calling hathe, fra this day furthe for the space of four yearis ordaint the new meikle mortclothe to pay tuentie schilling ilk friman ilk tyme they sall have to do theirwith, ten schilling for the litle new ane, ten schilling for the old meikle clothe, and fyve schilling for the litle old clothe.

In 1774 a partnership was entered into between the Incorporations of Tailors and Wrights and the Weavers, by which the stock of mortcloths was amalgamated, and the shares agreed on were five twenty-thirds to the Tailors, and nine twenty-thirds to each of the other two Incorporations, the Wrights and the Weavers—the co-partnery to last for fifty-seven years. The whole mortcloths of the trades seem to have been amalgamated at a later date, and last century the custom of using them at funerals died out.

XVI.
THE WEAVER IN PUBLIC AFFAIRS.

There have already been quoted allusions to the burden of the cost of education falling upon the craft, but no evidence is found of any direct contribution by the Incorporation. From the Burgh Records there is the following—probably the beginning of technical education in the city:—

In October, 1728, an interesting appointment was made. The Town Council then approved of a contract between the Magistrates and Susannah Smith, widow of the late Rev. Archibald Wallace, Minister of Cardross, by which Mrs Wallace was nominated Mistress of the publict school erected in the city for teaching girls "to spin flax into fine yarn fit for making thread or cambrick. The lady was to receive an annual "encouragement" of £30 sterling, granted by the Commissioners and Trustees of the Improvement of Fisheries and Manufactories in Scotland.

An entry appears showing that the Incorporation directly helped the early efforts in Sunday-school teaching. It was only fourteen years before this date that Robert Raikes began this movement:—

(21-2-1794)

There was then laid before the meeting a Petition of the Managers of the Sunday Schools in Glasgow signed in their name by William Wardlaw preses and John Muir secretary praying for aid to carry on the schools for the current year;—which, being read, the members of the Incorporation being fully sensible of the great utility of the Sunday Schools and that many poor people of this Incorporation have their children taught in them, unanimously did and hereby do vote five pounds sterling to be paid from the Incorporation's Funds to the collector of the said Sunday Schools, and authorize the said Alexander Wyllie collector to pay the same accordingly.

The Trades' House in 1808 started a boys' school for over 100 pupils, to which school this Incorporation had permission to send eight boys. In 1838 the school was extended to include girls, and these schools now exist as Hutchesons' Grammar Schools.

THE WEAVER IN PUBLIC AFFAIRS.

In civic affairs, especially in the early part of the eighteenth century, the Incorporation took an active interest. All movements in the way of Burgh Reform were carefully and critically examined. The craftsmen most jealously watched any enactment which gave power to individuals, and were always favourable to popular election of representatives. There is recorded a long and interesting deliverance at an early stage of the discussions and movement which ended in the repeal of the Corn Laws :—

> At the Trades Alms-House of Glasgow the 28 Oct. 1786 Convened Christopher Beck Deacon William Scott Collector with the masters and a great number of the other members of the Incorporation of Weavers in Glasgow the whole being duly warned as was verified by the officer.

The Incorporation being this day convened, in obedience to an act of the Trades House; in order to take into consideration a plan proposed by the Landed Interest of Mid-Lothian for altering the present laws regarding the Importation of Grain and Meal into Scotland and making their County the standard and a Jury of their own number the Judges of opening and shutting the Ports. After reasoning on the subject at great length were unanimously of opinion

1mo That in a Commercial and Manufacturing Country such as this; the hands employed ought to be plentifully supplied with provisions at moderate prices in order to enable us the more effectually to rival other countries in Commerce and Manufactures. To obtain which great end nothing can be more conducive than a free Importation of grain from other countries, which can afford it at a cheap rate, and as the price of grain regulates the price of Labour, our Manufactures in point of cheapness would be on a footing with those of other countries and we could easily go before them in point of quality.

2do It is a fact, that Scotland from its great increase of population cannot supply itself with provisions. Of the whole counties only eight can export corn besides serving themselves, and the overplus expected cannot be great. The necessity therefore of importing grain and meal from foreign countries is obvious. But the legislature has thought fit to restrict a free importation of grain, excepting at stated periods, when the internal high price and scarcity require it; by this the Landed Interest have always a certainty of a sufficient price for their grain with which they ought to rest satisfied and not by any innovation hurt their country's manufactures.

3tio By the great exertions of this country and some patriotic individuals the Fisheries on our coasts are put on a fair way of being a source of wealth to the

THE WEAVER IN PUBLIC AFFAIRS.

nation; But the present plan were it adopted, would not only effectually destroy the Fisheries, but ruin the whole Manufactures of the West.

4to It is highly unjust and unpolitical to allow one county to be the Judge and arbiter of supplying another with provisions, especially Mid-Lothian one of the most fruitful shires of Scotland; it would be more reasonable that the poorest county should be the rule of importing grain for the rest; It would be hard to deprive any County or the Manufacturing Interest of the Right of supplying themselves in provisions at as cheap a rate as possible. The trade and manufactures of this country are the sole support of it, as they pay eight-tenths of the National Taxes; to restrict them therefore in Provisions would be to ruin the country.

The Incorporation for these reasons are humbly confident the Legislature will never listen to the Plan of the Landholders of Mid-Lothian, which is calculated merely to promote their own Interest at the expense of their country; and unanimously resolve to oppose it to the utmost of their power and contribute their proportion of any expense. They return their thanks to the respectable Chamber of Commerce of this City for their watchful attention to the public Interest; they also request other Societies and Bodys Corporate would join them in the above measures. And appoint these resolutions to be advertised in the Edinburgh and Glasgow newspapers.

(Signed)   CHRISTOPHER BECK.

The weavers, however zealous in opposing privilege where the cost of their own food was concerned, did not show any disposition to abandon their own exclusive privileges. Early in the nineteenth century there were frequent movements for the enforcement of the rights of the craft; but the progress of the times led to Parliament, in 1846, withdrawing all such exclusive rights, and throwing open all trades and crafts to any one who chose to engage in them.

The following is the only entry found of anything in the Incorporation corresponding to the Freedom of the City being conferred on those who have done special service to the community, and, in passing, it may be remarked that the references to Rutherglen are, considering its proximity to Glasgow and its known importance as a weaving district, very infrequent:—

1 May 1730.

John Harvie Deacon of Rutherglen Weavers Incorporation was admitted "for his good services to the Toun of Glasgow and in particular at the election of Thos. Smith, M.P."

THE WEAVER IN PUBLIC AFFAIRS.

There have been several references to the Incorporation recognising, by exemption or modification of fees, services to the State in the Army or Navy. In very early days the deacon had to provide a musket, presumably for the arming of a civic guardian:—

The fourth day of November, 1629.

The quhilk day, it is statut and ordanit that in all tymes cumming qubaever fallis to be deacon and is subject to put in ane muskat that at sal be wpon his awin charges; and no help of the craft.

Mr. GEORGE STIRLING.

Another early entry shows that a musket was in pledge to the craft and released on payment of its value:—

Duodecimo February 1641 yeiris.

The quhilk day, William Rid, officer, hes presentlie delyverit to the deacon four pund for the price of ane muskat quhilk the said William ressevit frm the croft to apryise, and quhilk muskat belongit to Robert Haistie, and wes impignorat be the said Robert to the said croft for satisfactioun of his fyne and compositionne and the said William priefit- he wes fred thairof in tyme cuming.

The Incorporation made a special exemption as to voting, in favour of the defenders of the country:—

At the Tron Church of Glasgow the 18th day of Decr., 1755.

The said [day] it was unanimously enacted by the Trade and is hereby enacted that no freeman of the Trade shall hereafter be allowed to vote or be voted upon for any office-bearer of the Trade until he pay up his whole bygone quarter accounts and other debts due to the Trade whether he be living within or outwith the Town, unless he has been serving his Majesty in his Army or Navy.

A few years later they assessed themselves to the extent of £200, which had to be raised by a special addition to quarter accounts. The Regiment was probably the Highland Light Infantry:—

2-1-1778. £200 voted by a majority to raise Glasgow Regiment to be refunded by every freeman paying 1/ additional of quarter accounts.

The Volunteer movement at the end of the eighteenth century, when an invasion by the French was feared, was well supported by the weavers, as well as the other Incorporated Trades. The following entry gives the beginning of the movement:—

(1-6-1798).

The Deacon laid before, and read to the meeting a Report and Regulations of the Trades House of Glasgow remitted to him with regard to raising a Battalion of Craftsmen in the City upon the present emergency when the country is threatened with invasion by a cruel enemy, to consist of from three to five hundred men, to be termed the "Trades Battalion of Royal Glasgow Volunteers" to learn the use of Arms, and be ready at all times when called upon by the Lord Provost, Magistrates, Dean of Guild, and Convener, when the regular Military and Volunteer corps are called out of town, to stand forth and defend the City and suburbs.

The meeting taking the same into consideration approved of the resolution, and in order to give it full effect the masters in the meantime cheerfully offered, and agreed among themselves to join in forwarding the undertaking, and that a Committee shall be appointed to [have] the plan carried fully into execution.

(5-6-1798).

The meeting in pursuance of their former resolution of carrying the plan of the Trades Battalion for the defence of the City and Suburbs into effect resolved that a Printed offer of service (transmitted from the Trades House for the subscription of individuals) shall be presented to the several members of this Incorporation for their signature to engage in so necessary a service, and for that end appoint . . . . .

An elaborate scheme for personally calling on every member of the craft follows. The next entry preserved shows that funds were not so readily forthcoming as offers of personal service. No doubt in those days, as at the present day, it was felt that such charges should be borne by the whole community:—

(17-1-1804).

The Deacon laid before the meeting an extract act of the Trades house, dated the 11th inst., appointing the respective Deacons of the Incorporated trades to convene their incorporations in order to resolve whether they will contribute an additional sum out of their funds to be applied towards completing the Trades Regiment of Volunteers. The meeting order the same to be laid before a general meeting of the Incorporation in the Trades Hall on Tuesday first at 5 o'clock.

XVII.
LATER HISTORY.

In the previous chapter the later history has been somewhat led up to by detailing the action of the Incorporation at the time of the agitation against the Corn Laws. Throughout the closing years of the eighteenth and earlier half of the nineteenth century there is also frequent reference to Burgh and Parliamentary reform, the Slave Trade, and the Laws against Popery. On these subjects the Incorporation freely expressed its feeling and used its influence on the popular side.

An important factor in the later history of the trade was the introduction of the power loom. On that subject *Pagan's History of Glasgow* says:—

"The power loom was introduced to Glasgow in 1773, by Mr James Louis Robertson of Dunblane, who set up two of them in Argyle Street, which were set in motion by a large Newfoundland dog performing the part of a gin-horse." John Robertson, a Pollockshaws power-loom tenter, in several letters sent to the Glasgow Herald in Jany and Feby 1871 stoutly contests the accuracy of this statement, and, contending that Mr Pagan must have been misinformed, he says that a man named Adam Kinloch, whom he met in 1845, and who was then eighty-five years of age, "made the first two power-looms that ever were made in the world, and drove them with the use of a crank by his own hand, in a court off the Gallowgate" in 1793.

In *Gibson's History of Glasgow* (pp. 247, 8) there is an interesting detailed account of the classes and values of textile goods manufactured in the city during 1771. He shows that then cotton and linen fabrics largely preponderated over woollen, which in the earlier years had been the staple manufacture of Glasgow. The total value, however, only reached £156,456. The same volume has a very interesting reference to the effect of the loss of the American trade in 1776:—

"Perhaps no circumstance could have occurred more fortunate for the manufactures of Glasgow, than the stop which has for some time been put to the commerce with

LATER HISTORY.

America. Prior to this event the chief aim of the manufacturers was to procure a sale of their commodities to this market; and, as the returns for these were not made in less than eighteen months, the capital necessary to carry on any manufacturing branch of business, even to a tolerable extent, was considerable: by the shutting of. the American market, necessity has led them to make trial of others, and they now find that markets for their manufactures can be procured which will make them returns in six months, so that three times the quantity of business may be done on the same capital as formerly."

M'Gregor's History of Glasgow gives particulars of a serious trade disturbance as follows:—

"In the summer of 1787 the journeymen weavers in the Calton commenced an agitation for an increase of wages; and as they had been unable to obtain all the concessions they desired from their employers, their feelings overcame their judgment. Threatening letters were sent to those who opposed them; and towards the end of August acts of violence were committed—the rioters cutting the webs from the looms of those of their fellows who were working at the old rate, and the contents of warehouses were thrown into the streets as fuel for bonfires. The authorities of Glasgow at last found it necessary to take strict measures for the preservation of the peace; and on the 3d September, the city magistrates, with a force of officers, proceeded to the Calton. The mob attacked them with a variety of missiles and drove them citywards. A detachment of the 39th Regiment then quartered in Glasgow, marched, under the command of Lieut.-Colonel Kellet, to the assistance of the civil power. At Parkhouse, in Duke St., near the place where Tennant's Brewery is now, the rioters and the authorities came into collision, and a pitched battle ensued. The riot act had to be read; and a volley from the muskets of the military killed three of the weavers, and wounded several others. The crowd quickly dispersed. In the afternoon there were symptoms of further disturbances, but any outbreak was quelled by the immediate appearance of the soldiers. On the following day however, more wrecking of looms took place in Calton; but the presence of the military brought the community into a more orderly condition, and prevented a prolongation of the riots."

In the closing years of the eighteenth and first twenty years of the nineteenth century there was a rapid increase in the textile trade of Glasgow and neighbourhood. *M'Gregor's History*, already quoted, states that:—

In 1818 there were fifty-two cotton mills in Glasgow, containing 511,200 spindles, and employing an estimated capital of £1,000,000 stg. The amount of cotton cloth produced yearly in the city was computed to be upwards of 100,000,000 yards, of a total value of £5,000,000. During this period there were 64,803 packages of cotton wool imported into the city, and these packages were estimated to have contained

LATER HISTORY. 133

18,198,500 lbs., while there were exported 46,565 packages, leaving 18,238 on hand at the close of the year. Within the city there were eighteen steam weaving factories, containing 2,800 looms and producing 8,400 pieces of cloth weekly. Including the outlying districts of Partick, Pollockshaws, Rutherglen, Cambuslang, &c., there were 18,537 looms, and including in a grand sweep those looms in neighbouring towns which were usually kept employed by Glasgow merchants, the total mounts up to 32,000 steam and hand looms.

The question of maintaining the exclusive rights of the craft became acute about 1826, and there was frequent litigation: but the time had gone by for such restrictions, and in connection with a reform of the whole municipal government the exclusive privileges were swept away. Whether or not this freedom was a factor we cannot tell, but from 1846 onwards there was a very rapid expansion of the textile trade in Glasgow. Dr. John Strang, the City Chamberlain in 1856, states that:—

There were then about 30,000 cotton spinners and power loom weavers in the West of Scotland, "of which Glasgow is the central mart." In 1841 the average weekly wage of a cotton spinner was 21s. and of a power loom weaver 7s.; in 1851 21s. and 7s. 3d. respectively; and in 1856 20s. to 35s. in the one case, and 8s. 3d. in the other. The working hours were in 1841 69 hours per week, in 1851 60 hours per week.

And again, writing about ten years later, says that:—

The census returns of 1861 showed that in that year Textile products to the value of £25,121 were exported direct to France. There were employed in cotton, flax, and jute, wool and silk factories in Glasgow 1,104,472 spindles, 22,813 power looms, engines of 13,214 horse power, and 28,489 operatives.

Many new branches of textile manufacture have taken root and grown in the city during the latter half of the nineteenth century, while the grey cotton industry, which, as shown in the extract just quoted, gave employment to the great bulk of the operatives, has practically been given up.

The later history of the Incorporation itself has been placid and without outstanding incident. As in the other Incorporations, the membership in many cases has no connection with the trade, but a reference to the list of present members of the Master Court in

LATER HISTORY.

Appendix I. will show that even now the majority—and the Master Court may be taken to be fairly representative of the members—are closely connected with the weaving trade. Many surnames of frequent occurrence in the early records have completely disappeared. Such names as Fleikfield, Winzett, Snyip, and Schankschawe are unknown now. On the other hand, the same families, who wrought so faithfully and planned so broadly for the future of Glasgow, are still well represented in the life of the city. Such names as MacBrayne, Alston, Paul, Coats, Addie, Hunter, Glen, Kirkland, Dobbie, Ralston, Gemmell, Scott, Cuthbert, Muir, Anderson, and Kilpatrick were, one to two hundred years back, of frequent occurrence in the weavers' records. The Incorporation has ceased to have any direct connection with or control of the weaving trade, but the interest in and responsibility of caring for the poorer members is as great as ever, and it may fairly be claimed that the funds are now as usefully administered for that purpose as at any period in its long and interesting history.

APPENDIX.

APPENDIX I.
INCORPORATION OF WEAVERS,
1904-1905.

OFFICE-BEARERS.

Deacon.
ROBT. D. M'EWAN (No. 5),
Cotton and Woollen Manufacturer.

Collector.
JOS. P. MACLAY (No. 7),
Shipowner.

Masters.

ADAM WHITE (No. 1),
Chemical Broker.

JOHN SERVICE (No. 2),
Wholesale Warehouseman.

ALBERT HARVEY (No. 3),
Muslin Manufacturer (*retired*).

ROBERT KEDIE (No. 4),
Wholesale Warehouseman.

J. M. EASTON (No. 6),
Civil Engineer (*retired*).

JAS. G. MACPHERSON (No. 8),
Woollen Yarn Merchant.

NICOL P. BROWN (No. 9),
Muslin Manufacturer.

THOS. A. PAUL (No. 10),
Foreign Merchant (*retired*).

JAMES ARTHUR (No. 11),
Wholesale Warehouseman.

JOHN LYLE (No. 12),
Carpet Manufacturer.

R. G. PATERSON (No. 13),
Cotton Manufacturer.

A. L. HOLMES (No 14),
Cotton and Woollen Manufacturer.

FRED. L. MACLEOD (No. 15),
Foreign Merchant.

GEO. W. YOUNGER (No. 16),
Woollen Yarn Merchant.

CHAS. J. MACLEAN (No. 17), Writer,
Clerk to the Incorporation.

The numbers opposite the names refer to Plate VIII.
No. 10.—Col. Paul is in uniform of 1st Lanark Rifle Volunteers.

PLATE VIII.

APPENDIX II.
LAWS AND REGULATIONS.

I.—NAME AND DESIGNATION OF INCORPORATION.

The Incorporation shall be known, as heretofore, under the name and designation of the Incorporation of Weavers of Glasgow, and shall be governed, in time coming, as hereinafter provided for.

II.—ENTRANTS.

All applicants must be Burgesses and Guild Brethren of the Burgh of Glasgow, and produce their certificates as such on making their applications. Every person applying for admission as a member shall produce a certificate of his birth, or, failing this, make a declaration of age agreeably to a printed form to be furnished by the Clerk. These require to be lodged with the Clerk prior to the meeting of the Master Court at which the application is to be considered.

Far-Hand.—Applicants at the Far-Hand are those who have had no previous connection with the Incorporation. Every Entrant at Far-Hand must be approved of by three-fourths of the Master Court present when he is proposed for admission. The Master Court shall have the absolute power to admit or reject the application.

Near-Hand.—Sons and sons-in-law of Members shall be entitled to become Members, provided their father or father-in-law, as the case may be, shall have been entered a Member for a year and a day preceding the date of application, and provided, in the case of sons-in-law, that the wife, through whom the applicant claims admission, shall be in life. Apprentices of Members of the Incorporation in business as weavers, whose indentures have been booked with the Clerk of the Incorporation within three months of their date, shall be entitled to admission as Members at the Near-Hand on the termination of their apprenticeship.

The applicant, if found qualified, shall, upon payment of the Entry Money, as specified in the Schedule annexed, or on payment of such Entry Money as may from time to time be fixed by the Incorporation, be admitted a Member of the Incorporation, and to all the liberties and privileges thereof.

All persons joining the Incorporation shall be bound by the Rules and Regulations thereof in force for the time being.

III.—Office-Bearers and Management.

1.—Office-Bearers.

The affairs of the Incorporation shall be managed by a Master Court, consisting of the Deacon, Collector, late Deacon, late Collector, and twelve Masters, in all sixteen. The election shall take place as after provided, at a General Meeting of the Members specially convened for that purpose, on the first Friday after the 15th September in each year.

2.—Deacon.

Any Member of the Incorporation eligible to be elected to the office of Deacon must have held the office of Collector for at least one year, and been honourably discharged of his intromissions, and been a year out of that office. The Deacon shall hold office for one year, but may be re-elected.

3.—Duties of Deacon.

The Deacon shall act as Chairman at all Meetings of the Incorporation and Master Court, at which he is expected to wear his official medal and chain. In the absence of the Deacon, the late Deacon shall preside, and failing them the Meeting shall elect a Chairman for the time being, who must be a Member of the Master Court, and the Deacon, or the person acting as Chairman, shall, besides a deliberative vote, have also a casting vote in all cases of equality. The Deacon shall have power in any urgent case to grant a precept, not exceeding sixty shillings. The Deacon shall be the Director of the Old Man's Friend Society.

4.—*Collector.*

Any Member of the Incorporation eligible to be elected to the office of Collector must have been for one year at least a Member of the Master Court. The Collector shall hold office for one year, but may be re-elected.

5.—*Duties of Collector.*

The Collector shall manage the whole money transactions of the Incorporation, and shall keep regular and distinct accounts of his receipts and disbursements. He shall keep an open cash account (to be operated on by the Deacon and Collector jointly, or, in absence, any two senior Members of the Master Court) with such chartered or joint-stock bank as the Master Court may direct, and regularly deposit therein all monies belonging to the Incorporation, not retaining in his hands any sum exceeding £25 sterling. The Collector shall find security for his intromissions with the funds of the Incorporation to the extent of £200. The Bond of Caution shall be prepared by the Clerk, at the expense of the Incorporation.

The Collector shall at the end of each month submit his books to the Deacon, who shall subscribe the same.

The Collector shall, with the assistance of the Clerk, annually, as at the 15th day of August, make up a correct statement of his intromissions, embracing an account of the Revenue and Expenditure during the preceding year, a Stock Account, and an Abstract or Balance, exhibiting the whole properties and moneys belonging to the Incorporation, which shall be examined and compared with the relative vouchers by a Committee appointed by the Master Court to examine the same, along with a Committee of three Members of the Incorporation appointed at the Meeting in August, and who shall submit the statement, with their report thereon, to the Meeting of the Incorporation in September, and if said statement is approved of by the Meeting, the Collector shall be discharged and acquitted.

and his Bond of Caution delivered up. Any Collector not being so honourably discharged shall not be entitled to sit in the Master Court.

6.—*Representatives to the Trades House.*

The Incorporation being entitled to send four Representatives to the Trades House, of whom the Deacon and late Deacon are two, *ex officiis*, the other two shall be elected at the General Meeting in September, and must be Members of the Master Court. One of the Representatives shall also be elected at said Meeting to be a Member of the Trades House Committee on Education. The Deacon shall be the Member for the Incorporation of the Trades House Committee on Buildings.

In the event of the re-election of the Deacon, the late Deacon shall be eligible for re-election as one of the four Representatives to the Trades House.

Representatives who have been elected Deacon Convener or Collector of the Trades House, must be returned as Representatives so long as they hold such offices, or are entitled to sit in the House as late Deacon Convener or late Collector.

7.—*Qualifications of Deacon, Collector, and Trades House Representatives.*

It shall not be lawful to any person who now is, or who shall hereafter be, a Member of the Incorporation, to hold office as Deacon, or to be elected a Representative of the Incorporation to the Trades House, or a Member of the Trades House Committee on Education, unless he is a Burgess and Guild Brother of Glasgow *qua* Weaver, or shall have paid, or shall pay, to the Collector of the Trades House, two guineas, or such other sum exigible at the time as the Entry Money to the funds of the House. Representatives to the Trades House must have a dwelling house or place of business within the Municipal boundaries of the City of Glasgow, as defined by Act of Parliament.

8.—*Election of Office-Bearers.*

The election of Office-Bearers shall be conducted in the following manner, at the Annual General Meeting in September, and the voting shall be by direct vote:—

1. The Member of the Master Court duly qualified who, on being proposed and seconded, receives the greatest number of votes of the Members present, shall be declared elected Deacon of the Incorporation for one year.

2. The Meeting shall then in the same manner elect a Collector for one year.

3. The five Masters at the top of the list shall annually retire, but are eligible for re-election. At the General Meeting of the Incorporation on the first Thursday in August, Members shall be proposed and seconded to fill the vacancies in the Master Court. In the event of there being only five nominated, they shall be declared duly elected at the Annual General Meeting in September. In the event of more than five being nominated, the names of the persons so nominated shall be printed on a slip of paper, and a copy of the slip shall be handed to each Member of the Incorporation on the qualified roll present at the Annual General Meeting in September. Each Member present shall mark with a X the persons, not exceeding five, for whom he votes, and shall sign his slip, which shall be handed in to the Clerk at the Meeting. The votes shall be counted by two or four scrutineers appointed at the Meeting, and the five on the list having the greatest number of votes shall be declared by the Deacon as elected to fill the vacancies. In the event of one of the nominees on the list being chosen as Collector, then the Meeting shall only elect four Masters. The Deacon shall thereafter, by virtue of his office, elect two Members of the Incorporation to serve in the Master Court for the ensuing year as Deacon's Masters.

4. Two Representatives to the Trades House from the Master Court shall be elected at the Annual General Meeting, and one to represent the Incorporation for the year on the Trades House Committee for managing the Gorbal Lands.

5. A Representative to the Trades House Committee on Education shall be elected from among the Representatives to the Trades House.

6. The qualified roll, consisting of all free Members, viz., those who have been joined a year and a day, and are not recipients from the funds, shall be laid upon the table at the commencement of the Meeting, and no person shall be entitled to vote whose name shall not appear on said roll. No minor shall be qualified to vote, or hold office in the Incorporation.

7. On the election of a Member to the office of Deacon, Collector, or Master of the Incorporation, he shall, on accepting said offices, take the oath *de fideli*, as use is.

8. It shall not be competent to elect any Member to hold office in the Incorporation who at the same time is an office-bearer in any other of the Trades' Incorporations.

9. The Deacon and Collector on retiring from office shall have their names added at the foot of the list of Masters, the Deacon's Masters being placed immediately above them.

10. Any Master who is not present at the Meeting at which he is elected to office shall appear at the first Meeting of the Master Court thereafter, and take the oath. If he does not so appear his election shall be held to have fallen, but he may be re-elected by the Master Court.

9.—*Vacancies during Term.*

In the event of the death, resignation, or other disqualification of the Deacon, or the Collector, or any of the Representatives to the Trades House, a General Meeting of the Incorporation shall be called by the Master Court, at which the vacant office shall be filled up, *ad interim*, until the next Annual Meeting for election purposes; and in the event of a vacancy occurring in any of the offices of Master, Clerk, or Officer, the Master Court shall fill up such vacancy until the next Annual General Meeting.

10.—*Clerk.*

At said Annual General Meeting a Clerk to the Incorporation shall be elected. He must be a member of the legal profession, and if not a Member of the Incorporation at the time of his election, he must undertake to enter within three months thereafter. The duties of the Clerk shall be to conduct the business and correspondence of the Incorporation and Master Court. Among other things, he shall write, or cause to be written out, minutes of the proceedings, call all Meetings, as instructed by the Deacon, assist the Collector in making up his yearly accounts, and the Master Court in all the ordinary administration of the affairs of the Incorporation, and give his legal advice upon such when required, meet and give information to all persons applying for admission as Members, and also to Members and their widows and others applying for relief; for all which he shall be paid such yearly salary and dues as the Master Court may fix from time to time, but exclusive of the usual professional fees for preparing all legal deeds and documents, which shall be prepared by him as heretofore, and for conducting legal business of the Incorporation.

11.—*Officer.*

At said General Meeting an Officer to the Incorporation shall be elected. In making such appointment, it shall not be necessary that the person so elected be a Member of the Incorporation. His salary shall be fixed and his duties defined by the Master Court.

IV.—MEETINGS OF INCORPORATION.

There shall be two fixed Meetings of the Incorporation held in each year. These Meetings shall be as follows, viz.:—(1) The Annual General Meeting, which happens on the first Friday after the 15th of September, when the Office-Bearers for the year are elected, and the other business transacted as herein provided; and (2) On the first Thursday of August, called the Lammas Court, for general business.

Special Meetings of the Incorporation may be called for the despatch of business, or for the consideration of any matter or subject affecting the Incorporation, by the Deacon, the Master Court, or on a requisition subscribed by not less than 16 qualified Members. Should the Deacon fail to call such Special Meeting within ten days after the requisition has been put into his hands, it shall be competent for the requisitionists to convene such Meeting through the Clerk, who shall be bound to call it.

No motion shall be made, considered, and decided on at the same Meeting of the Incorporation at which it shall be introduced; but each motion shall lie over for further consideration and decision at the next Ordinary General Meeting, or at a Special General Meeting called for the purpose, except as after provided in Section VI., clause 2.

At all Meetings of the Incorporation any 16 of the Members on the qualified roll shall be a quorum. After the Minutes are read, if approved of, they shall be signed by the Chairman.

The fixed Meetings of the Incorporation shall be called by advertisement in the newspapers and by circular posted to the known addresses of the Members, and Special Meetings by circular only.

V.—THE MASTER COURT AND ITS MEETINGS.

The whole affairs of the Incorporation, except as is otherwise provided for by these Laws and Regulations, shall be managed by the Master Court, who may, whenever they deem it necessary, call a Meeting of the Incorporation for the consideration of any special matter or matters.

The Ordinary Meetings of the Master Court shall be five in number, and shall be held as follows:—(1) On the Friday immediately after the Annual General Meeting; (2) On the first Friday of November; (3) On the second Thursday of February; (4) On the first Thursday of May; and (5) On the first Thursday of August; but it shall be competent for the Deacon to call Special Meetings of the Master Court at any other time. The last four fixed Meetings of the Master Court shall be named Quarterly Meetings. Both the Ordinary and Special Meetings of the Master Court shall be called by circular delivered to the Members by the Officer, or through the Post-Office.

The first Meeting of the Master Court shall be held on the Friday immediately following their election, as above arranged. At that Meeting the Master Court shall elect the Key Keepers—three for the Deacon's and three for the Collector's Box—who shall be as follows:—For the Deacon's Box, the Deacon, the late Deacon, and one Member of the Court; for the Collector's Box, the Collector, the late Collector, and one Member of the Court. The Meeting shall appoint the following Committees:—(1) To look after and let the Incorporation property; (2) To provide for the education of the children of such Members as may require it; (3) To arrange for the visitation of those receiving aid from the Incorporation residing in the city, and obtaining information regarding those at a distance; and (4) To examine the securities of the Incorporation.

At the four Quarterly Meetings the general business shall be transacted, such as—the admission of Members, revision of the Roll of Pensioners, and any other business competent to be dealt with by the Master Court.

At all Meetings of the Master Court seven shall be a quorum.

VI.—THE FUNDS.

1. The Funds of the Incorporation shall be applied for the support of decayed Members of the Incorporation, and of deceased Members' widows in indigent circumstances, at the discretion of the Master Court; and also, of unmarried daughters, as provided in Section VII., clause 10 hereof; for aids, by donation or otherwise, to public institutions and benevolent objects; and for the promotion of public measures for the advantage of the Incorporation and the good of the community of Glasgow, if voted at a Meeting of the Incorporation duly called.

2. The Funds of the Incorporation shall be managed under the direction and superintendence of the Master Court, who shall have all the powers, privileges, and immunities of gratuitous Trustees, by Statute or at Common Law, and particularly, but without prejudice to said generality, the Funds may be invested in the purchase of lands, houses, feu-duties, or ground annuals, or in Government annuities, or may be lent upon first heritable bonds to an amount not exceeding two-third parts of the estimated value of the property mortgaged, in addition to the personal security of the borrowers, or upon the security of the dues of the River Clyde, under the Acts

constituting the River Trust, or to the City Corporation, or to the Police or Statute Labour Board for Glasgow, or may be deposited in any Chartered or Joint-Stock Bank, but shall not be lent on personal security, or to any Member of the Master Court. No motion for any grant of money exceeding £20 shall be entertained, except by the consent of two-thirds of the Meeting at which the motion is made, unless notice of the same has been tabled and read at a previous Meeting of the Incorporation, excepting always the grant to unmarried daughters, for which no previous notice of motion is required. The investments of the Incorporation shall be taken in name of the Deacon and Collector for the time being, and their successors in office, as Trustees for behoof of the Incorporation.

VII.—THE PENSIONERS.

1. The right to enrol, and to remove from the Pension Roll, any person whatever, rests with the Master Court.

2. It shall not be competent to enrol any person as a Pensioner on the funds of the Incorporation who is a Member of the Master Court of any Incorporation.

3. Pensioners on the funds of the Incorporation shall not be entered upon the qualified roll, and shall not vote or be voted upon.

4. All pensions shall be payable during the pleasure of the Master Court, and no person shall have, or shall acquire, a legal right to share the funds of the Incorporation as Pensioners or otherwise.

5. Pensions may be awarded by the Incorporation to decayed Members and the widows of deceased Members in indigent circumstances to such extent as the Master Court shall consider suitable.

6. No pension shall be awarded until the expiry of five years after the admission of the person in respect of whose Membership the aid is asked, unless under exceptional circumstances to be judged of by the Master Court.

7. All applications for pensions or aid from the funds of the Incorporation must be lodged with the Clerk, stating the age, means of support, residence, and other circumstances of the applicant, according

to a printed form to be furnished by the Clerk. If entertained, the application shall be remitted to one or more of the Master Court, who shall carefully consider the same, and report thereon to next Meeting of the Master Court.

8. Pensioners shall be paid quarterly in advance. The pensions shall be paid by the Collector on Saturday immediately after each of the four Quarterly Meetings of the Master Court in the Trades House or other place duly appointed and intimated, or may be remitted to the pensioners.

9. On due intimation of the death of any pensioner being received by the Deacon or Collector, an allowance of £3 may be given for funeral charges.

10. It has been customary for many years for the Master Court to ask from the Incorporation a sum yearly from the funds to be distributed among the necessitous unmarried daughters of deceased Members, and this custom may be continued.

11. As heretofore, the Master Court shall have the privilege of recommending persons as pensioners on the funds of the Trades House, according to the enactments made, or to be made, by the Trades House to that effect.

VIII.—ALTERATION OF RULES AND REGULATIONS.

These Laws or Regulations shall not be altered or rescinded in any respect until the proposed alteration or repeal has been tabled and read at one Meeting of the Incorporation, and considered at another Meeting, at least one month subsequent to that at which it was tabled and read, and then agreed to by two-thirds of the Members present at such latter Meeting, and until such alteration or repeal has been sanctioned by the Trades House.

APPENDIX.
INCORPORATION OF WEAVERS OF GLASGOW.

ENTRANCE FEES SANCTIONED BY TRADES' HOUSE,
18th MAY, 1905.

Age Next Birth-day.	Near-Hand.	Far-Hand.	Age Next Birth-day.	Near-Hand.	Far-Hand.
	£ s. d.	£ s. d.		£ s. d.	£ s. d.
25 years and under	10 0 0	40 0 0	48 years and under	21 10 0	66 0 0
26 ...	10 10 0	40 0 0	49 ...	22 0 0	68 0 0
27 ...	11 0 0	40 0 0	50 ...	22 10 0	70 0 0
28 ...	11 10 0	40 0 0	51 ...	23 0 0	72 0 0
29 ...	12 0 0	40 0 0	52 ...	23 10 0	74 0 0
30 ...	12 10 0	40 0 0	53 ...	24 0 0	76 0 0
31 ...	13 0 0	40 0 0	54 ...	24 10 0	78 0 0
32 ...	13 10 0	40 0 0	55 ...	25 0 0	80 0 0
33 ...	14 0 0	40 0 0	56 ...	25 10 0	82 0 0
34 ...	14 10 0	40 0 0	57 ...	26 0 0	84 0 0
35 ...	15 0 0	40 0 0	58 ...	26 10 0	86 0 0
36 ...	15 10 0	42 0 0	59 ...	27 0 0	88 0 0
37 ...	16 0 0	44 0 0	60 ...	27 10 0	90 0 0
38 ...	16 10 0	46 0 0	61 ...	28 0 0	92 0 0
39 ...	17 0 0	48 0 0	62 ...	28 10 0	94 0 0
40 ...	17 10 0	50 0 0	63 ...	29 0 0	96 0 0
41 ..	18 0 0	52 0 0	64 ...	29 10 0	98 0 0
42 ...	18 10 0	54 0 0	65 ...	30 0 0	100 0 0
43 ...	19 0 0	56 0 0	66 ...	30 10 0	102 0 0
44 ...	19 10 0	58 0 0	67 ...	31 0 0	104 0 0
45 ...	20 0 0	60 0 0	68 ...	31 10 0	106 0 0
46 ...	20 10 0	62 0 0	69 ...	32 0 0	108 0 0
47 ...	21 0 0	64 0 0	70 ...	32 10 0	110 0 0

APPENDIX III.

TABULATED STATEMENT,

Showing Membership, Income, Expenditure, and Capital Funds of the Incorporation of Weavers of Glasgow from 1866 to 1904.

Year.	Income from Investments.			Members Admitted.	Entry-Money and Quarters' Accounts.			Total Income.			Expenditure.			Recipients of Aid.	Increase in Capital.			Total Capital.		
	£	s.	D.		£	s.	D.	£	s.	D.	£	s.	D.		£	s.	D.	£	s.	D.
1866-67	810	2	7½	15	69	17	4	879	19	11½	733	4	4	65	146	15	7½	13,987	6	8½
1867-68	711	3	1½	15	93	5	0	804	8	1½	757	7	4	74	47	0	9½	16,334	7	6
1868-69	741	13	4	6	29	13	8	771	7	0	685	12	3½	77	85	14	8½	16,420	2	2½
1869-70	787	3	4½	9	70	5	0	857	8	4½	643	6	11	71	214	1	5½	16,718	10	0
1870-71	786	6	8	27	196	3	0	982	9	8	637	2	6½	69	345	7	1½	17,063	17	1½
1871-72	777	15	4	19	139	6	4	917	1	8	720	6	6½	76	196	15	1½	17,260	12	3
1872-73	765	6	8½	10	55	7	0	820	13	8½	738	18	4	77	81	15	4	17,342	7	7
1873-74	822	4	9½	10	65	16	10	888	1	7½	737	17	3½	73	150	4	4	17,492	11	11
1874-75	792	16	11½	12	153	14	8	946	11	7½	723	16	3½	74	222	15	4	17,715	7	3
1875-76	920	0	3½	29	213	14	2	1133	14	5½	898	11	1	75	235	3	4½	17,950	10	7½
1876-77	866	2	6½	20	296	18	8	1163	1	6½	801	3	6	75	361	18	0½	18,312	8	8
1877-78	893	15	0½	25	226	14	5	1120	9	5½	918	11	10½	79	201	17	7	18,514	6	3
1878-79	857	13	7	19	171	11	2	1029	4	9	895	2	3	88	134	2	6	18,648	8	9
1879-80	850	0	7½	18	216	3	6	1066	4	1½	865	7	4½	86	233	3	7	18,881	12	4
1880-81	896	5	2½	22	210	13	5	1106	18	7½	909	5	9	88	197	12	10½	19,079	5	2½
1881-82	860	11	0	13	80	13	4	941	4	4	862	18	1	83	78	6	3	19,157	11	5½
1882-83	967	17	9½	17	176	6	7	1144	4	4½	805	0	2	78	339	4	2½	19,496	15	8
1883-84	911	13	11½	13	143	12	10	1055	6	9½	830	0	10½	77	244	2	2	19,740	17	10
1884-85	966	2	0½	53	793	8	2	1759	10	2½	810	13	5½	85	948	16	9	20,689	14	7
1885-86	1022	9	10	15	193	14	10	1246	4	8	872	11	2	81	343	13	6	21,033	8	1
1886-87	925	4	7	11	145	16	9	1071	1	4	1036	8	10	81	217	5	7	21,250	13	8
1887-88	1006	3	8	9	90	1	6	1096	5	2	1118	7	2	80	82	19	8	21,167	14	0
1888-89	1026	17	5½	10	117	8	7	1144	6	0½	1021	18	4½	79	215	9	7	21,383	3	7
1889-90	953	18	11	11	235	9	9	1189	8	8	864	2	5	70	325	6	3	21,708	9	10
1890-91	980	14	0½	4	98	19	3	1079	13	3½	930	11	8	64	149	1	7½	21,857	11	5½
1891-92	1032	5	7	11	104	11	4	1136	16	11	891	3	9½	70	245	13	1½	22,103	4	7
1892-93	969	2	1½	15	163	9	6	1132	11	7½	947	5	6½	69	185	6	1	22,288	10	8
1893-94	968	12	2½	13	184	12	10	1153	5	0½	922	15	4½	75	230	9	8	22,519	0	4
1894-95	1040	2	11	41	548	17	11	1589	0	10	968	18	3	62	620	2	7	23,139	2	11
1895-96	990	6	9	14	125	19	10	1116	6	7	1045	8	6	76	70	18	1	23,210	1	0
1896-97	976	17	4	13	188	16	8	1165	14	0	1005	3	2	74	160	10	10	23,370	11	10
1897-98	1076	1	6	11	245	6	2	1321	7	8	1003	19	3	74	317	8	5	23,688	0	3
1898-99	949	10	9	17	323	5	3	1272	16	0	936	1	9	75	336	14	3	24,024	14	6
1899-00	979	11	5	13	184	11	1	1164	2	6	944	3	9	71	219	18	9	24,244	13	3
1900-01	1137	15	3	21	163	0	6	1300	15	9	1017	4	10	69	283	10	11	24,528	4	2
1901-02	1101	2	8	11	383	9	2	1484	11	10	930	3	5	72	554	8	5	25,082	12	7
1902-03	1106	16	5	49	894	1	11	2000	18	4	987	4	6	74	1013	13	10	26,096	6	5
1903-04	1441	19	11½	35	660	8	7	2102	8	6½	1014	3	0½	71	1088	5	6	27,184	11	11

APPENDIX IV.

LIST OF PERSONS
WHO HELD THE OFFICE OF DEACON OF THE
INCORPORATION OF WEAVERS.

Year	Name	Year	Name
1591-92	Johnne Glen.	1632-33	Johnne Falcouner.
1592-93	Do.	1633-34	Thomas Andirsoune.
1593-94	Archibald Patersone.	1634-35	John Falcouner.
1594-95	Do.	1635-36	William Falcouner.
1595-96	Richard Kirkland.	1636-37	Thomas Andirsoune.
1596-97	Archibald Paterson.	1637-38	Patrik Clark.
1597-98	Richard Kirkland.	1638-39	Do.
1598-99	Do.	1639-40	Thomas Andirsoun.
1599-1600	Do.	1640-41	Richard Flaikfeild.
1600-01	Finlaye Schankschawe.	1641-42	Patrik Clark.
1601-02	Archibald Patersone.	1642-43	Johne Falconer.
1602-03	Richard Kirkland.	1643-44	Johne Baird.
1603-04	Archibald Patersoun.	1644-45	Patrik Clark.
1604-05	Richard Kirkland.	1645-46	Johne Baird.
1605-06	Archibald Paterson.	1646-47	Patrik Clark.
1606-07	Richard Kirkland.	1647-48	Johne Baird.
1607-08	John Clerk.	1648-49	Patrik Bryce.
1608-09	Archibald Patersoune.	1649-50	Do.
1609-10	Richert Kirkland.	1650-51	Do.
1610-11	Johne Clark.	1651-52	Patrik Clark.
1611-12	Williame Kirkland.	1652-53	Do.
1612-13	Johne Clark.	1653-54	Archibald Glen.
1613-14	Georg Schirilaw.	1654-55	Patrik Clerk.
1614-15	Johne Clark.	1655-56	Michaell Watsone.
1615-16	Georg Schirilaw.	1656-57	John Falconer.
1616-17	Johne Baird.	1657-58	Michaell Watsone.
1617-18	Do.	1658-59	Johne Falconer.
1618-19	Archibald Patersoune.	1659-60	Do.
1619-20	Williame Kirkland.	1660-61	Archibald Glen.
1620-21	Johne Clark.	1661-62	Johne Falconer.
1621-22	Johne Baird.	1662-63	Do.
1622-23	Johne Clark.	1663-64	Johne Clark.
1623-24	Thomas Andirsoune.	1664-65	Patricke Bryce.
1624-25	John Baird.	1665-66	Johne Falconer.
1625-26	Patrick Clark.	1666-67	Walter Stewart.
1626-27	James Grahame.	1667-68	Johne Clark.
1627-28	James Weinzet.	1668-69	Walter Stewart.
1628-29	John Falconer younger.	1669-70	Archibald Glen younger.
1629-30	James Grahame elder.	1670-71	John Flaickfeild younger.
1630-31	John Falconer younger.	1671-72	Walter Stewart.
1631-32	Patrik Clairk.	1672-73	John Patersone younger.

APPENDIX.

Year	Name	Year	Name
1673-74	Robert Flaikfeild.	1728-29	Robert Machliu.
1674-75	Robert Gilmour.	1729-30	John Lang.
1675-76	Patrick Lang.	1730-31	John M'Endoe.
1676-77	Robert Flaikfeild.	1731-32	Robert Manchlin.
1677-78	Patrick Lang.	1732-33	Wm. Buchanan.
1678-79	John Fleackfeild elder.	1733-34	James Boyll.
1679-80	Gawine Stevine.	1734-35	James Campbell.
1680-81	William Paislay.	1735-36	John Goudie.
1681-82	Robert Barbour.	1736-37	Wm. Watson.
1682-83	William Boill.	1737-38	Thomas Brown.
1683-84	William Paslay.	1738-39	John M'Eldoe.
1684-85	Do.	1739-40	James Smith.
1685-86	Johne Stevine younger.	1740-41	Andrew Millar.
1686-87		1741-42	
1687-88		1742-43	
1688-89	John M'Gilchrist.	1743-44	
1689-90	Do.	1744-45	
1690-91	James Findlay.	1745-46	
1691-92		1746-47	
1692-93		1747-48	Robert Barbour.
1693-94		1748-49	James Stewart.
1694-95		1749-50	Do.
1695-96	Robert Dobbie.	1750-51	William Aitken.
1696-97	John Loch.	1751-52	James Henderson.
1697-98		1752-53	Patrick Brisbane.
1698-99		1753-54	Thomas Coats.
1699-1700		1754-55	Patk. Cummin.
1700-01	Wm. Haddin.	1755-56	John Robertson.
1701-02		1756-57	David Dalglish.
1702-03	Wm. Haddin.	1757-58	Do.
1703-04		1758-59	John Barbour.
1704-05		1759-60	William Knox.
1705-06		1760-61	James Gibson.
1706-07		1761-62	Alex. Riddell.
1707-08	Robert Loch.	1762-63	James Davidson
1708-09		1763-64	Robert Winning.
1709-10		1764-65	James Bogle.
1710-11	James Boyll.	1765-66	Wm. M'Farlane.
1711-12		1766-67	John Robertson.
1712-13	Robert Wood.	1767-68	Thomas Adam.
1713-14	William Haddin.	1768-69	David Lennox.
1714-15	James Bole.	1769-70	Richard Millar.
1715-16	William Brysonne.	1770-71	William Bell.
1716-17	Thomas Cochran.	1771-72	Alexr. Scott.
1717-18	William Ritchie.	1772-73	Francis Reid.
1718-19	William Haldin.	1773-74	William Boyle.
1719-20	Robert Wood.	1774-75	David Dalglish.
1720-21	John Robertson.	1775-76	William Bell.
1721-22	Robert Loch.	1776-77	Malcolm Dun.
1722-23	James Boylle.	1777-78	John Simson.
1723-24	Wm. Bryson.	1778-79	Patrick Salmon.
1724-25	John Lang.	1779-80	Christopher Beck.
1725-26	James Boyll.	1780-81	William Ritchie.
1726-27	Robert Wood.	1781-82	Alex. Campbell.
1727-28	James Campbell.	1782-83	John Reid.

APPENDIX.

1783-84	John Reid.		1838-39	John Hendry.
1784-85	John Paul.		1839-40	William Lyall.
1785-86	William Shaw.		1840-41	James M'Lellan.
1786-87	Christopher Beck.		1841-42	James Scott.
1787-88	Jas. Richardson.		1842-43	John Hendry.
1788-89	John Kirkland.		1843-44	John Turner.
1789-90	William Scott.		1844-45	John Orr.
1790-91	Jas. Richardson.		1845-46	Alexander Bartholomew.
1791-92	John Turner.		1846-47	James Service.
1792-93	Neil M'Brayne.		1847-48	Robert Cooper.
1793-94	William Hunter.		1848-49	James Service.
1794-95	Thomas Alston.		1849-50	John Knox.
1795-96	Alexr. Wyllie.		1850-51	William Fraser.
1796-97	John Coats, Junr.		1851-52	Allan M'Dougall.
1797-98	Andrew Adie.		1852-53	Andrew Wilson.
1798-99	James Paul.		1853-54	George Thomson.
1799-1800	John Duncan.		1854-55	William Fraser.
1800-01	Robert Cullen.		1855-56	John Morrison.
1801-02	James Watson.		1856-57	Joseph Ewing.
1802-03	Thomas Alston.		1857-58	John Orr.
1803-04	John Wright.		1858-59	Andrew Marshall.
1804-05	William Scott, Junr.		1859-60	James Smart.
1805-06	John Coats.		1860-61	Henry Bruce.
1806-07	Robert Easton.		1861-62	Andrew Wilson.
1807-08	Thomas Alston.		1862-63	Henry Bruce.
1808-09	John M'Nair.		1863-64	Andrew Marshall.
1809-10	William Buchanan.		1864-65	James Gourlay.
1810-11	John Alston, Junr.		1865-66	Joseph Ewing.
1811-12	John Graham.		1866-67	Forrest Frew.
1812-13	Alexander Wylie.		1867-68	J. W. Anderson.
1813-14	William Blackburn.		1868-69	John Mair.
1814-15	William Snell.		1869-70	William Johnston.
1815-16	James Watson.		1870-71	James Downie.
1816-17	Laurence Phillips.		1871-72	Robert Gourlay.
1817-18	Robert Miller.		1872-73	John Mair.
1818-19	Cornelius Brown.		1873-74	James Anderson.
1819-20	Laurence Phillips.		1874-75	George Gibson.
1820-21	William Frew.		1875-76	James Alexander.
1821-22	William Buchanan.		1876-77	Alexander Begg.
1822-23	John M'Whannell.		1877-78	Alexander Birrell.
1823-24	James Graham.		1878-79	Matthew Fairley.
1824-25	Robert Wilson.		1879-80	William Duncan.
1825-26	Alexander Campbell.		1880-81	William Newlands.
1826-27	William Craig.		1881-82	John Millen.
1827-28	William Frew.		1882-83	James Thomson.
1828-29	William Patrick.		1883-84	George Younger.
1829-30	Robert Wilson.		1884-85	James Wilson.
1830-31	James M'Lellan.		1885-86	David Paterson.
1831-32	John Blackie.		1886-87	*Angus Mitchell.*
1832-33	John Neill.		1887-88	*James Hutton.*
1833-34	John Walker.		1888-89	John Miller.
1834-35	Thomas Waddell.		1889-90	*Andrew Paterson.*
1835-36	William Patrick.		1890-91	*John Knox.*
1836-37	David Goudie.		1891-92	*Peter Steven.*
1837-38	John Houston.		1892-93	John B. Wingate.

APPENDIX.

1893-94	James Waddel.	1899-1900	*John G. Couper.*
1894-95	*John S. Mair.*	1900-01	*John Service.*
1895-96	*Adam White.*	1901-02	Do
1896-97	*M. Pearce Campbell.*	1902-03	*Albert Harvey.*
1897-98	*James A. Duncan.*	1903-04	*Robert Kedie.*
1898-99	*Robt. F. Alexander.*	1904-05	*R. D. M'Ewan.*

NOTE.—The surviving Deacons in above list have the names printed in *italics*.

CLERKS TO THE INCORPORATION.

1600-02	J. Allinson.	1679-90	Robert Finnisone.
1602-06	J. Craig.	1690-1716	Thomas Falconer.
1606-08	J. Allinson.	1716-	John Robertson.
1608-27	W. Fleming.	1788	Thomas Sivert.
1627-31	Geo. Stirling.	1789-1821	James Robb.
1631-42	Patrick Baird.	1821-43	James Wilson.
1642-59	Wm. Yair.	1843-56	Adam Monteith.
	(Also Town Clerk of Glasgow.)	1856-65	John Earston.
1659-69	M. Rowand.	1865-99	William MacLean.
1669-78	Patrick Clark.	1899-	Chas. J. MacLean.

In the earlier years the dates are approximate; it is probable that the appointments were not permanent, and that the Clerk did not attend all meetings.

APPENDIX V.

ALPHABETICAL ROLL

OF THE

INCORPORATION OF WEAVERS.

GLASGOW, 1905.

NOTE.—An asterisk (*) indicates last known Address.

No. on the Roll	Name.	Craft.	Address.	Year of Entry.
2275	Arnott, Archibald	W	*221 St. Vincent Street	1871
2283	Alexander, R. F.	H & W	105 Clyde Street, Anderston	1871
2284	Alexander, William	W	Solicitor, Dunblane	1871
2285	Alexander, James	H & W	105 Clyde Street, Anderston	1871
2339	Anderson, David H.	W	Atlantic Mills, Bridgeton	1874
2406	Alston, William M.	W	24 Sardinia Terrace	1878
2418	Auchinvole, John	W	113 Virginia Street	1878
2461	Anderson, Robert	W	12 Princes Square	1880
2463	Andrew, Alexander	W	22 Westminster Terrace	1881
2501	Alexander, Rev. A. B. D.	W	Langbank	1883
2523	Anderson, John	Dyer	44 Maxwell Drive, Pollokshields	1884
2534	Alexander, James	W	78 Miller Street	1884
2550	Allardyce, Charles	Hammer	12 Kidston Street, S.S.	1885
2551	Allardyce, Archibald M'N.		75 Buchanan Street	1885
2560	Aitken, James G.	W	30 George Square	1885
2562	Allan, Alexander	W	20 Montgomerie Cottages, Scotstoun	1885
2570	Arthur, Andrew	W	78 Queen Street	1885
2571	Arthur, James	W	78 Queen Street	1885
2572	Arthur, Thomas G.	W	78 Queen Street	1885
2573	Arthur, Sir Matthew, Bart.	W	78 Queen Street	1885
2582	Allan, William E.	W	43 Overdale Street, Langside	1885
2602	Allan, E. J. M.	W	70 South Portland Street	1886
2622	Adam, William	W	5 Main Street, Anderston	1888
2626	Allan, William Hadyn	W	223 New City Road	1889
2636	Allan, William	W	117 Golfhill Terrace, Dennistoun	1890
2685	Allan, James	W	13 John Street	1894
2714	Alexander, Jas. M.	W	11 Belmont Crescent, W.	1895

APPENDIX.

No. on the Roll.	Name.	Craft.	Address.	Year of Entry.
2715	Alexander, David D.	W	11 Belmont Crescent, W.	1895
2781	Anderson, Dr. William	W	The Shrublands, Leytonstone, London, N.E.	1899
2849	Auchinvole, Stewart P.	W	113 Virginia Place	1903
2872	Andrew, James	W	160 West George Street	1903
2895	Alexander, Robt. G.	W	11 Belmont Crescent, Glasgow	1904
2896	Arthur, J. Cecil	W	Fullarton, Troon	1904
2324	Bruce, Henry	W	161 Roman Road, Bow, London, S.	1873
2354	Brodie, Robert	C	77 St. Vincent Street	1876
2357	Bannerman, Robert	W	16 Blythswood Square	1876
2428	Brown, John	W	Enderly, Bridge of Weir	1879
2429	Brown, Daniel	W	705 Shields Road, Pollokshields	1879
2430	Brown, David R.	W	Victoria	1879
2431	Brown, Frank H.	W	40 St. Enoch Square	1879
2465	Barclay, Robert B.	W	Local Government Board, Edinburgh	1881
2470	Brown, Thos.	W	57 Cochrane Street	1881
2512	Brown, Alex. T.	W	6 Olrig Terrace, Pollokshields	1882
2513	Brown, John H.	W	57 Cochrane Street	1883
2514	Brown, Thomas H.	W	57 Cochrane Street	1883
2589	Brown, Hugh	W	9 Clairmont Gardens	1885
2610	Buchanan, William	W	21 North St. Mungo Street	1887
2616	Buchanan, John	W	40 Clyde Street, Calton	1888
2617	Buchanan, James		91 Abbott Road, Poplar, London, E.	1888
2677	Baillie, James	B	12 Wilson Street, Hillhead	1894
2678	Buchanan, John	S	27 Randolph Gardens, Partick	1894
2684	Brown, David S.	W	130 Greenhead Street, Bridgeton	1894
2722	Baillie, J. G. A.	Gardener	Kentlodge, Ramsgate	1895
2730	Booth, James	W	13 Windsor Street	1895
2731	Brown, Hugh, jun., C.A.	W	58 St. Vincent Street	1896
2732	Brown, Laurence R.	W	9 Clairmont Gardens	1896
2748	Brown, Nicol P.	W	22 Belhaven Terrace	1897
2758	Boyd, Wm., jun., C.A.	W	116 St. Vincent Street	1898
2763	Brown, Thos.	B	352 Main Street, Bridgeton	1899
2771	Bryce, Chas. C.		43-45 Great Tower Street, London, E.C.	1899
2778	Brodie, Wm.	Cord	77 St. Vincent Street	1899
2782	Barr, John	W	51 Camphill Avenue, Langside	1899
2830	Brown, Hugh T.	W	111 French Street, Bridgeton	1902
2855	Brodie, John M'Clure	W	23 Belhaven Terrace	1903
2856	Brodie, Thomson	W	23 Belhaven Terrace	1903
2859	Blackie, Walter W., B.Sc.	W	17 Stanhope Street	1903
2878	Blyth, Robt. Oswald	W	1 Montgomerie Quadrant	1903
2898	Black, William G.	W	88 West Regent Street	1904
2903	Bissett, Jas. G.	W	Netherpark, Largs	1904
2939	Baird, David	B	139 Greenhead Terrace	1905
2940	Baird, Harry	B	Mossbank, Gallowflat, Rutherglen	1905
2296	Crawford, Thomas	W	113 Somerville Drive, Mount Florida	1871
2325	Campbell, James	W	c/o Robert Kennedy, Argyle Villa, Alloway, Ayr	1873

APPENDIX.

No. on the Roll.	Name.	Craft.	Address.	Year of Entry.
2335	Couper, John	S	Copeland Villa, 22 Kelvinside Gardens	1874
2336	Couper, James	W	599 Duke Street	1874
2364	Campbell, The Right Hon. J. A., LL.D., M.P.	W	Stracathro, Brechin	1876
2365	Clavering, Thomas	W	24 George Square	1876
2427	Cunningham, James	Gardener	20 Clarendon Place, Mount Preston, Leeds	1879
2456	Crawford, David	W	5 Clifton Road, Eccles, Manchester	1880
2459	Cubie, Alexander P.	W	142 Main Street, Bridgeton	1880
2488	Carrick, James	W	62 Argyle Street	1882
2497	Clarke, William	W	245 Buchanan Street	1882
2517	Caldwell, John	W	Maryville Lodge, Uddingston, West	1883
2518	Clark, C. E.	W	Hayfield, Dunoon	1883
2542	Caldwell, Alex. S.	W	Maryville Lodge, Uddingston, West	1885
2552	Campbell, William A.	W	137 Ingram Street	1885
2553	Campbell, M. Pearce	W	137 Ingram Street	1885
2555	Couper, John G.	W	21 Glassford Street	1885
2598	Caskie, Dr. W. A.	W	1 Beechwood Drive, Jordanhill, Glasgow	1886
2620	Chesney, Benjamin	W	22 Caledonia Road	1888
2627	Craighead, William	W	51 Whitevale Street	1889
2646	Craig, Hugh J.	W	12 Hamilton Drive, Hillhead	1892
2673	Cuzen, Francis G.	W	Buchanan Retreat, Bearsden	1893
2706	Campbell, Colin	W	1313 Pollokshaws Road, High Shawlands, Glasgow	1895
2711	Cherry, Jas. S.	Maltman	Mexico	1895
2712	Cherry, Wm.	Maltman	102 Bath Street	1895
2713	Cherry, Gavin S.	Maltman	70 Bath Street	1895
2741	Carrick, Peter M.	W	9 Cartvale Road, Langside	1897
2744	Crosland, Stanley P.	W	*Glenville, Gledholt, Huddersfield	1897
2745	Caldwell, John, jun.	W	4 Kennyhill Gardens, Dennistoun	1897
2795	Caldwell, Jas. T.	W	1 Kennyhill Gardens, Dennistoun	1900
2826	Campbell, Jas. C.	W	9 Lynedoch Crescent	1902
2834	Couper, David	W	Bridgend Works, Dalry, Ayrshire	1903
2835	Couper, Thomas	W	21 Glassford Street	1903
2836	Couper, William H.	W	21 Glassford Street	1903
2837	Couper, Jno. Graham, jun., C.A.	W	The Hollies, Langbank	1903
2838	Couper, James H.	W	21 Glassford Street	1903
2843	Crabb, David	W	36 North Frederick Street	1903
2887	Craig, Arch. M.	W	7 Robertson Lane	1904
2894	Campbell, Adair	W	137 Ingram Street	1904
2911	Craig, A. Blackburn	W	41 St. Vincent Place	1905
2912	Carmichael, Rev. Wm.	W	Crossknowe, Torrance	1905
2918	Cooke, David	W	631 Alexandra Parade	1905
2919	Cooke, James	W	93 Hutcheson Street	1905
2930	Connell, John	W	Bonnington, Busby	1905
2294	Downie, James	W	57 Ingram Street	1871
2341	Dodd, Robert T.	M	61 Westmoreland Street	1875
2409	Duncan, James A.	Hammer	Coltness Iron Co., 138 West George Street	1878
2410	Duncan, Robert	Hammer	Whitefield Works, Govan	1878

APPENDIX. 157

No. on the Roll.	Name.	Craft.	Address.	Year of Entry.
2487	Davidson, Arthur	W	22 Argyle Street	1882
2601	Dawson, John	W	274 Lincoln Place, Partick	1887
2606	Drysdale, James T.	W	103 Bath Street	1887
2619	Dreghorn, David	Mason	Greenwood, Nithsdale Drive, Pollokshields	1888
2623	Drysdale, John W. W.	W	183 Fordneuk Street	1889
2675	Dunn, David	S	7 Royal Bank Place	1894
2683	Downie, John A.	W	57 Ingram Street	1894
2704	Downie, Robert	W	111 Finlay Drive, Dennistoun	1895
2710	Downie, James M.	W	Sunnyside, Lenzie	1895
2740	Docherty, James	W	94 George Street, Paisley	1897
2762	Downie, John S.	W	School House, Newton-Mearns	1899
2768	Danskin, William R.	W	25 Glencairn Drive	1899
2808	Danskin, John A.	W	Ardgowan, Broadloan, Renfrew	1901
2827	Dow, John Graham	W	207 Ingram Street	1902
2829	Dickson, William M.	W	Glenroy House, Princes Town, Trinidad	1902
2840	Dunn, Herbert	W	20 Park Circus	1903
2841	Dunn, Bannatyne	W	20 Park Circus	1903
2869	Dunn, James D.	W	20 Park Circus	1903
2885	Dunn, John	H	29 Bellgrove Street	1904
2886	Dick, Robt.	W	19 Waterloo Street	1904
2905	Docherty, And.	W	8 Miller Street	1904
2906	Downie, Dr. J. W.	W	4 Woodside Crescent	1904
2907	Downie, A. M.	W	4 Strathmore Gardens, Hillhead	1904
2921	Downie, Robert, jun.	W	111 Finlay Drive, Dennistoun	1905
2384	Ewing, John	W	148 Renfrew Street	1877
2408	Easton, John M.	W	Tordarroch, Helensburgh	1878
2420	Easton, Frederick J.	W	London	1878
2580	Eason, Robert	W	*674 Gallowgate	1885
2656	Easton, William C.	W	Tordarroch, Helensburgh	1893
2657	Easton, Duncan T.	W	Tordarroch, Helensburgh	1893
2788	Eadie, John	W	69 Eglinton Street	1900
2240	Fleming, Michael W.	W	*97 Montrose Street	1870
2299	Findlay, James	W	Gallowflat House, Rutherglen	1871
2482	Ferguson, Alexander	Barber	116 St. Vincent Street	1881
2498	Finlayson, William	W	67 Roslea Drive	1883
2536	Frew, James	W	15 Royal Terrace, Crosshill	1884
2537	Fulton, John	W	31 Hanover Street	1884
2539	Forrest, R. W., M.D.	W	319 Crown Street	1884
2547	Finlayson, Wm., jun.	W	67 Roslea Drive	1885
2581	Fyfe, Henry B.	W	115 St. Vincent Street	1885
2604	Fleming, E. B.	W	50 Renfrew Street	1887
2637	Fleming, William	W	138 Duke Street	1890
2676	Findlay, Wm. M.	W	261 West George Street	1894
2696	Fisken, James J.	W	73 Virginia Street	1894
2785	Frame, Wm.	W	5 Walmer Terrace	1900
2815	Fraser, John	W	177 Reid Street, Bridgeton	1902
2821	Filshill, Jas.	W	420 Gallowgate	1902
2874	Forrest, Thos.	W	1 Moray Place, Glasgow	1903
2875	Forrest, Wm.	W	114 Dixon Avenue, Crosshill	1903

APPENDIX.

No. on the Roll.	Name.	Craft.	Address.	Year of Entry.
2876	Forrest, Jas. Dick	W	114 Dixon Avenue, Crosshill	1903
2877	Forrest, Robt. W.	W	114 Dixon Avenue, Crosshill	1903
2883	Fyfe, Alex., M.A.	W	16 Montgomerie Quadrant	1904
2884	Fyfe, Henry H.	W	16 Montgomerie Quadrant	1904
2933	Fleming, John	W	138 Duke Street	1905
2942	Fyfe, Walter W.	W	16 Montgomerie Quadrant	1905
2943	Fyfe, John E.	W	16 Montgomerie Quadrant	1905
2161	Graham, Peter	M	8 Albany Street, North Kelvinside	1861
2185	Gourlay, Robt., LL.D.	W	5 Marlborough Terrace	1862
2288	Galloway, Wm.	Baker	52 Glassford Street	1871
2426	Gemmell, Wm. M.	Gardener	44 Princes Street, Pollokshields	1879
2479	Gemmell, Adam	W	57 West Nile Street	1881
2503	Gemmell, William	W	139 Greenhead Street	1883
2519	Graham, Hugh	W	*198 New City Road	1884
2531	Gibson, George	W	17 Victoria Crescent	1884
2545	Galbraith, Robert B.	Dyer	35 Glassford Street	1884
2642	Gibb, Andrew	Wright	Garthland, Westcombe Park Road, Blackheath, London, S.E.	1891
2665	Gray, John	W	3 Maxwell Terrace, Pollokshields	1893
2666	Gartshore, Alex.	W	43 Virginia Street	1893
2695	Gardiner, Wm.	W	The Rachan, Helensburgh	1895
2699	Graham, David J.	W	109 St. Peter's Road, Leicester	1895
2707	Gemmell, John	W	211 Greenhead Street	1895
2743	Gray, Wm.	W	44 Maxwell Drive	1897
2809	Gourlay, Jas.	W	11 Crown Gardens, Dowanhill	1901
2810	Gourlay, John W., C.A.	W	124 St. Vincent Street	1901
2879	Galbraith, Robt. J.	W	4 West Regent Street	1904
2880	Galbraith, Chas.	W	35 Glassford Street	1904
2897	Guthrie, And. J.	W	29 West George Street	1904
2908	Gourlay, Robt. C.	W	Caledonian Engine Works, Paisley	1905
2909	Gourlay, Robt. J.	W	Bank of Scotland, Glasgow	1905
2928	Graham, Arthur H.	W	107 Buchanan Street	1905
2944	Gray, Alex. S. T.	W	3 Maxwell Terrace, Pollokshields	1905
2183	Henry, E. W.	M	The City Liberal Club, Wallbrook, London, E.C.	1862
2262	Hutton, James, C.A.	W	203 West George Street	1869
2303	Hennedy, David	W	10 Prince's Square	1872
2313	Hunter, John	W	54 London Road, Kilmarnock	1872
2361	Harvey, Albert	W	2 Park Terrace, East	1876
2483	Henderson, John	Barber	34 Dunearn Street	1881
2521	Horn, Alex. R.	W	Clydesdale Bank, Limited, Glasgow	1884
2566	Halliday, George	W	1 Broomhill Terrace, Partick	1885
2658	Hamilton, James	W	19 Wilson Street	1893
2679	Hewat, Wm.	W	22 Queen Mary Avenue, Crosshill	1894
2681	Houston, Wm.	W	59 St. Vincent Street	1894
2687	Holmes, A. L.	W	13 John Street	1894
2723	Hewat, John	W	22 Queen Mary Avenue	1895
2724	Hewat, Wm., jun.	W	22 Queen Mary Avenue	1895
2725	Hewat, Henry A.	W	22 Queen Mary Avenue	1895
2759	Hunter, John	W	79 Fotheringay Road, Maxwell Park	1898
2769	Houston, John S.	W	59 St. Vincent Street	1899

APPENDIX. 159

No. on the Roll	Name	Craft	Address	Year of Entry
2791	Harvey, Wm. A., C.A.	W	2 Park Terrace, East	1900
2792	Harvey, Geo. T.	W	2 Park Terrace, East	1900
2793	Harvey, Wilson	W	2 Park Terrace, East	1900
2794	Harvey, Thos.	W	2 Park Terrace, East	1900
2796	Hamilton, Robert	W	Lochend, Glengarnock	1901
2804	Houston, Jas. E.	W	1 Seyton Avenue, Langside	1901
2904	Headrick, Robt.	W	21 Bothwell Street	1904
2935	Hirst, Fred. W.	W	Mountjoy Road, Huddersfield	1905
2947	Holmes, Jas. A.	W	13 John Street	1905
2476	Inglis, Lawrence R.	W	34 Garturk Street, Crosshill	1881
2820	Innes, Gilbert	W	21 Glassford Street	1902
2824	Inverclyde, Lord	W	Castle Wemyss, Wemyss Bay	1902
2250	Johnston, William	W	11 Derby Crescent, Kelvinside	1868
2251	Johnston, John	W	6 Fitzroy Place, Sauchiehall Street	1868
2298	Johnstone, T. R.	W	Italy	1871
2460	Jenkins, Thomas	W	27 Pitt Street	1880
2717	Johnston, John D.	W	6 Fitzroy Place, Sauchiehall Street	1895
2718	Johnston, Wm.	W	6 Fitzroy Place, Sauchiehall Street	1895
2193	Knox, John	W	Airedale Shed, Silsden, via Keighley, Yorks.	1863
2421	Knox, Robert A.	W	5 Park Quadrant	1878
2575	Kay, John R.	W	78 Queen Street	1885
2576	Kedie, Robert	W	146 Argyle Street	1885
2590	Knox, Robert M.	W	47 Crownpoint Road, Mile End	1886
2591	Knox, John S.	W	10 Clayton Terrace, Dennistoun	1886
2615	Kidston, James B.	Barber	50 West Regent Street	1888
2624	Kyd, Alexander	W	980 Pollokshaws Road	1888
2628	Kidston, William	Barber	50 West Regent Street	1889
2643	Kerr, John E.	Skinner	Harviestoun Castle, Dollar	1891
2753	Kirkpatrick, Hubert V.	W	5 Park Terrace	1898
2738	Kirkpatrick, Duncan T.	W	5 Park Terrace	1896
2739	Kirkpatrick, Thomas A.	W	5 Park Terrace	1896
2787	Kidd, Alex.	T	239 Ingram Street	1900
2832	Kay, Arthur	W	78 Queen Street	1903
2868	Kidd, Henry A.	W	571 Sauchiehall Street	1903
2899	Knox, John, jun.	W	Silsden, Yorks.	1904
2900	Knox, Wm.	W	Silsden, Yorks.	1904
2922	Kinghorn, John P.	Wright	105 West George Street	1905
2217	Leggatt, Rev. Wm.	W	2 James Street, Greenhead	1865
2446	Lyle, George	W	Clelland's Land, Bishopbriggs	1880
2472	Leggat, Robt.	W	107 Bishop Street, North	1881
2481	Logan, Lieut.-Col. C. A.	W	Denovan House, Denny	1881
2535	Legate, James	M	1 Queensborough Drive, Hyndland	1884
2584	Laughland, James	W	71 Mitchell Street	1885
2663	Logan, David	W	Thrums, Shettleston	1893
2737	Lumsden, Harry, M.A., LL.B.	W	105 West George Street	1896
2751	Lyle, John	W	10 Fordneuk Street	1897
2772	Legate, Francis	W	1 Queensborough Drive, Hyndland	1899
2773	Legate, Alex. B. S.	W	1 Queensborough Drive, Hyndland	1899

APPENDIX.

No. on the Roll.	Name.	Craft.	Address.	Year of Entry.
2789	Laird, Alex.	W	24 Dixon Avenue, Crosshill	1900
2852	Lindsay, Malcolm W.	W	2 West Regent Street	1903
2860	Lyle, John E.	W	10 Fordneuk Street	1903
2215	Miller, Alex.	W	3 Windsor Quadrant, Kelvinside	1865
2232	Mair, John S.	W	Mount Hermon, Helensburgh	1869
2261	Mitchell, Andrew	W	6 Lilybank Gardens, Hillhead	1869
2267	Miller, Robert	W	186 Trongate	1870
2270	Maltman, Thomas	W	34 Wilton Gardens	1870
2297	Murdoch, Robert	Hammer.	National Bank, Dundee	1871
2302	Muir, Robert	W	London	1872
2348	Mair, Charles S.	W	Tigh-na-mara, Bone, Algeria	1875
2392	Mitchell, Angus	C & W	35 Miller Street	1877
2405	Minnoch, Wm. H.	W	17 Park Terrace, Stirling	1878
2411	Murray, Robert	W	128 Bothwell Street	1878
2412	Murray, John T.	W	309 Golfhill Drive	1878
2473	Miller, John	W	105 Buccleuch Street	1881
2495	Mitchell, Angus, jun.	W	8 Clarence Drive, Hyndland	1881
2496	Mitchell, John M'P.	W	177 Ledard Road, Langside	1882
2529	Marshall, John	W	Alma Place, Shawlands	1884
2554	Mann, James	W	21 Glassford Street	1885
2588	Munsie, Robert G.	W	34 Gray Street, W.	1885
2600	Mason, Thomas	Mason	21 Clyde Place	1886
2603	Muir, James B.	W	471 Rutherglen Road	1886
2655	Morrice, James	W	104 Cecil Street, Manchester	1892
2682	Mitchell, Wm.	W	Glencairn, Crosshill	1894
2701	Manson, And. D.	B & D	104 Hydepark Street	1895
2726	Millen, James A.	W	33/35 Commerce Street	1895
2746	Milne, James	W	Upper Craigwells, Netherley, by Stonehaven, Kincardineshire	1897
2750	Mann, Robert M.	W	21 Glassford Street	1897
2761	Mitchell, James T.	C	137 Ingram Street	1898
2783	Monro, Thos. K., M.A., M.D.	W	10 Clairmont Gardens	1899
2790	Marshall, David	W	Horrockses, Crewdson & Co., Ld., 107 Piccadilly, Manchester	1900
2844	Mason, Thos., jun.	M	Craigiehall, Bellahouston	1903
2845	Mason, Robt. W.	M	Craigiehall, Bellahouston	1903
2850	Manson, Wm. Hyslop, M.A.	W	Avenue Villa, Mansion House Road, Langside	1903
2888	Muir, Rev. Wm., B.D.	W	St. Andrews U.F. Manse, Blairgowrie	1904
2902	Mowat, Joseph G.	H	50 Wellington Street	1904
2917	Morton, David S.	W	309 Dobbie's Loan	1905
2920	Marshall, Geo. B.	W	703 Cathcart Road	1905
1952	M'Lellan, Malcolm	M	3 Clairmont Gardens	1838
2110	M'Lellan, Donald	W	Ardmay, 1 Eglinton Drive	1851
2141	M'Lintock, Walter	W	25 Sydney Street, Saltcoats	1858
2156	M'Lellan, George	W	Allan Bank, Kilmalcolm	1861
2186	Macpherson, Henry S.	W	62 Queen Street	1862
2234	M'Laren, Alexander	W	532 East Prospect Street, Cleveland, Ohio, U.S.A.	1867
2282	Macfarlane, John	W	19 Sydney Street	1871

APPENDIX. 161

No. on the Roll	Name	Craft	Address	Year of Entry
2387	Maclean, David, C.A.	Maltman	10 Somerset Place	1877
2433	MacLean, Chas. J.	W	115 St. Vincent Street	1879
2489	M'Connell, Robt.	W	5 Clyde Street, Helensburgh	1882
2490	M'Connell, Thomas	W	*20 Windsor Terrace	1882
2491	M'Connell, William	W	Royal Laundry, Whiteinch	1882
2492	M'Connell, John	W	c/o Cruickshanks, 325 Hutcheson Square	1882
2500	M'Dougall, Robert	W	133 West Regent Street	1883
2524	Macfarlane, Mal., M.A.	Barber	School House, Bridge of Allan	1884
2530	Macpherson, James G.	W	62 Queen Street	1884
2568	Macfarlane, Thomas	W	39 Miller Street	1885
2596	M'Allister, W. S.	W	96 Renfield Street	1886
2608	M'Lintock, Walter, jun.	W	*112 Parson Street	1887
2614	M'Dougall, James	W	27 Caird Drive, Partick	1888
2629	M'Kinnon, Archibald	W	*139 Greenhead Street	1890
2640	M'Leod, Thos. C.	W	142 St. Vincent Street	1891
2641	M'Ewan, Robt. D.	W	22 Montrose Street	1891
2644	M'Culloch, John L.	W	15 Castle Street	1891
2645	M'Kechnie, James	W	79 John Knox Street	1891
2654	M'Lean, John Allan	H	Havanna, Cuba	1892
2661	Macfie, Wm.	W	26 Bishop Street, Rothesay	1893
2680	M'Culloch, John	W	421 Gallowgate	1894
2697	M'Nish, Geo. S.	W	55 Washington Street	1895
2698	M'Nish, John S.	W	55 Washington Street	1895
2702	Maclay, Jos. P.	W	21 Bothwell Street	1895
2703	Maclay, Wm. P.	W	104 Hydepark Street	1895
2716	M'Dougall, Wm.	W	284 Bath Street	1895
2719	Maclay, Wm.	B	5 Waterloo Street	1895
2736	M'Culloch, David W.	W	*66 Evelyn Street, Dennistoun	1896
2742	M'Dougall, Allan	W	149 West George Street	1897
2749	MacNaughton, Rev. Geo. F. A.	W	The Manse, Carsphairn	1897
2764	M'Nair, Thomas	Wright	27 St. Vincent Place	1899
2770	M'Allister, Jas.	W	541 Duke Street	1899
2774	M'Kenzie, John	W	103 Burnside Street	1899
2779	MacDougall, Jas., jun.	W	27 Caird Drive, Partick	1899
2780	MacLeod, Fred. L.	W	142 St. Vincent Street	1899
2805	M'Kenzie, John, jun.	W	103 Burnside Street	1901
2806	Macpherson, Thomas W.	W	62 Queen Street	1901
2813	Maclay, R. M., C.A.	W	209 West George Street	1901
2814	MacLean, Wm.	W	3 Grosvenor Crescent	1901
2857	MacLean, Archd. Campbell H.	W	The Royal Scots, Kamptee C.P., India	1903
2867	M'Kay, George H.	W	40 Dumbarton Road	1903
2870	M'Intyre, Thos. W.	H	21 Bothwell Street	1903
2881	Mackinlay, Chas. A.	W	28 Dobbie's Loan	1904
2901	Macindoe, Alex.	C	104 West George Street	1904
2913	Maclay, John C.	B	5 Waterloo Street	1904
2914	Maclay, Kenneth	B	21 St. Vincent Place	1905
2923	Macalister, David R.	W	106 Cowcaddens Street	1905
2938	Maclay, Arthur A.	B	Thornwood, Langside	1905
2945	Macleod, D. Macfarlane	W	47 Mornington Road, Bow, London	1905
2946	Macnair, Donald F.	W	41 St. Vincent Place	1905

x

APPENDIX.

No. on the Roll	Name.	Craft.	Address.	Year of Entry
2435	Newlands, James	W	Rio, Brazil	1879
2436	Newlands, Joseph F.	W	105 West George Street	1879
2442	Ness, Robert	W	19 Woodside Place, W.	1879
2454	Newstead, Thomas	W	Dilston, Bertrohill, Shettleston	1880
2721	Noble, Walter D.	W	21 Glassford Street	1895
2882	Newlands, Geo. F.	W	135 St. Vincent Street	1904
2579	O'May, Thomas	W	14 Circus Drive, Dennistoun	1885
2652	Orr, Thomas	W	22 Fox Street	1892
2669	Orr, Wm. Yuille	W	22 Fox Street	1893
2833	Ogilvie, Herbert	W	78 Queen Street	1903
2889	Ogilvie, Cecil	W	78 Queen Street	1904
2301	Paterson, Wm. Scott	W	21 Kelvinside Terrace, South	1872
2311	Paterson, Andrew	W	Hapland, Helensburgh	1872
2321	Patrick, George	W	15 Smith's Court, Candleriggs	1873
2383	Pollock, Rev. John	W	7 Glandon Park, Belfast	1877
2453	Paterson, John	M	Shettleston	1880
2468	Paterson, Robt. G.	W	c/o Jas. Paterson & Co., Newhall Street, Bridgeton	1881
2504	Paterson, James	W	69 Park Drive South, Whiteinch	1883
2516	Paterson, Robert	W	John Street Public School	1883
2526	Paterson, James C., C.A.	W	63 St. Vincent Street	1884
2527	Paterson, Robert S.	W	22 West Nile Street	1884
2593	Paul, Thomas A.	W	Dunarden, Helensburgh	1885
2612	Paterson, Wm. M.	W	27 Baskerville Road, Wandsworth Common, London, S.W.	1888
2621	Peebles, James	W	*13 Wellfield Street, Springburn	1888
2631	Paterson, Alexander N., M.A., A.R.I.B.A.	W	266 St. Vincent Street	1890
2662	Place, James	Cordiner	42 Kersland Street, Hillhead	1893
2688	Pomphrey, Geo. G.	W	137 Ingram Street	1894
2767	Peebles, Wm.	W	*5 Dunchattan Street	1899
2890	Parker, Jas. H., C.A.	W	89 West Regent Street	1904
2941	Paterson, George	W	376 St. Vincent Street	1905
2264	Robson, James	W	Flower Bank, Clynder	1870
2320	Robb, William	W	*Ailsa Tower, Dunoon	1873
2401	Rae, William	W	818 New City Road	1878
2484	Reid, Robert, C.A.	W	40 St. Vincent Place	1881
2586	Robertson, John	W	Clydebank Finishing Works, Rutherglen	1884
2609	Ramsay, William S.	W	6 Ruthven Street, Hillhead	1887
2651	Russell, William	W	Woodend, Langside	1892
2690	Reid, Robert A.	W	125 Buchanan Street	1895
2696	Robertson, James	W	137 West Regent Street	1895
2705	Rae, John B.	W	818 New City Road	1895
2727	Robertson, Andrew	W	Trearne Cottage, Wellshothill, Cambuslang	1895
2729	Reid, John	W	61 Henderson Street	1895
2752	Reid, Henry A.	W	108 West George Street	1898
2777	Reid, James A.	Wright	172 St. Vincent Street	1899
2811	Reid, A. Roger	Wright	1 Derby Crescent, Kelvinside	1901

APPENDIX. 163

No. on the Roll.	Name.	Craft.	Address.	Year of Entry.
2812	Reid, Robert A. M.	Wright	1 Derby Crescent, Kelvinside	1901
2816	Robertson, Archibald	W	51 James Street, Calton	1902
2817	Reid, Hugh	W	13 Victoria Buildings, Shettleston	1902
2831	Reid, John	Hammer	Hydepark Locomotive Works, Springburn	1903
2842	Rew, Angus,	W	2 Wellfield Terrace, Springburn	1903
2848	Ritchie, Wm.	W	77 Queen Street	1903
2892	Reid, Geo. L.	W	Windsor Place, Shettleston	1904
2893	Reid, Hugh Y.	W	13 Victoria Buildings, Shettleston	1904
2915	Reid, Rev. Edward T. S.	W	St. Cuthbert's Church, Hawick	1905
2925	Russell, James	W	23 Fortis Green Road, East Finchley, London	1905
2931	Russell, William E.	W	32 Fortis Green Road, East Finchley, London	1905
2932	Russell, John	W	Woodend, Lethington Avenue, Langside	1905
2274	Stewart, John Gilchrist	W	Hilda, Balshagray Avenue	1871
2329	Stobo, David	W	205 Langside Road	1873
2350	Stewart, James T.	W	96 Byres Road	1875
2373	Scott, Innes W.	W	*12 Princes Terrace	1876
2377	Steele, Robert I.	Barber	137 Ingram Street	1876
2378	Steven, Alex. F.	W	43 Queen's Square, Queen's Park	1876
2379	Steven, Robert M.	W	176 Ingram Street	1876
2382	Smith, William	W	119 Argyle Street	1877
2389	Steven, Peter	W	Applegarth, Helensburgh	1877
2395	Steven, Andrew	Wright	3 Granville Gardens, Newcastle-on-Tyne	1877
2414	Sandeman, Boswell	W	St. Ronan's, Lenzie	1878
2416	Seton, William C.	W	*283 High Street	1878
2448	Salmon, Peter	W	Sandyhills, Shettleston	1880
2485	Smith, William, jun.	W	*Torwood, Helensburgh	1882
2505	Stewart, George	W	68 Mitchell Street	1883
2515	Sturgeon, William	W	205 Albert Road, Pollokshields	1883
2520	Sloan, James	M	*7 Royal Bank Place	1884
2525	Sloan, George	W	8 Gordon Street	1884
2545	Stewart, John S.	W	21 Buchanan Street	1885
2546	Stewart, Ninian B.	W	21 Buchanan Street	1885
2558	Smith, William A.	W	6 South Hanover Street	1885
2563	Stout, John S.	Cordiner	c/o Mrs. Thomson, 129 Whitehill Street	1885
2564	Service, Andrew G.	Gardener	27 St. Vincent Place	1885
2577	Sloan, James R.	W	Southfield, Queen's Drive	1885
2587	Service, John	W	71 Mitchell Street	1885
2613	Speirs, Archibald	W	74 Canning Street	1888
2632	Stewart, James B.	W	96 Byres Road	1890
2633	Stewart, William H.	W	205 Hope Street	1890
2634	Stewart, John L.	W	96 Byres Road	1890
2653	Sutherland, George	W	34 Granby Terrace	1892
2691	Smith, John B.	W	12 Waterloo Street	1895
2692	Smith, Alex. D.	W	96 Springfield Avenue	1895
2720	Service, William S.	Gardener	208 St. Vincent Street	1895
2734	Smith, George	W	141 St. Vincent Street	1896

164   APPENDIX.

No. on the Roll.	Name.	Craft.	Address.	Year of Entry.
2735	Smith, Robert W.	W	141 St. Vincent Street	1896
2747	Stirling, Hugh A.	W	133 St. Vincent Street	1897
2755	Steven, John M.	W	115 Stirling Road	1898
2756	Steven, William D.	W	Supt., India General Steam Navigation Co., Calcutta	1898
2757	Steven, Peter A., M.D.	W	Ripon	1898
2766	Smith, James W.	W	73 Earl's Park Avenue, Newlands, Glasgow	1899
2776	Scott, Thomas	W	153 Queen Street	1899
2786	Stockdale, H. F.	Barber	38 Bath Street	1900
2819	Stewart, R. B.	W	146 Argyle Street	1902
2839	Suttie, Robert	W	10 Prince's Square, Buchanan Street	1903
2846	Strang, Andrew S.	W	201 Greenhead Street	1903
2853	Smart, A. Wilson, C.A.	W	66 Bath Street	1903
2854	Smart, Lewis A.	W	Birkbeck Bank Chambers, Holborn, London	1903
2916	Shaw, James	W	101 St. Vincent Street	1905
2295	Thomson, John Shaw	W	16 Watling Street, London, E.C.	1871
2375	Taylor, Gilbert	W	46 West George Street	1876
2376	Thom, James	W	150 Ingram Street	1876
2438	Thomson, George	W	100 Great Hamilton Street	1879
2455	Thomson, James	W	Mount Royd, Park Drive, Huddersfield	1880
2522	Taylor, William	W	16 Whitehill Street, Dennistoun	1884
2557	Thomson, John	W.	394 Paisley Road, W.	1885
2569	Tillie, William J.	W	39 Miller Street	1885
2594	Telford, Robert	W	Arouca, Rutherglen	1886
2605	Tod, Alexander W.	W	112 Nithsdale Road, Pollokshields	1887
2828	Taylor, William	W	180 West George Street	1902
2858	Thomson, H. J.	W	147 Bath Street	1903
2891	Turner, John	W	27 King Street, Liverpool	1904
2926	Taylor, Frederick	W	49 Jamaica Street	1905
2927	Todd, Thomas C.	W	30 Gordon Street	1905
2934	Tod, Thomas	W	26 Queen Street	1905
2936	Taylor, John	W	40 Queen's Square, Strathbungo	1905
2502	Urquhart, Robert D.	Maltman	42 India Street, Edinburgh	1883
2223	Watson, Joseph	W	3 Mansfield Place, High Street, Rothesay	1866
2272	Winning, James	W	1 Prince's Square, 48 Buchanan Street	1870
2290	Wilson, Samuel	W	Greenkerse, Corntan, Bridge of Allan	1871
2314	Wallace, James	W	45 Arlington Street	1872
2332	Woodrow, Alex.	W	75 Glassford Street	1874
2333	Wilson, Peter B.	W	114 Trongate	1874
2340	Wilson, John, jun.	W	121½ Duke Street	1875
2380	Watson, Thomas	M	9 Belhaven Terrace	1876
2419	Wallace, John	W	229 Norfolk Street, Dorchester, Boston, U.S.A.	1878
2439	Wright, Robert H.	W	188 South Woodside Road	1879

APPENDIX. 165

No. on the Roll.	Name.	Craft.	Address.	Year of Entry.
2457	Wilson, James	W	15 Cleveland Street	1880
2458	Wilson, Michael	W	13 John Knox Street	1880
2493	Wylie, David V.	W	102 Bath Street	1882
2508	Wilson, William	W	15 Edmund Street, Dennistoun	1883
2509	Wilson, Robert	W	Mayfield, Falkirk	1883
2510	Wilson, James, jun.	W	Bantaskin, Falkirk	1883
2511	Wilson, Gilbert T.	W	Bantaskin, Falkirk	1883
2528	White, Adam	W	104 West George Street	1884
2567	Wilson, Thomas M.	Hammer	42 Glassford Street	1885
2599	Wylie, Robert	Mason	354 Paisley Road	1886
2611	Watson, James M.	W	7 Kenilworth Avenue, W. Didsbury, near Manchester	1888
2647	Wallace, John B.	Maltman	60 Bidston Road, Birkenhead	1892
2648	Waddel, Alex.	W	Aldworth, Kilmalcolm	1892
2649	Waddel, John	W	Invereck, Kilmalcolm	1892
2650	Wilson, Andrew M.	Cooper	168 Oxford Street	1892
2664	Woodrow, Alex. N.	W	75 Glassford Street	1893
2668	Wright, David C.	Hammer	87 Meadowpark Street	1893
2689	Wilson, Edwin C.	W	Bantaskin, Falkirk	1895
2694	Watson, Hugh, jun.	W	61 North Craigpark Street, Dennistoun	1895
2700	Wallace, Arch. C.	Hammer	71 West Nile Street	1895
2708	Winning, Henry D.	W	1 Prince's Square, 48 Buchanan Street	1895
2733	Woodburn, William D.	F	22 Eldon Street, Greenock	1896
2754	Wollheim, Chas. L.	W	*Bath House, Buxton	1898
2760	Wright, Daniel	H	11 Bannatyne Avenue	1898
2784	Wilkie, Connal A.	W	72 Tobago Street	1901
2807	Wright, John G. G.	W	10 New Burlington Street, London	1901
2822	Webster, James	W	103 West George Street	1902
2823	Wilson, David, D.L., D.Sc.	W	Of Carbeth, Killearn	1902
2825	Walker, Andrew	Gardener	43 Glassford Street	1902
2851	Watson, Jas. Muir	W	13 Bellgrove Street	1903
2861	Watson, Walter M.	W	Airedale Shed, Silsden, York	1903
2862	Wilson, Jas., tertius	W	Mayfield, Falkirk	1903
2863	Wilson, John Ross	W	Mayfield, Falkirk	1903
2864	Wilson, Tom Taylor	W	Mayfield, Falkirk	1903
2865	Wilson, Robert, jun.	W	Mayfield, Falkirk	1903
2866	Wilson, Cecil Guy	W	Mayfield, Falkirk	1903
2871	Wishart, John	H	Oakbank Oil Co., 39 St. Vincent Place	1903
2910	Woodburn, Wm. H.	W	17 Carlton Place, S.S.	1904
2924	Wright, David	W	57 Reidvale Street	1905
2929	Weston, John H.	W	17 West Register Street, Edinburgh	1905
2937	Webster, Jas. Manuel	W	103 West George Street	1905
2355	Young, James	W	92 Union Street	1876
2356	Young, John E.	W	92 Union Street	1876
2425	Young, James	Skinner	52 Dundas Street, Kingston	1878
2543	Younger, George W.	W	14 Prince's Square, Buchanan Street	1885
2544	Younger, Robert T.	W	Advocate, Edinburgh	1885
2548	Yuill, William	W	39 Finlay Drive, Dennistoun	1885
2596	Young, William G., M.D.	W	22 Monteith Row	1886

APPENDIX.

No. on the Roll.	Name.	Craft.	Address.	Year of Entry.
2728	Young, Robt. F.	W	Dunkeld, Buchanan Drive, Cambuslang	1895
2797	Young, James H.	W	92 Union Street	1901
2798	Young, R. M.	W	92 Union Street	1901
2799	Young, Harry A.	W	24 Belhaven Terrace	1901
2800	Young, John E., jun.	W	2nd Lieut., R.S.F.	1901
2801	Young, John R.	W	53 Mill Street, Bridgeton	1901
2802	Young, George R.	W	8 Claremont Terrace	1901
2803	Young, Robert F.	W	8 Claremont Terrace	1901
2847	Yuill, Hugh	W	34 Finlay Drive, Dennistoun	1903
2873	Yuill, Arthur	W	93 Candleriggs	1903

APPENDIX VI.

INVENTORY OF OLD MINUTE BOOKS, CHARTERS, DEEDS, AND OTHER RECORDS BELONGING TO THE INCORPORATION OF WEAVERS.

BY GEORGE NEILSON, ESQ., LL.D., F.S.A., ETC.

I.—ORIGIN AND EARLY HISTORY OF THE CRAFT.
Minute Books, Charters, and Records.

1.—Minute Book, 1591–1611. } For extracts see Chap. I. *et seq.*
2.—Minute Book, 1611–1686. }
3.—Minute Book, 1791–1795.
4.—Minute Book, 1795–1810.
5.—Register indicating brethren's payments of quarter compts, 1712-1744.
6.—Collector's Account Book, 1671-1732.
7.—Collector's Account Book, 1743-1780.
8.—Memorandum Book, containing Acts of Trade, references to Petitions, Lawsuits, and other craft and public affairs, 1796-1839.
9.—Act Book, 1786-1821.
10.—Enrolment Book for Apprentices and Journeymen, 1717-1817.
11.—Letter Book, 1839.
12.—Collector's Book, for noting papers put into the box or taken from it, 1818-1844.
13.—Copy Letter of Guildry of 9th February, 1605 (see p. 42).
14.—Seal of Cause by the Provost, Bailies, and Community of Glasgow to the Weavers, dated 16th February, 1605 (see p. 2).
15.—Charter by the Archbishop of Glasgow in favour of the Weavers, dated 19th July, 1681 (see p. 5).
16.—Ratification by Parliament, dated 17th September, 1681 (see p. 6).

II.—CONSTITUTION.

See Division I., *supra*.

III.—APPRENTICESHIP AND FREEMANSHIP.

Acts anent Booking of Apprentices and Admission of Strangers as Freemen, together with Indentures of Apprentices.

1.—Extract Act of Trades' House, dated 11th December, 1671, ratifying a former Act regulating the booking of apprentices (see pp. 31, 32).

2.—Extract Act of Trades' House ratifying an Act of the Weavers of date 2nd May, 1673, fixing the freedom fine for strangers entering freemen (see p. 33).

3.—Extract Act of Trades' House anent an Act of Town Council as to the placing of boys on apprenticeship under the Auldhouse Mortification, dated 28th February, 1746.

4.—Agreement between John Cochrane and Duncan Lorne, whereby the said John is to be taught " double cuveringis," dated 16th July, 1656 (see p. 28).

5.—Indenture of David Muir, son of Abraham Muir in Craigend, dated 24th December, 1657.

6.—Indenture of John Bryson, son of the late John Bryson, weaver burgess of Glasgow, dated 27th July, 1658 (see p. 22).

7.—Indenture of Andrew M'Indoe, son of James M'Indoe, indweller in Dintraith, dated 17th October, 1694.

8.—Indenture of John Bruce, son of Wm. Bruce, weaver in Airdrie, dated 17th November, 1729, with Memorandum on back, dated 7th February, 1735, bearing that the Indenture is " given up," the apprentice being convicted of theft.

9.—Assignation of John Bruce's Indenture in favour of a new master, dated 26th April, 1733.

10.—Indenture of George Humphrey, son of Robert Humphrey, weaver in Glasgow, " one of the poor boys under Hutchesons' Mortification," dated 9th October, 1732.

11.—Indenture of John Lang, son of the late John Lang, maltman burgess, " one of the poor boys on the Laird of Scots Tarbett's Mortification," dated 26th January, 1734.

12.—Indenture of John M'Millan, son of the late John M'Millan, weaver at Lochfine, dated 10th December, 1737.

13.—Indenture of James Stevenson, son of John Stevenson, stabler in Glasgow, dated 1st January, 1737.

APPENDIX.

14.—Indenture of Duncan M'Farlane, son of the late Patrick M'Farlane, land labourer in Buchanan, dated 2nd November, 1738.

15.—Indenture of John M'Arthur, son of the late Duncan M'Arthur, tailor in the Parish of Kilmore, dated 16th May, 1738.

16.—Indenture of James Dougall, son of Henry Dougall, land labourer in Glasgow, dated 8th November, 1738.

17.—Indenture of Andrew Gray, son of the late Andrew Gray, land labourer in the Parish of Linlithgow, dated 2nd September, 1741.

18.—Indenture of James Marshall, son of Alexr. Marshall, workman in Glasgow, dated 17th March, 1742.

19.—Indenture of Wm. Reid, son of the late Michael Reid, wright in Glasgow, dated 28th September, 1743.

20.—Indenture of John Sutherland, son of Alexr. Sutherland, chairman in Glasgow, dated 30th September, 1743.

21.—Indenture of Robert Anderson, natural son of the late John Anderson, surgeon in Arran, dated 17th November, 1743.

22.—Indenture of James Gray, son of Archibald Gray, workman in Glasgow, dated 13th July, 1743.

23.—Indenture of Daniel Shaw, son of John Shaw, servant to Alexr. M'Donald in the Isle of Uist, dated 18th July, 1743, with Memorandum on back that he had " run away from his master with the rebells."

24.—Indenture of John M'Farlan, son of the late Wm. M'Farlan, gardener at Ruchhill, dated 27th January, 1744.

25.—Indenture of Wm. Wright, son of Dougal Wright, workman in Glasgow, dated 5th March, 1744.

26.—Indenture of James Aiken, son of Wm. Aiken, " maltcaer " in Glasgow, dated 27th June, 1744.

27.—Indenture of James Marshall, son of John Marshall, coalheaver in Muir of Gorbals, dated 23rd February, 1744.

28.—Indenture of Robert Smart, son of John Smart, journeyman weaver in Glasgow, dated 5th October, 1744.

29.—Indenture of Hugh Wilken, son of James Wilken, merchant in Glasgow, dated 15th January, 1745.

30.—Indenture of Charles Pirrie, son of Charles Pirrie, wright in Gorbals, dated 5th June, 1745.

APPENDIX.

31.—Indenture of James Thomson, son of the late George Thomson, workman in Glasgow, dated 7th August, 1745.

32.—Indenture of Robert Chambers, son of the late James Chambers, smith in Cumbernauld, dated 9th April, 1745.

33.—Indenture of John M'Farlane, son of R. M'Farlane, land labourer in the Parish of Lochgoilhead, dated 6th March, 1746.

34.—Indenture of John Brown, son of Hugh Brown, farmer in the Parish of Kilbrinnan, dated 26th May, 1747.

35.—Indenture of John M'Kenzie, son of the late John M'Kenzie, coalheaver in Gorbals, dated 21st October, 1775.

36.—Indenture of Andrew Liddel, son of Andrew Liddel, labourer in Gorbals, dated 17th January, 1788.

37.—Assignation of the Indenture of date 14th March, 1732, between Wm. Young and James Moy, weaver, in favour of a new master, dated 27th April, 1733.

IV.—TRADE PRIVILEGES.

Burgess Tickets, Records of Privileges of Freemen Craftsmen, and of Penalties incurred by Strangers infringing the liberties of the Craft.

1.—Burgess Ticket of John Boyd, tailor, dated 8th August, 1678 (see p. 36).

2.—Burgess Ticket of John Murray, merchant, dated 16th June, 1692.

3.—Burgess Ticket of James Stark, weaver, dated 18th September, 1734.

4.—Burgess Ticket (not legible), dated 1643.

5.—Extract Act of Town Council in favour of the Weavers as to the working of webs in a Manufactory, dated 5th May, 1638 (see p. 35).

6.—Bond by Patrick Aikenhead, weaver at Provane-mylne, to pay 58 shillings Scots yearly for liberty to take weaver work in Glasgow to work at his home, dated 29th July, 1657.

7.—Extract Act of Trades' House anent a Petition by the Coopers against the partners of the East Suggary for employing an unfreeman cooper, dated 1st June, 1687.

8.—Act of the Lords of the Exchequer as to privileges given to the masters of the East Suggary, dated 5th July, 1687 (see p. 37).

APPENDIX. 171

9.—Extract Act of the Weavers refusing the prayer of a Petition by certain freemen weavers anent the booking of stranger journeymen, dated 14th November, 1746.

10.—Representation to the Trades' House on behalf of the Petitioners anent the booking of stranger journeymen, dated 2nd December, 1746, having endorsed thereon Minute of the Weavers' consideration of the representation which had been transmitted to them by the Trades' House for answers, dated 13th February, 1747.

11.—Complaint and Representation to the Weaver craft by their collector against two freemen weavers contravening the Acts of the Trade by giving work to unfreemen, dated 21st January, 1747 (see p. 40).

12.—Copy Petition to the Lord Provost and Council by Wm. Gemmill and James Sym, freemen weavers, to have an Act of the Weavers of date 23rd May, 1735, referring to the employment of unfreemen, rescinded, dated 26th January, 1747.

13.—Obligations by certain persons found guilty of acting contrary to the Acts of the Weaver craft by taking freemen's work outwith the town to work, binding themselves never again to infringe upon the liberties and privileges of the craft under specified penalties:

John Pettigrew, weaver in Dykehead, dated 8th March, 1675.
John Ker, weaver in Titwood, dated 9th November, 1681.
James Barton, weaver in Meikle Govan, dated 16th November, 1682.
James Duncan, weaver in Gourock, dated 20th December, 1682.
John Stewart, weaver in Partick, dated 9th August, 1683.
Wm. Wilson, weaver in Easter Cunchlie, dated 9th August, 1683.
David Shanks, weaver in Auchiniron, dated 14th March, 1683.
John Wark, weaver in Kinmuir, dated 31st January, 1683.
Wm. Morton, in Middle Quarter of Shettleston, dated 24th January, 1683.
Wm. Gilmour, younger, weaver in Meikle Govan, dated 27th September, 1687.
Thomas Spreull, weaver in Netherpollock, dated 22nd August, 1688.
Wm. Stark, in Gartsherry, dated 30th July, 1697.
John Gardner, weaver in Keppoch, dated 26th June, 1724.
Alexr. Jamieson, weaver in Boghall, dated 28th September, 1726.
James Steven, weaver in Craigends, dated 1st October, 1731.

14.—Petition to the Magistrates to concur in the prosecution of Wm. Robertson, journeyman weaver to John Biggar, in Glasgow, for taking freemen's stuff out of the town contrary to an article in the Weavers' Charter; dated 4th January, 1711.

15.—Petition to the Magistrates to grant warrant to summon John Anderson and Matthew Barr to answer to the charge of doing craft work within the city, they not being freemen; warrant granted; dated 1st March, 1780, having endorsed thereon Decreet of Magistrate fining each in 5s. stg., and ordering them to give bond to cease working until they enter as freemen; dated 9th March, 1780.

V.—RECORDS OF THE INCORPORATION OF WEAVERS IN RELATION TO THE TRADES' HOUSE OF GLASGOW.

1. —Receipt for 40 pounds Scots paid by the Craft as part of the expenses incurred in obtaining the "Ratification of the Guildry," dated 11th November, 1672 (see p. 42, and Craufurd's *Sketch of the Trades' House*, p. 84).
2. —Receipt for £6 stg. paid by the Craft towards defraying the expenses of the "plea between the four and the ten trades," dated 18th September, 1776 (see p. 84, and *Sketch of the Trades' House*, pp. 109, 110).
3. —Receipt for £9 10s. paid by the Craft "as their proportion of extracting the Decreet that the four got against the ten," dated 14th July, 1777 (see *Sketch of the Trades' House*, p. 110).
4. —Extract Act of the Trades' House, in answer to a Petition from the Maltmen anent quarter compts, dated 5th June, 1744.
5. —Extract *Acts of the Trades' House* :
   Confirming Acts of the Cordiners, dated 6th March, 1781.
   Anent Reform of Burgh Set, dated 10th January, 1788.
   Anent the Gorbal Lands, dated 12th August, 1788.
   Anent Funds to oppose Police Bill, dated 2nd March and 3rd June, 1790.
   Anent Appropriation of Funds, dated 11th June, 1790, and 25th January, 1793.
   Anent protest against proceedings of 25th January, 1793.
   Anent the Bill for Regulating the Importation of Corn, etc., dated 26th January, 1791.
   Anent Augmentation of Pensions, dated 7th March, 1791.
   Anent the Building of a Hall, dated 11th June, 1791 ; 26th January, 1792.
6. —Minute of the Weavers anent the proposal to build a Hall, dated 17th March, 1792, following upon an Extract Act of the Trades' House, dated 10th March, 1792.
7. —Extract Act of Trades' House anent a Petition from the Dyers and Bonnetmakers "for restoration to their dormant privileges," dated 18th August, 1791, having endorsed thereon Minute of the Weavers, dated 26th August, 1791.
8. —Extract Act of the Trades' House anent the state of the Funds, dated 3rd April, 1795, having endorsed thereon Minute of the Weavers, dated 15th May, 1795.
9. —Extract Acts of the General Committee on the Lands of Gorbals, dated 1st November, 21st December, 1790 ; 7th March, 1791 ; 16th February, 27th February, 2nd March, 1792 ; 11th September, 1794.
10. —Receipt for payment to the Trades' House of the Weaver Craft's share of loss sustained on Grain brought in for the years 1766 and 1767, dated 5th September, 1772.
11. —Receipt for payment by the Weavers of £10 stg. as their first share of advance for following out the question whether the Trades' House have management of their own Funds, dated 18th August, 1791.

APPENDIX.

VI.—SUPERVISION OF TRADESMANSHIP.

See Divisions III. and IV.

VII.—MEETINGS AND PLACES OF MEETING.

See Minute Books, Division I.

VIII.—DISCIPLINE.

Records of cases of Defaulters granting obligations not to repeat the offence.

1.—Obligation by Wm. Turner, merchant in Glasgow, convicted before a magistrate " for misdemeanour and scandalous expressions " against the Weavers, dated 11th October, 1703.
2.—Obligation by Archibald Menzies, horse-hirer in Glasgow, found guilty of scandalising the Weavers, dated 6th March, 1706.
3.—Obligation by Wm. Crawfurd, weaver, convicted by the Deacon of slandering James Wright, weaver, dated 6th June, 1712.
4.—Obligation by Thomas Barr, journeyman weaver to Wm. Fleckfield, to pay, when required, 12 pounds Scots, in which he was fined by the Deacon and masters for deserting his master.

IX.—MONEY MATTERS.

1.—A bundle of Bills granted to the Weavers in payment of reeds, freedom fines, house rents, quarter compts, etc., between the years 1721 and 1788.
2.—Extract Registered Protest against Robert Steven, reedmaker in Kirkintilloch, for non-payment of bill, dated 20th August, 1724.
3.—Extract Registered Protest against Wm. Reid, weaver in Glasgow, for non-payment of bill, dated 12th September, 1728.
4.—Protest against John Miller, weaver in Glasgow, for non-payment of bill, dated 1st October, 1731.

APPENDIX.

5.—Extract Registered Protest against James King, reedmaker in Paisley, for non-payment of bill, dated 1st May, 1731, and Execution of charge for payment, dated 22nd May, 1731.

6.—Extract Registered Protest against Wm. Alexander, weaver in Glasgow, for non-payment of bill, dated 5th March, 1733 ; and Execution of charge, dated 14th March, 1733.

7.—Extract Registered Protest against Patrick Lang, reedmaker in Glasgow, for non-payment of bill, dated 12th August, 1736 ; and Execution of charge, dated 10th August, 1741.

8.—Extract Registered Protest against James Eglinton, reedmaker in Paisley, for non-payment of bill, dated 20th September, 1737 ; and Execution of charge, dated 12th April, 1740.

9.—Extract Registered Protest against James Aird, weaver in Gorbals, for non-payment of bill, dated 13th June, 1746.

10.—Extract Decreet before a magistrate of the Burgh, at the instance of the Weavers against certain weavers for payment of certain sums due by bill, dated 2nd March, 1761 ; and Execution of charge in virtue of Decreet, dated 25th March, 1761.

11.—Testament Dative and Inventory of umquhill Andrew Graham, manufacturer, Glasgow, dated 8th June, 1774.

12.—A small bundle of Bills granted by the Weavers for money received on loan " for behove of the Incorporation," 1742-1798.

13.—Receipt by Margaret Houston, relict of Michael Watson, weaver burgess, in favour of the Weavers, for their payment of one year's interest on a 400 merks bond, dated 5th August, 1668.

14.—Receipt for payment by Weaver Craft of 100 merks, being one half of a 200 merks bond, dated 11th November, 1693.

15.—Receipt for payment by Weaver Craft of interest on a hundred pounds Scots bond, dated 31st August, 1742.

16.—Receipt for payment by Weaver Craft of one year's interest on a 200 merks bond, dated 24th June, 1746.

17.—Receipt for payment by Weaver Craft of one year's interest on £80 stg. bond, dated 8th June, 1767.

18.—A bundle of Receipts acknowledging payments made by Weaver Craft of tradesmen's and other accounts, 1746-1750.

19.—Receipt for 15 pounds Scots paid to the Trades' House for 4 quarter compts, dated 25th August, 1660.

APPENDIX. 175

20.—Receipts for payment of a half-year's and a quarter-year's rent due by the Weavers for the Chapel in the Castle of Glasgow, dated 2nd November, 1731, and 2nd May, 1732.

21.—Receipt for payment made to the College of ground annuals due from the Weavers' lands of Bowastie, dated 20th February, 1661.

22.—A bundle of Receipts for payments of ground annuals to the College, 1774-1812.

23.—A bundle of Receipts for payments made by Weavers, of Land Stent and Trade Stent, for years 1749-1814.

24.—Receipt in favour of the Weavers and Andrew Galloway and John Stirling, portioners in Auchinairn, for part payment of tradesmen's account for casting a ditch between their lands and the lands of George Scot of Wester Limloch, dated 6th June, 1720.

25.—Execution of Arrestment in the hands of James Stevenson, portioner in Auchinairn, at the instance of the Weavers against John Stirling, portioner of Auchinairn, for 20 pounds Scots; dated 9th November, 1721.

26.—Memorandum of Expenses in connection with certain Letters of Horning.

27.—Fragment of an Account in connection with "spinnells."

28.—Invoice from Archibald Boyd, Hamilton, for yarn and worsted, sent per carrier, dated 8th December, 1701.

29.—Invoices from Richard Meikle, Strathaven, for worsted, etc., sent per carrier, dated November and December, 1701, and February, 1702.

30.—Account of sum due to John Knox for yarn, dated 10th December, 1701.

31.—Receipt for £2 paid by the Craft to the widow of Daniel Morrison, officer to the Weavers, dated 10th April, 1792.

32.—Warrant to the collector to pay the officer 4s. stg. for "overplus" services, dated 19th February, 1779.

33.—Receipt for £10 10s. paid to the clerk as his year's salary, dated 31st August, 1810.

34.—A few Accounts for legal expenses, 1762-1810.

35.—Warrant of the Magistrates to summon James Wilson, late collector of Weavers, to answer the complaint by the deacon and masters that he refuses to make compt of his intromissions with the Craft funds, dated 9th November, 1719.

36.—Letters of Horning passed at the instance of David Robb, elder, maltman, against James Wilson, principal in a bond for 100 merks Scots, dated 10th November, 1719; and Execution of charge, dated 11th November, 1719.

APPENDIX.

37.—Letters of Inhibition passed as in foregoing, dated 10th November, 1719 ; and Execution of charge, dated 11th November, 1719.

38.—Execution of charge in virtue of Letters of Inhibition at the instance of the Weavers against James Wilson, late collector, dated 13th November, 1719.

39.—Execution of charge in virtue of Letters of Inhibition containing arrestment at the instance of the Weavers against James Wilson, arresting in the hands of Robert Dobie and others, weavers, 3000 merks and all goods, etc., belonging to James Wilson, dated 14th November, 1719.

40.—Extract Decreet before the Magistrate at the instance of the Weavers ordaining Robert Dobie and others to pay to the Weaver Craft certain sums borrowed from James Wilson, to which the Weaver Craft has right by assignation from the said James, dated 30th November, 1719 ; and Execution of charge, dated 9th December, 1719.

41.—Charge and Letters of Horning at the instance of the Weavers against James Wilson on a heritable bond to the Incorporation for 1100 merks Scots, with 300 merks of penalty, dated 31st May, 1720.

42.—Warrant of Caption by the Lords of Council at the instance of the Weavers against James Wilson, who has been put to the horn for a debt of 1100 merks Scots under a heritable bond with relative rents and penalty, dated 9th August, 1720.

43.—Discharge by David Robb, maltman, to James Wilson and his cautioners in a 100 merks bond for payment of 40 pounds Scots; and Assignation by David Robb to the Weavers (in consideration of payment made) of the sum of 43 pounds 5s. 4d. Scots and the annual rents thereon, with full power to them to uplift sum assigned ; dated 1st October, 1720.

44.—Assignation by Janet Robertson, relict and Executrix Dative, decerned and confirmed, to the deceased James Ferguson, collector to the Weavers, of the sums contained in 4 bills payable to the deceased James, and allowed to the Weavers by interlocutor pronounced at the instance of the Weavers before the Magistrates of Glasgow ; dated 20th February, 1724.

45.—Bundle of 42 Bonds granted by the Weavers for sums of money borrowed on behalf of the Craft, with some discharges for annual rents and principal sums, 1666-1757.

46.—Bundle of 6 Bonds granted in favour of the Weavers, 1631-1778 (see p. 77).

47.—Extract Registered Assignation by James Boyle, weaver, to the Weavers, in and to the whole annual rents of the sum of money lent on bond of 8th January, 1748, to Wm. Millar and Hugh and John Stewart, merchants ; dated 15th December, 1760.

APPENDIX. 177

X.—LEGISLATION AND LITIGATION.

1.—Copy Act of Privy Council discharging the exportation of linen yarn, dated 13th January, 1603 (see p. 86).

2.—Letters by King James VI. against the transportation of linen yarn, dated 12th March, 1612 (see p. 87).

3.—Copy Supplication by the Weavers of Scotland to the Lords of the Privy Council, praying for the Suspension of the Act of Parliament passed in 1661 regulating the breadth of linen cloth ; dated 21st November, 1666 (see p. 88).

4.—" xliii Act discharging the exportation of linen yarn and regulating the breadth of linen cloth, etc.," 1641 (see p. 90).

5.—Information for the Weavers of Glasgow, Gorbals, and Rutherglen against David Weymes (see p. 91).

6.—Instrument of Protest by the Weavers of Glasgow and of Gorbals against James Bryce, messenger, dated 8th October, 1667 (see p. 93).

7.—Instrument of Protest by the Weavers of Rutherglen against James Bryce, messenger, dated 9th October, 1667.

8.—Copy of Letters from Wm. Brown, agent to the Burghs, to Wm. Anderson, late Provost of Glasgow, concerning the Weavers' cause against David Weymes, dated at Edinburgh, 7th, 9th, and 14th May, 1668.

9.—Extract Act of the Lords of Exchequer in answer to a Petition given in by the Royal Burghs anent the xliii Act of 1641, discharging, until further order, David Weymes from " further prosecuting of his Gift " against contraveners, dated 9th May, 1668.

10.—Contract and Agreement by the Weavers of Glasgow and of Bridgend in favour of the Weavers in Kirkintilloch and the parts within the Parish of Lenzie, with regard to privileges under the foregoing Act ; dated 29th May, 1668.

11.—Discharge by Wm. Paisley and Thomas Davidson, weaver burgesses of Paisley, to the Weavers of Glasgow and Gorbals, discharging them (without payment) of a bond of 40 pounds Scots advanced for helping in the defence in the action intended against them at the instance of David Weymes, " in regard that through the just and diligent defence the said David was discouraged in the pursuit against us " ; dated at Paisley, 28th October, 1670.

12.—Letter from Wm. Wilson, jun., acknowledging receipt of £15 stg. " to account of the Weavers," making reference to an Interlocutor of the Lords, and mentioning that although the Decreet is not yet extracted application may be made to the magistrate " for getting every silk weaver fined who has not entered with the Incorporation " ; dated at Edinburgh, 2nd March, 1778.

APPENDIX.

13.—Receipt for Craft payment of £24 stg. to account of expense of extracting a Decreet against the silk weavers in Glasgow, dated 13th November, 1778.

14.—Receipt granted to the Weavers by John Marshall for payment of £3 3s. for his " trouble in the Processes " for and against the Weavers before the Magistrates of Glasgow and the Lords of Session with relation to the silk weavers, dated 27th November, 1778.

15.—Receipt for £3 10s. in payment of expenses decerned to be paid by defenders in the Process before the Magistrates, at the instance of Robert Craig against the Weavers, dated 16th April, 1793.

16.—Letter from David Campbell, Ayr, desiring a copy of the Address to Parliament anent the " Linnen Manufactor," dated 29th December, 1719.

17.—Account of what was received from the country Weavers " about the calicoes," and account of expenses in connection therewith (undated).

XI.—RELATIONS WITH GORBALS AND BRIDGEND WEAVERS, AND ALSO WITH EDINBURGH WEAVERS.

Gorbals and Bridgend Weavers.

1.—Agreement between the Weavers of Glasgow and the Weavers of Gorbals, dated 8th May, 1605 (see p. 95).

2.—Contract and Agreement between the Weavers of Glasgow and the Weavers of Gorbals, dated 10th April, 1657 (see p. 98).

3.—Copy of foregoing Contract and Agreement, dated 1710.

4.—List of the " deficiency of the non-payers' quarters for 1688-1694," containing the names of the Weavers of Gorbals, the number of looms, " payment of quarter compts, deficiencies and quota thereof in money."

5.—Extract Act of the Magistrates and Council of Glasgow, dated 3rd October, 1692, as to certain privileges in the Contract and Agreement of 10th April, 1657 (see p. 103).

6.—Extract Decreet of Gorbals Bailie with concurrence of Magistrates and Council of Glasgow, at the instance of the Glasgow Weavers against the Gorbals Weavers for contravening the 1657 Contract and Agreement; dated 18th March, 1695.

APPENDIX. 179

7.—Execution of charge in virtue of Letters of Horning raised at the instance of the Glasgow Weavers against Gorbals Weavers, dated 4th April, 1695.

8.—Bill of Suspension to the Lords of Session by the Weavers of Gorbals against the foregoing Decreet; Stay of Execution granted and answers called for; dated April, 1695.

9.—Answers for the Weavers of Glasgow to the Reasons of Suspension given in by Weavers of Gorbals, in which reference is made to the Contract between the Weavers of Edinburgh and of Westport " as the rule and method " upon which the Contract between the Weavers of Glasgow and of Gorbals follows.

10.—Summons of Declarator by the Lords of Session at the instance of the Weavers of Glasgow, dated 22nd April, 1695.

11.—Execution of Summons in virtue of Summons of Declarator, dated 27th April, 1695.

12.—Memorandum for the Weavers of Glasgow in Summons of Declarator.

13 —Letters of Arrestment, pending caution, in the action at the instance of the Weavers of Glasgow against Weavers of Gorbals, dated 23rd April, 1695.

14.—Execution of Arrestment in the hands of various merchants, weavers, etc., in Gorbals, dated 4th May, 1695.

15.—Minute for the Suspenders, 1695.

16.—Execution of charge in virtue of Letters of Horning raised at the instance of the Weavers of Glasgow against the Weavers of Gorbals, dated 4th December, 1719.

17.—Extract Act of Weavers, and Agreement between Weavers of Glasgow and Weavers of Gorbals for defending their rights against out-of-the-town weavers, dated 3rd February, 1722.

18.—Petition by Weavers of Gorbals to the Weavers of Glasgow for an alteration in the articles of their Agreement of 1657, having reference to the payment of quarter accounts, dated 1735, having endorsed thereon Minute of Weavers appointing a committee to consider the Petition, dated 14th November, 1735.

19.—Memorial for the Weavers of Glasgow reviewing their relations with the Weavers of Gorbals since 1657, in which reference is made to the Decreet of the Gorbals Bailie being affirmed by a Decreet of the Lords of Session of 7th February, 1696; reference also being made to the Petition of Gorbals Weavers of 1735.

20.—Memorandum of Papers sent to Wm. Wilson, W.S., in connection with a Bill of Suspension raised by Charles Wallace, weaver, who set up in Gorbals as a militiaman, against a Decreet of the Gorbals Bailie; dated 4th July, 1750.

APPENDIX.

Edinburgh Weavers.

21.—Copy of the Act of the Magistrates and Council of Edinburgh anent transporting of webs and yarn to Westport and other suburbs for weaving, of date 27th November, 1584; copied 5th June, 1694.

22.—Copy Extract Decreet granted by the Lords of Session at the instance of the Weavers of Edinburgh against certain "wobster indwellers in Cannongate," of date 11th February, 1614.

23.—Copy Agreement between the Weavers of Edinburgh and the Weavers of Westport, of date 5th April, 1650.

24.—Copy of Articles agreed on conform to foregoing Contract.

25.—Discharge by the Weavers of Edinburgh to the Weavers of Glasgow of all debts and claims due to the Weavers of Edinburgh "for money disbursed by them, and information and instruction given concerning the enlargement of their liberties against unfreemen living in the suburbs of Glasgow several years ago"; dated 18th April, 1661.

26.—Declaration by the Weavers of Edinburgh anent the Contract made between themselves and the Weavers of Westport, dated 14th February, 1698.

XII.—RELATIONS OF THE WEAVERS OF GLASGOW WITH THE WEAVERS IN CALTON AND BLACKFAULDS.

1.—Agreement between Weavers of Glasgow and Wm. Miller, weaver in Blackfauld, dated 19th October, 1710 (see p. 107).

2.—Contract and Agreement between the Weavers of Glasgow and the Weavers in Calton and Blackfauld, dated 23rd February, 1725 (see p. 108).

3.—Extract Act of the Magistrates and Council of Glasgow ratifying the foregoing Contract and Agreement, dated 29th April, 1725.

4.—Petition to the Weavers of Glasgow by certain weavers residing in Calton for admission to the liberties and privileges of the Craft, and Act of Weaver Craft granting same, dated 11th September, 1733 (see pp. 113, 114).

5.—Obligation by these weavers so admitted binding themselves to perform "the haill articles and conditions" of admission, dated 11th September, 1733.

6.—Copy of Acts of Trades' House of dates 7th December, 1723; 21st January, 1724; and 3rd August, 1730, anent the purchase and sale of Bortowfield and Blackfauld, wherein is a double of Mr. John Orr's proposals.

APPENDIX. 181

7.—Copy Memorial for the Weavers of Glasgow in settlement of all disputes and lawsuits between them and Mr. John Orr [1732].

8.—Execution of Summons in virtue of Summons of Reduction, Declarator and Payment before the Lords of Session at the instance of the Weavers in Calton and Mr. John Orr against the Weavers in Glasgow, dated 15th January, 1734.

9.—Copy of Letters from the Weavers to John Bogle, W.S., instructing him as to the defence and employment of Counsel in foregoing action, dated 6th February, 1734

10.—Copy Minute in the action.

11.—Memorial for the Weavers in Glasgow.

12.—Copy Petition to the Trades' House by the Weavers for assistance in the action against them at the instance of Weavers of Calton and Mr. John Orr.

13.—Copy Petition of Weavers, with concurrence of the Trades' House, to the Provost and Council of Glasgow for assistance in their defence.

14.—Copy Petition of Weavers to the Convention of Burghs for assistance in their defence.

15.—Account of Expenditure by the Weavers of Glasgow " anent the Calton affair."

16.—Memorandum anent the Weavers in Calton taking fines " without owning the Weavers in Glasgow "; and anent Mr. John Orr discharging an oversman chosen by the deacon and masters according to contract.

XIII.—SOCIAL MATTERS.

See Minute Books, Division I., *et passim.*

XIV.—PROPERTIES HELD BY THE INCORPORATION.

Rottenrow, Calton, Weaver Street, Old Wynd, Drygate, Gorbals, etc.

Bowastie, Rottenrow.

1.—Instrument of Sasine in favour of Matthew Muirhead, burgess of Glasgow, in a waste tenement on the north side of Rottenrow, bounded by the Manse of Eddleston on the west, dated 14th March, 1537 (see p. 118).

2 —Instrument of Sasine (under Contract of Marriage) on the resignation of Matthew Muirhead in favour of Catherine Fleming, daughter of the Laird of Boghall, in the tenement above described; dated 30th May, 1539.

APPENDIX.

3.—Instrument of Sasine in favour of John Muirhead, son of Matthew Muirhead, in the tenement above described, dated 3rd March, 1544.

4.—Instrument of Sasine on the resignation of Thomas Muirhead, procurator, in name of John Muirhead, in favour of John Nichol and Mariota Muirhead, his spouse, in the property above described, dated 20th April, 1563 (*Glasgow Protocols*, No. 742).

5.—Disposition (under Contract of Marriage) by Jean Nichol to Wm. Fergus, of the assignation made to her by her father, with a view to the redemption of that waste tenement with yard in Rottenrow, wadset by her father to Jean Boyd, dated 28th November, 1589.

6.—Contract between Wm. Nichol, tailor burgess, and Nicholas Watson, his wife, on the one part, and Robert Lang, weaver burgess, on the other, relative to that yard, etc., called Bowastie, on the north side of Rottenrow ; dated 30th January, 1612.

7.—Instrument of Sasine on the resignation of Wm. Nichol and his spouse in favour of Robert Lang and his wife, in Bowastie ; dated 15th April, 1613.

8.—Disposition by George Lang, son of deceased Robert Lang, in favour of Patrick Lang, his brother, of that yard, etc., called Bowastie ; dated 23rd August, 1625.

9.—Discharge by Patrick Lang to Elizabeth Nichol, daughter of Nicholas Watson and Wm. Nichol, for 200 merks Scots due under contract of 30th January, 1612 ; dated 4th November, 1625.

10.—Minute of Appointment of Judges and Arbiters in the division of lands (including Bowastie) belonging to the late David Warden, maltman burgess, amongst his three daughters ; dated 3rd June, 1657.

11.—Decreet Arbitral of Judges in foregoing reference, dated 2nd July, 1657.

12.—Disposition by Elspeth Warden and Christian Warden in favour of Walter Neilson, present deacon-convener of the Trades' House of Glasgow, in the orchard, etc., called Bowastie ; dated 6th August, 1657.

13.—Disposition by Walter Neilson to Janet Warden, of the orchard, etc., called Bowastie, dated 14th August, 1658.

14.—Bond and Disposition in security, by Janet Warden to James Gairner at Provanmylne, and Margaret Williamson his wife, dated 1658 (incomplete).

15.—Instrument of Sasine on the resignation of Janet Warden in favour of James Gairner and his wife, in that yard, etc., called Bowastie, dated 14th August, 1658.

16.—"Account of the Weavers' disbursements" for the buying of Bowastie, with memorandum, dated 5th September, 1664.

17.—Discharge by Patrick Jackson to Janet Warden for fulfilment of her bond, granted 5th January, 1633.

18.—Receipt by the factor to the College to Janet Warden for payment of bygone ground annuals furth of her tenement in Rottenrow, dated 2nd June, 1664.

APPENDIX. 183

Rottenrow Tenement.

19.—Instrument of Sasine on the resignation of John Robertoun and his wife in favour of John Robertoun, their son, in a tenement, with yard and pertinents thereto, situated on the north side of Rottenrow, and bounded on the west by the lands of John Nichol, dated 7th September, 1574 (*Glasgow Protocols*, No. 2082).

20.—Retour of Service of John Robertoun as heir of his brother Archibald (who died July, 1628), son of James Robertoun of Ernok, in all and whole a tenement of land in Rottenrow, bounded on the west by the lands belonging to the heirs of Wm. Nichol, dated 31st July, 1629.

21.—Bond by John Robertoun, son of James Robertoun of Ernok, for the sum of 500 merks money borrowed from his brother, Andrew Robertoun, dated at Leith, 14th July, 1630.

22.—Assignation of foregoing Bond (in consideration of payment now made) by Andrew Robertoun to his brother, Wm. Robertoun, dated 2nd December, 1639.

23.—Decree by the Commissioners for Administration of Justice in Scotland charging the Regent of the College of Glasgow to infeft Wm. Robertoun of Prestonpans, in a tenement of land in the Rottenrow of Glasgow, dated August, 1655 ; with proceedings in the Court of Apprising.

24.—Instrument of Sasine on the resignation of Wm. Robertoun in favour of the Weavers of Glasgow, in that tenement of land in the Rottenrow of Glasgow, bounded on the west by the lands of old belonging to the deceased Wm. Muirhead, thereafter to the heirs of the deceased Wm. Nichol, and now to the Weavers of Glasgow ; dated 20th February, 1665.

25.—Memorandum for the Weavers, being apparently an instruction as to steps to be taken to cause Wm. Robertoun to procure the service and retour of John Robertoun as heir of his father, and the said John's (or his curator's) ratification of the Disposition by the said William (*circa*, 1666).

26.—Extract Decreet Wm. Robertoun against John Robertoun declaratory of pursuer's heritable and irredeemable right to the tenement in Rottenrow, dated 7th February, 1666.

27.—Extract Registered Disposition by Wm. Robertoun to the Weavers, of a tenement of land on the north side of Rottenrow, dated 17th November, 1666.

28.—Letters of Inhibition at the instance of the Weavers against Wm. Robertoun, dated 1st January, 1667.

29.—Execution of charge, at the Mercat Cross of Edinburgh, in virtue of Letters of Inhibition against Wm. Robertoun, dated 21st January, 1667.

30.—Execution of charge at the Mercat Cross of Haddington, in virtue of Letters of Inhibition against Wm. Robertoun, dated 31st January, 1667.

31.—Receipt by Andrew Ralston, gardener burgess of Glasgow, to the Weavers, for payment of 34 pounds 16 shillings Scots " for his pains in going to Prestonpans " with the deacon, to buy the tenement of land on the north side of Rottenrow, from Wm. Robertoun, dated 13th March, 1667.

32.—Extract Decreet before the Dean of Guild at the instance of the Weavers against Margaret Anderson and others to cause them to repair their hedges and dykes neighbouring complainers' lands, dated 25th February, 1669.

33.—Execution of charge " to fulfil and obey " foregoing Decreet, dated 26th February, 1669.

Calton.

34.—Bond by Alex. Muirhead, maltman in Calton, in favour of John Purdon, portioner in Partick, for the sum of 200 merks Scots borrowed money, dated 17th May, 1738.

35.—Assignation by John Purdon to the Weavers of Glasgow of foregoing Bond granted in his favour by Alex. Muirhead, maltman in Calton, dated 25th November, 1747.

36.—Decreet before the Justices for Lanark at the instance of the Weavers against Colin Keith for payment of his rent of the house in Calton lately belonging to Alex. Muirhead, dated 27th February, 1745.

37.—Decreet before the Magistrates at the instance of the Weavers against Colin Keith, giving warrant for arrest of the said Colin's effects ; and Execution of warrant; dated 1st March, 1745.

38.—Declaration by Colin Keith " in corroboration of a Decreet " obtained against him, empowering the Weavers to uplift effects belonging to him in the hands of Daniel Clark, dated 24th April, 1745.

39.—Warrant by Agnes Hill for payment to the Weavers of a bill due by Colin Keith, dated 24th May, 1745.

40.—Inventory of Effects found in the house of Agnes Stewart, in Calton, sequestrated by warrant at the instance of the Weavers for security of a year's rent, dated 22nd August, 1751.

41.—Precept by the Weavers for the warning of Peter Baird and his wife from the house in Calton, heritably possessed by the Weavers from the late Alex. Muirhead, maltman, dated 20th March, 1752.

42.—Articles and Conditions of Sale of tenement of land, houses, etc., on the west side of the High Street of Calton, belonging to the Weavers of Glasgow, dated 1st May, 1759 (sold to James Freebairn, Calton).

43.—Double of Accounts concerning the debts due to the Weavers by the estate of the late Alex. Muirhead, 1759 and 1762.

APPENDIX.

Eddleston Manse.

44.—Titles of Eddleston Manse, dated 10th April, 1568 (see p. 119).
45.—Disposition by Mr. John Hay, late parson of Renfrew, to Thomas Crawford, younger, merchant burgess, of that tenement of land on the north side of Rottenrow, belonging of old to the Prebendar of the Prebendary of Eddleston, dated 21st August, 1660.
46.—Precept of Clare Constat granted by the College of Glasgow to Mr. John Hay, in foregoing tenement, dated 28th August, 1660 ; with Memorandum, endorsed, bearing that Mr. John Hay was infeft by Ninian Hill, bailie.
47.—Discharge by Mr. James Findlay, parson of Eddleston, to Thomas Crawfurd of Crawfurdsburne, for complete payment of feu-duties payable to the parson of Eddleston, dated 6th June, 1678.
48.—Disposition by Thomas Crawfurd in favour of Robert Brock, goldsmith in Glasgow, of that tenement of land belonging of old to the Prebendar of the Prebendary of Eddleston, dated 28th September, 1692.
49.—Declaration by George Ross, of Galston, of delivery of Disposition to the Weavers, of foregoing tenement, dated 17th June, 1706.
50.—Instrument of Sasine in favour of the Weavers in that tenement on the north side of Rottenrow, formerly called the Prebendal Manse of Eddleston, dated 20th June, 1706.
51.—Discharge by Wm. M'Rae, baxter in Glasgow, to George Ross, of Galston, in full satisfaction of the Bond granted by the said George on 9th May, 1700 ; dated 12th June, 1706.
52.—Articles and Conditions of Sale of tenement of old belonging to the Prebendar of the Prebendary of Eddleston, and now to the Weavers, dated 27th March, 1766.

Weaver Street.

53.—Tradesmen's Estimates for workmanship in connection with the buildings to be erected for the Craft in Weaver Street, April, 1795.
54.—Extract Decreet of Lining granted to the Weavers for a new tenement of land to be built at the corner of Weaver Street and Rottenrow Street, dated 2nd July, 1795.

Old Wynd.

55.—Articles and Conditions of the Roup of that barn and yard, and tenement on the south side of it, all situated on the west side of the Old Wynd, and belonging heritably to the Weavers of Glasgow ; with Minute of Sale of same at 1190 merks Scots ; dated 20th September, 1720.
56.—Receipt by Robert Rankin, carter in Glasgow, to the Weavers, for the writs of the tenement in Old Wynd.

APPENDIX.

Drygate.

57.—Testament of Barbara Lennox, wife of David Fleming, constituting the said David sole executor, dated 4th September, 1596.
58.—Discharge by John Fleming, on behalf of his brothers Patrick and Thomas, to Malcolm Fleming, of Woodilee for 500 merks Scots in satisfaction of their heritable right in the lands of Robrestoun, dated 22nd December, 1607.
59.—Extract Registered Obligation by John Drew in favour of John Fleming for 100 merks Scots, dated 8th June, 1612.
60.—Disposition by John Drew, maltman burgess of Glasgow, to Thomas Pettigrew and James Lightbody, of a tenement of land, etc., on the north side of the Drygate of Glasgow, dated 21st January, 1614.
61.—Instrument of Sasine in favour of John Fleming and his wife in a tenement on the north side of Drygate, dated 19th July, 1616.
62.—Letters of Inhibition at the instance of Malcolm Fleming, of Woodilee, and Lilias Fleming, his daughter, against John Fleming, dated 23rd June, 1620.
63.—Execution of charge in virtue of foregoing Letters of Inhibition, dated 17th January, 1621.
64.—Disposition by John Fleming and Elizabeth Shaw, his wife, to John Shaw, of Bargarran, of that tenement of land, etc., situated in the Drygate on the north side of the High Street, dated 5th March, 1622.

Gorbals.

65.—Charter by the Magistrates and Town Council of Glasgow in favour of the Weavers for their $\frac{1}{6}$ part of the lands of Gorbals, dated 15th July, 1650.
66.—Instrument of Sasine in favour of the Weavers in their share of the lands of Gorbals, dated 17th July, 1650.
67.—Letter from James Hill, acting for Hutchesons' Hospital, requesting the loan of "the Writings of the Weavers to their $\frac{1}{6}$ parts of the Lands of Gorbals," he being engaged in preparing "a State of the Method"; dated 8th February, 1790.

General.

68.—Extract Sasine on the resignation of the Weavers in favour of Andrew Young, weaver in Glasgow, in a piece of ground in Rottenrow, dated 13th February, 1752; and extracted 21st August, 1771.
69.—Disposition by Andrew Young to Robert Craig, farmer, High Possil, of a piece of ground in Rottenrow, dated 11th May, 1774.

APPENDIX.

70.—Sasine on the resignation of Andrew Young in favour of Robert Craig, dated 6th March, 1786.

71.—Sasine on the resignation of Robert Craig in favour of the Weavers, in a piece of ground in Rottenrow, with houses thereon, bounded on the west by the tenement belonging to the Weavers, and on the north by the ground now converted into Weaver Street, dated 8th March, 1793.

72.—Agreement and Contribution by the proprietors in Weaver Street for taking in Robert Craig's property, " in order that the street shall be straightened," dated 3rd September, 1792.

73.—Letter from Mr. John Herbertson giving a guinea towards the contribution, dated at Grangemouth, 5th September, 1792.

74.—Measurements of the Weavers' lands on the north side of Rottenrow, dated 27th January, 1792—29 steadings in all.

75.—Contracts (" in implement of the Articles of Roup of the steadings ") of Ground Annual between the Weavers of Glasgow and the purchasers of the steadings, dated 1792-1800.

76.—Feu Contracts between the Weavers and the purchasers of certain steadings, dated 1792.

77.—Minute of Weavers anent a road to be made through two of the steadings, dated 1st March, 1793.

78.—Measurement of ground, dated 29th November, 1793.

79.—Plan of part of Weaver Street, 20th June, 1794.

80.—Receipt for £5 stg. in name of damages due to Andrew Adie, in connection with the alteration of Canal Road, dated 23rd April, 1793.

Tacks of Lands, Dwelling-houses, etc.

81.—Tack by John Gairner, merchant, to John M'Lom, gardener, of a large yard lying on the north side of the Rottenrow, dated 15th December, 1706.

82.—Tack by the Weavers to Janet Anderson, relict of Patrick Tennent, gardener, of a large yard, and a " little yard at the head of it," newly taken in by the Weavers, dated 20th December, 1717.

83.—Bundle of Tacks (1731-1792) by the Weavers of their large yard and small yard in Rottenrow to Hugh Tennent, late visitor of the gardeners; James M'Lom, gardener; Archibald M'Cousland, gardener; Thomas Barton, gardener; John Jamieson, gardener; James Stewart, late deacon of the Weavers; James Stewart, and Walter, his son; and John Allan, gardener.

84.—Discharge of Tack by the widow of John Allan, gardener, owing to the sale of the grounds by the Weavers, a payment of £6 10s. 6d. being made to her in name of damages for manure laid on the ground, dated 20th March, 1792.

85.—Discharge by John Dougal, gardener, to the Weavers for a payment of £9 12s., made to him in name of damages, dated 14th February, 1792.

86.—Tack by the Weavers to James M'Indoe, gardener, of that dwelling-house and yard at the back thereof, commonly called Bowastie, on the north side of Rottenrow, dated 29th November, 1682.

87.—Tack by the Weavers to Robert Dougald, gardener, of dwelling-house and yard on the north side of Rottenrow, dated 19th October, 1703.

88.—Bundle of Tacks by the Weavers of that tenement of land and pertinents on the north side of Rottenrow, " commonly called Galston's Lodging," to Charles Dunlop, weaver; John Girvan, weaver; George Umphray, weaver; Charles Lyle, weaver; and Margaret Nichol, relict of John Dougal, gardener; and several Decreets against tenants for payment of rent (1719-1748).

89.—Bundle of Tacks (1728-1764) by the Weavers of that tenement on the east side of the High Street of Glasgow, below the Wyndhead, to Wm. Taylor, merchant; Thomas Stewart, gardener; and Wm. Findlay, weaver.

90.—Bundle of Tacks (1742-1743) by the Weavers of that tenement on the west side of the New Wynd of Glasgow, to John Goudie, late deacon of Weavers; Duncan M'Farlan, weaver; George Goudie, weaver; Gavin Marshall, weaver; and James Watson, weaver.

91.—Tack by the Weavers to Archibald M'Auley, gardener, of the housing, yard and pertinents, on the south side of the street below the Wyndhead, only to be used as garden grounds, dated 17th September, 1754.

92.—Precept on Decreet at the instance of the Weavers against John Baird, weaver, for a year's rent of a dwelling-house in the tenement in the Wynd, called "Lindsay's Easter Wynd," dated 27th October, 1752.

XV.—MORTCLOTHS.

1.—Contract of Co-partnery between the Incorporations of Tailors, Wrights, and Weavers, under which their Mortcloths are united into a common stock, dated 8th February, 1774 (see p. 125).

2.—" Compt of the several things contained in the Mortcloths box " (*circa*, 1670).

APPENDIX. 189

XVI.—PUBLIC AFFAIRS.

1.—Receipts granted by the Treasurer of the City of Glasgow to the Weavers for payment of £200, being the Craft's contribution towards raising the Regiment of Royal Glasgow Volunteers, dated February and April, 1770.

2.—Receipt for payment of account for advertising the Resolutions of the Incorporation of Weavers against the Police Bill, dated 9th May, 1792.

3.—Receipt for payment of £105, being Weavers' Subscription to the Glasgow Infirmary, dated 20th September, 1792.

XVII.—MISCELLANEOUS.

1.—Feu Charter by Thomas Robson, burgess of Rutherglen, and James Robson to John Hamilton, in Newton, of "Melvinis orchard," situated between Rutherglen and Ferme, dated 22nd October, 1589.

2.—Copy Charter of Erection in favour of the Faculty of Physicians and Surgeons of the City of Glasgow, dated 29th November, 1599.

3.—Discharge by Colonel Walter Whitefurd, son of the deceased Lord Bishop of Brechin, to James Nisbit, portioner of Auchinairn, of all duties due by him under the Decreet obtained before the Lords of Council at the instance of Walter Whiteford against the "heritors and possessors of lands within the subdeanrie of Glasgow," dated 16th March, 1670.

4.—Assignation by Christian Hastie, relict of Wm. Watson, weaver, to her youngest daughter, Barbara, of the Bond granted on 18th August, 1709, in her favour by Robert Dobbie; dated 5th September, 1717.

5.—Extract Decreet before Matthew Gilmour, bailie, at the instance of Christian Hastie against Robert Dobbie, dated 11th December, 1718.

6.—Assignation by Barbara Watson to James Wilson, weaver, of a Bond for 100 merks Scots assigned to her by her mother, dated 6th February, 1719.

7.—Extract Registered Bond granted by John M'Kie, gardener, and his wife in favour of Wm. Morrison, younger, gardener, and his wife, for 1300 merks Scots borrowed money, dated 8th October, 1605.

8.—Disposition in Security of Bond, by John M'Kie, gardener, to Wm. Morrison, younger, and his wife, of his lands lying within the burgh of Glasgow, dated 18th September, 1706.

APPENDIX.

9.—Bond of Provision by Francis Reid, weaver in Glasgow, to the Weaver Craft, making provision for the sum of £100 being paid to the Weavers at his death, upon condition that they oblige themselves to pay £5 yearly to a poor weaver burgess to be nominated by Janet Reid, his wife, and failing her by his nearest male relative, dated 18th February, 1774.

10.—Letter of Presentation of James Scott to the benefit of Francis Reid's Mortification, dated 7th April, 1807.

11.—Letters of Presentations made to the benefit of John M'Indoe's Mortification, 1770-8.

12.—Memorial for the Committee appointed by the Manufacturers and Operative Weavers in and about Glasgow in connection with the state of the trade, dated 13th March, 1801.

13.—Complainer's Reply and Defender's Duply in the dispute between Andrew Galloway (in Auchinairn) and James Stevenson, complainers, and Wm. Lyle, defender (see IX., 24).

14.—Three Embossed Prints wrapped up in paper, which bears the following endorsement in an 18th century hand: "Inclosed are three valuable pictures of our Saviour Jesus Christ and the Virgin Mary, etc., which are sealled up by order of the Deacon and masters of the Weavers in Glasgow, and all persons are discharged to open or breack up the same under their highest perrill, 1563."

APPENDIX VII.

ROLL OF MEMBERS

OF

THE INCORPORATION OF WEAVERS.

Revised Lammas, 1863, and brought down to June, 1908.

NOTE.—The addresses given in this list are in nearly all cases those of members as at the date of their joining the Incorporation. These original addresses have been retained for the purposes of identification. More recent addresses will in many cases be found in the alphabetical list appearing on page 154 *et seq.* For the sake of brevity the word " Glasgow " has been omitted after the streets, etc., in Glasgow, and for the last twenty years the occupations of members have also been omitted.

Year of Membership.	Names of Members.
95–96	James Paton.
98–99	David Stevenson.
1901–02	William Lee.
1903–04	James Brodie.
1907–08	John Gardner.
	Samuel Easton, 82 Mitchell Street.
	William Hunter, jun.
	Thomas Alston, jun., 52 Weaver Street.
	Robert Buchanan.
	John Scouller.
1908–09	John Mitchell.
	James Fleming.
	John Blackie, 36 North Frederick Street.
1909–10	David Blackburn, 5 Lynedoch Crescent.
	Donald M'Gregor.
	Robert Brown.
	David Davidson, Berwick.
	Hugh Tennent, sen., of Wellpark.

Year of Membership.	Names of Members.
1809–10	Thomas Kirkpatrick.
	John Boyd.
1810–11	William Corbett, 2 Mansfield Place.
	William Morrison.
	Robert White, jun., 256 West George St.
	James Henderson.
	Thomas Goodwin, Canada.
1811–12	John Cooper, 9 Mansfield Place.
	David M'Kinlay, of Oswald Bank.
1812–13	Robert Kirkwood, 40 Miller Street.
	David M'Gown.
	John Gray, Helensburgh.
	Duncan M'Nee, Partick.
	George Miller.
	James Muir.
1813–14	William Buchanan, Perth.
	William Gray.
	Thomas Thomson.
	James Graham.

APPENDIX.

1813-14 John Barbour, Manchester.
Henry Corbett.
Jas. Brown, 1 St. James Street, P. Road.
Thomas Nicolson.
Andrew Grant, 32 Parson Street.
James Provan.
John Tollan.
William Armour.
Donald Campbell, Stirling.
William Carlyle.
Duncan Buchanan.
George Ross Wilsone, Endrick Bank.

1814-15 John Heriot, Greenock.
Robert Forrester.
Hugh Brown, jun., 104 Virginia Place.
Robert Freeland, jun., of Gryfe Castle.
Andrew Buchanan.
John Brown.
James Paterson, 17 Virginia Street.
Thomas Taylor.
William Brown.
Archibald Kelso.
Samuel Harper, 99 Waterloo Street.

1815-16 Alexander Stevenson, 93 So. Portland St.
Hugh Stevenson.
Andrew Waters, Edinburgh.
John Fairie.
Robert M'Lauren.
James Mutrie.
Duncan Cameron, Helensburgh.
George Burns, 9 Buchanan Street.
Thomas Davidson, 46 John Street.
John Robertson, son of Matthew.
Duncan M'Nab, son of Robert.

1816-17 David M'Gown.
Robt. Wilson, 96 Regent Terrace.
James Campbell,
Thomas Muir, Madeira.
George Watson, Hogganfield.
Robert M'Indoe, 9 Exchange Square.
John Allan, Partick.
Robert Walker, of Lethamhill.
John Graham, 64 Buccleuch Street.
Richard John Mayne.
Alexander Glasgow, Ireland.
Thomas Jardine.
John Jamieson, 58 Dundas Street.
Matthew Alexander, 2 Burnbank Gardens.
James Towers.

1817-18 William M'Lean, of Plantation.
William Robertson.
John Lenney.
Robert M'Limont.
William Marshall, 8 Scotia Street.
Joseph Shankley.
Thomas Waddell, Ayr.
Archibald Fraser.
William Anderson.
Daniel Wright, 13 Glebe Street.
James Miller, jun.
Jonathan Thomlinson.
David Smith, St. Rollox.
John M'Lellan, Paisley.

1818-19 John Bartholomew, jun., 1 Dundas S
William Austin, 24 St. Vincent Place.
Robert Goodwin, Rock Villa, Melbou
Hugh Ritchie.
Robert Urquhart, of Moss, Govan.
David Miller, jun.
Alexander Buchan, Cambuslang.
Peter Dallas, 17 Cochrane Street.
Rev. Matthew Barclay, Old Kilpatric
John Fleming, 104 Virginia Street.
Andrew Buist, Ireland.

1819-20 John Gibson.
John Murray.
John Smith, 3 Burnbank Place.
Robert Hamilton.
Robert M'Haffie, of Eastwood.
James M'Haffie, 37 Garnethill Street.
Walter W. Whiteman, Dunoon.
James Fleming, Dunoon.
John M'Kinlay.

1820-21 George Lyon Walker, 117 Candleriggs
William Patrick, Cathedral Lodge.
John Cree, 22 St. George's Road.
John Cowan, Union Bank.
John Baird, America.
Thomas Dickson.
James Gray, 16 Hamilton Park Terra
Alexander Cowan, 47 Scott Street.
Robert Stewart, 1 West Regent Stree

1821-22 William Mutrie, 28 St. Enoch Squar
of David.
Robert Mutrie, son of David.
Robert Black, 9 Royal Exchange Squ
son of James.

APPENDIX.

Year of Membership.	Names of Members.
-22	John Niven, son of David. Sir James Campbell, of Stracathro. William Campbell, of Tilliechewan. George Smith, 208 Argyle Street. Thomas Speir, of Blackstone, son of Robert. James Anderson. Robert Ferguson, son of James. James Somerville. David Anderson, 80 Queen Street, son of John. Thomas H. Herbertson, Port Dundas, son of John. Herbert Buchanan, 241 West George St. William Bankier, 66 George Square, son-in-law of William Dennistoun. John Adam, son-in-law of a Member. David Campbell. Robert Finlayson, jun., London, son of Robert.
-23	John M'Lymont. John Meikle, America. John Moffat. James Hamilton, Ascog Bank, son of Patrick. John Hamilton, Canada, son of Patrick. Alexander Reid. John Smith, 155 Queen Street.
-24	William Meikle, 28 Eglinton Street. John Russell. Gilbert Weir, 220 West Regent Street. Robert Gilmour, 184 Buchanan Street. Andrew Hamilton, Hillhead. Andrew Harvey. John Donaldson, 68 Argyle Street. Peter Donaldson, London. Robert Cairnduff, 29 Houston Street. John Gardner. David Wright, son of a Member. Andrew Galbraith, 4 Bothwell Street. John Kerr, jun., 12 Queen's Crescent. Andrew Smith, jun., 3 Burnbank Place.
-25	James Stevenson. Gavin Walker, 5 George Square. John Morris. Alexander Guthrie, 103 Hill Street. Walter Lees, 43 Renfield Street. James Morris, America. Sir James Anderson, 3 Blythswood Square. John M'Farlane, M.D., Helensburgh.
1824-25	Hugh Smith, 94 Miller Street. Daniel M'Kay, 1 Dixon Street. James Spreull, 182 Trongate. Samuel Spreull, Toronto. Andrew Wilson, 20 South Frederick St. John MacFarlane, E. John White. James Hart, 25 Cochrane Street. Patrick Stevenson, Australia. James Cochran Miller, John Liddell, 50 St. Ninian Street. Alexander Buchanan, America. Johnstone Thomson, America.
1825-26	Robert Craig. Walter Graham M'Adam, Easterhouse. Robert Buchanan, 19 Cochrane Street. Henry Gray, London. Walter Buchanan, M.P., of Shandon. John Alexander, London. George Graham. Alexander Couper, 193 Bath Street. Daniel Riddell, Bothwell. Alexander M'Lean, 98 Fyfe Place. Alexander Field, Lanark. John Smith, Helensburgh. Peter Murdoch.
1826-27	James Watson, 343 High Street. William Gemmell, America. Robert Bell. Alexander Abercromby, 1 Prince's Court.
1827-28	Robert Ferguson. William Turnbull. John Clark, 10 Walworth Terrace. Peter M'Dowall. Hugh Barclay, LL.D., Sheriff of Perth. William C. Alston, Australia. John Alston, Helensburgh. James Frew, Australia. John Miller. John Calder, 69 Ingram Street. Frederick Hope Pattison, Duntocher. William Blackwood, 34 Kent Street. Thomas White, 28 St. Vincent Place. William Lyall, 170 Kent Road. James Scott, 66 Hutcheson Street. Alexander Cameron, Sydney. Robert Laing. William Ewing, Saltcoats. Henry Knox, jun., London.

APPENDIX.

Year of Membership.	Names of Members.
1827-28	Henry Pollock.
	Joseph Watson.
	James Papillon Jamieson, Gourock.
	Edward Broughton.
1828-29	George Grant, Mile-end.
	Archibald Mitchell.
	Duncan M'Larty.
	John Steven, 59 Maxwell Street.
	James Stiven, 82 West Nile Street.
	James Corsan, America.
	John Buchanan, 108 Hutcheson Street.
	John Jack, Carluke.
	William Muir.
	David Wilson, 145 Eglinton Street.
	George Campbell.
	Andrew Campbell.
	James Douglas, Prince's Square.
	Andrew Campbell, 80 Drygate Street.
	John M'Allister, jun., 159 West George St.
	John Houston, 105 Miller Street.
	James M'Intosh.
	Archibald M'Lymont.
	James Broom, Sanquhar.
1829-30	William Thomson.
	John Steel, 1 North Claremont Street.
	Peter Morrison.
	Robert Scott.
	Charles M'Kenzie, 21 Bath Street.
	John M'Lellan.
	David Boyd.
	James Martin.
	William Craig, Rothesay.
1830-31	William Paterson.
	James William Alston, 142 W. George St.
	David Gowdie, jun., Arran.
	David Woodrow Martin, 180 W. Regent St.
	Thomas Wilson, 145 Ingram Street.
	Gavin Rae, jun., 35 Montrose Street.
	John M'Haffie, London.
	Robert Bartholomew, 1 Dundas Street.
	William Martin, 34 Hutcheson Street.
	William Mitchell,
	Dugald Bannatyne.
	Robert Penney.
	John Murdoch, 38 Queen Street.
	Allan Burnside, Crossmyloof.
	James M'Allister.
	William Moir, Manchester.
	William Ritchie, 184 Crown Street.

Year of Membership.	Names of Members.
1830-31	James Fleming.
	John Blackie, jun., 36 North Freder
1831-32	Arthur Scouller, Australia.
	Robert Cogan, 32 West George Stree
	Andrew Paterson, 201 Gt. Eastern R
	David Stow, Port Eglinton.
	John Forsyth, 39 Drygate.
	William King, 78 Queen Street.
	Hugh Morton.
	John Anderson, 80 Queen Street.
	John Muir, 133 Drygate.
	William Bisset, 15 Scotia Street.
	William M'Lean, jun., 15 Cochrane S
	Fergus Ferguson, 11 Walmer Crescen
	Matthew Perston Bell, Glasgow Pott
	William Duguid Hill, Neilston.
	John James Muir, 1 So. Hanover St.
	James Shaw, 12 Royal Exchange Sq
1832-33	Alexander Robertson, 38 Queen Stre
	William Robertson, 38 Queen Street.
	Robert M'Michael, Australia.
	John Bell Lowry.
	Alexander Lowrie, Australia.
	Alexander Purdie, America.
	Walter Alexander, 2 Burnbank Gard
	William Walker.
	Lorraine Wilson, Port Eglinton.
	Thomas Kennedy, 1 Woodlands Roa
	John Hood, 20 Union Street.
	John Gibson, 134 Queen Street.
	James Graham, jun., 184 George Stre
	Robert Smith, 208 Argyle Street.
	George Smith, jun., 208 Argyle Stree
	Robert Walker.
	Humphrey E. Crum Ewing, M.P., of S
	Leven.
	Alexander Ferguson, 27 Balmano Str
	John Finlay, 12 Renfield Street.
	James Somerville.
	William Hinshaw, 17 John Street.
	Robert Jeffrey, 110 Brunswick Street
	John Auchinvole, 4 Montrose Street.
	James Colquhoun.
	James Scott Kelly.
	John Brebner.
	James Richmond, 2 Park Quadrant.
1833-34	John Howatt.
	Alexander Anderson, 16 Prince's Squ
	Thomas Steel, Stirling.

APPENDIX.

Year of Membership	Names of Members
3-34	John Armour, America.
	William Burnside.
	George Morrison, 62 Queen Street.
	Alexander Giffen, 161 Hope Street.
	Alexander Malcolm, 13 Dundas Street.
4-35	Samuel R. Brown, Paris.
	Thomas Brown, 80 Queen Street.
	Archibald Glen, 124 Hope Street.
	Peter Wilson.
	Matthew Hamilton, Dunoon.
	James Swan, 159 W. George Street.
	William Service, of Culcreuch.
	Alexander Mather, Edinburgh.
	Thomas Jackson.
	William Hutton, 9 Belgrove Street.
	John Graham, 196 North Street.
	James Dunlop.
	Allan M'Dougall, 127 Brunswick Street.
	Walter Carswell.
	William Fleming.
	James M'Alpine, Town's Hospital.
	William Aitken, 20 St. George's Road.
5-36	John Rae, 130 Broomielaw.
	Andrew Morrison, Manchester.
	John Orr, 137 New City Road.
	Peter Drew, 66 Wilson Street.
6-37	William Alston, 95 West George Street.
	Duncan Hunter, jun., 105 Douglas Street.
	James Smith.
	Charles M'Naught.
	Alexander Burns.
	William Brown.
	James Lang, 100 Crown Street.
7-38	George Grant, ter., Mile-end.
	Malcolm M'Lellan, 3 Claremont Gardens.
	Allan Ralston.
	Alexander Bartholomew, 111 Ingram St.
	William Chisholm, jun.
	John Foulds, Johnstone.
	John Walker, jun., London.
	Francis Moore, 13 Little Hamilton Street.
	William Allan.
	Robert Allan.
	William M'Allister, Paisley.
	George Jasper Lyon, Arran.
	Thomas Ross, jun., 87 South Portland St.
8-39	Andrew Thomson, 52 West Nile Street.

Year of Membership	Names of Members
1838-39	William Govan, 15 Renfield Street.
	Robert Shaw.
	John Broadley, 145 Queen Street.
	Robert Kerr, jun., Liverpool.
	George Lyle, 19 Montrose Street.
	Matthew Letham, London.
	Giles Dickson, Australia.
	Alexander M'Kean, 35 Renfrew Street.
	John Russell.
	James Lawrie.
	William Richard Paterson, of Balornoch.
	Alexander Turner, 124 Hope Street.
	Andrew Wilson, 167 Stirling Road.
1839-40	William M'Leod, Edinburgh.
	James Russell.
	Robert Wylie, 130 Paisley Road.
	James Dalrymple.
	William Morrison, 135 Buchanan Street.
	Daniel Walker, Australia.
	John Walker, Australia.
	David M'Donald, America.
	William Christie, 153 Queen Street.
	William Kirkland, Manchester.
	James Kirkland.
1840-41	Alexander Speirs, Houston Street.
	James Church, Liverpool.
	Alexander Beith.
	John Brown, Paisley.
	James Tait, Moffat.
	James Perston, 10 Greyfriar Wynd.
	Edward Alexander, 43 West Campbell St.
	Patrick Ewing, Belfast.
	John Wyse.
	Robert Watt, jun.
	James Clark, Manchester.
	Duncan Turner, 229 Argyle Street.
	George Martin, 124 Hope Street.
1841-42	Nathaniel Templeton, 20 Monteith Row.
	James Hutchison, or M'Hutcheson, Australia.
	William M'Dougall, Weaver Street.
	James Russell, 38 Paterson Street.
	John Morrison, Govan.
	James Cowan, 72 Virginia Street.
	Charles Campbell, Campsie.
1842-43	Joseph Ewing, 57 Miller Street.
	John Graham, Dunoon.
	Henry Baincaves, 178 Castle Street.

APPENDIX.

Year of Membership.	Names of Members.
1842–43	Anthony Wigham Nicholson, Manchester. Robert Muir Steven, 15 Cochrane Street. William Graham. James Laird Morrison, 62 Queen Street.
1843–44	George Thomson, 69 Ingram Street. James Paul, 110 Buchanan Street. William Somerville, 116 St. Vincent Street. James Wotherspoon, Perth. William Peebles.
1844–45	Alexander Broadfoot. James Howie Young, 64 Gordon Street. Lewis Park. Charles Park. John Knox, 73 Brunswick Street. Thomas Finlayson, 41 Brunswick Street. William Fraser, 45 Buccleuch Street. John Clapperton, 26 Exchange Square. David Scott, 82 West Nile Street.
1845–46	John Coulter, 52 Tylefield Street. David Brock. James Leck, Carmyle. John Stewart, 22 Ingram Street.
1847–48	John White, 161 Eglinton Street.
1848–49	William M. Turner, 111 Ingram Street.
1849–50	Robert Muir, 116 St. Vincent Street. James Smart, Police Buildings. William Kidston, 50 West Regent Street. John Kidston, 50 West Regent Street. James B. Kidston, 50 West Regent Street. Michael Kidston, Melbourne. John M'Farlane, LL.D., London.
1850–51	John M'Lellan, 341 St. Vincent Street. Donald M'Lellan, 341 St. Vincent Street. William Speirs, 2 St. Andrew's Square. David Yuille, 40 Miller Street. Robert Douie, 77 Renfield Street, son-in-law of R. Urquhart. James Ritchie M'Nair, son of Ritchie, 173 Buchanan Street. John Russell, Dunoon.
1851–52	James Fraser, America. Andrew Marshall, 48 London Street. Arthur Bryson.

Year of Membership.	Names of Members.
1853–54	Henry Bruce, 123 St. Vincent Street
1854–55	David Wright, 44 Trongate.
1855–56	Ebenezer Bryson, 101 Green Street. John Wilson, 45 Drygate. Andrew Harvey, 15 Morrison Street. William Andrew, 45 Drygate.
1856–57	James Millen, 116 George Street. George Blackwood, 56 Old Vennel. John Murray, 167 Stirling Road. James Downie, 91 Hutchison Street. John Eason, 390 Duke Street. Robert Dalglish, M.P., of Kilmardin
1857–58	David Hutcheson, 22 Struthers Stre Joseph Service, 48 Gordon Street. John Morrison, 29 Spoutmouth. William Johnston, 52 Howard Stree Walter M'Lintock, City Hall. John Earston, 69 St. Vincent Street
1858–59	James M'Lintock, 5 St. John's Place William M'Kinlay, 54 Union Street.
1859–60	Donald Simpson M'Nair, 16 Turner's James Gourlay, Bank of Scotland. Forrest Frew, 6 Hampton Court Te Alexander M'Kay, 113 Virginia Plac John Miller, 18 High Street.
1860–61	Andrew M'Gregor, Carmichael Castle William Stobo, 60 Rottenrow. William Wright, Phœnix Foundry. William Henry Alston, Australia. Andrew Steven, 151 Gallowgate. George M'Lellan, 341 St. Vincent St James Bain, 141 Argyle Street. William Renney Findlay, 62 Queen William Cowan, 64 St. Vincent Stree William MacLean, 41 West George S Peter Graham, 1 West Milton Street Alexander Finlay, 22 Adam's Court James Wallace Anderson, 62 Queen William Govan, jun., 15 Renfield St James Main, Airdrie. John Murchie, Merchant, Glasgow. Andrew Cumming, 179 Argyle Street Alexander Woodrow, 75 Glassford S John Mair, 106 Argyle Street.

APPENDIX.

Year of Membership.	Names of Members.
0-61	Hugh Wilson, 75 Glassford Street. Joseph M'Culloch, 15 Castle Street.
1-62	Peter Burn, 9 Exchange Place. James Stirling, 116 Rottenrow. James Harvey, Bridgeton. George Scott, Alnwick. Peter Walker, 59 St. Vincent Street. John M'Cubbin, Innellan. David M'Cubbin, 93 West Regent Street. John Fraser, 4 St. Andrew's Square. Thomas Millen, 3 Ronald Street. James Barr, Parkhead.
2-63	Ebenezer Henry, 51 Buchanan Street, son-in-law of Matt. Walker. Ebenezer Walker Henry, son of Ebenezer. Matthew Henry, son of Ebenezer. Robert Gourlay, Edinburgh, son of Jas. Gourlay. Henry Shaw M'Pherson, 80 Gordon Street, son-in-law of James Gourlay. Robert Gourlay, 12 Howard Street, son-in-law of James Gourlay. William M'Queen, 29 Dobbie's Loan, son of William. James Anderson, 4 St. Vincent Place. Thomas Whyte, 6 Union Street, Calton, son of Francis. Thomas Williamson, 179 West George St. William Scott, 33 Renfield Street. John Knox, jun., 73 Brunswick Street, son of John. William Millar, High Street, son of John. William Muir Ferguson, Mercantile Advertiser, son of Alexander.
3-64	David Auchinvole, son-in-law of John Turnbull. Matthew Fairley, 47 Queen Street. Thomas Mabon, son of David. Walter Muir, Collector of Police Rates, son of John. James Fleming, Wright, son of John. James Danskin, 24 Garscadden Street, son-in-law of And. Hardie. Thomas Forsyth, Storekeeper, Motherwell, son of John. Alexander Birrell, 4-5 George Square. John Danskin, 306 Argyle Street, son of James. George Gibson, Merchant, 163 Ingram St.
1864-65	Adam Moffat, son-in-law of David Ewing. David Bryce, Stationer, son of David. James Alexander, Merchant. Joseph Bayley, Merchant. John Robertson, son of John. Rev. John Dick Fleming, son of Rev. Wm Robert Fleming, Merchant, son of Rev. Wm Wm. M'Bride, Manufacturer. Alex. Miller, Merchant, son of Alexander *deceased*. Alex. Miller, jun., Merchant, son of Alex. George M'Leod, Manufacturer. Rev. Wm. Leggatt, Buchanan Institution Hugh Corbett Taylor, M.D., son-in-law o And. Marshall.
1865-66	John Thos. Herbertson, Merchant, Cana Office, son of Thos. Hopkirk Herbert son. James Paul, Skinner, son of William. Daniel Wright, Hammerman, younger so of Daniel. Robert Leckie, Warper, 7 Stanhope Stree eldest son of John Leckie. Joseph Watson, Merchant, 16 Sauchieha Street, son of William. James Barr, Merchant, 157 Rutherglei Loan, son of James. Wm. Bankier, Merchant, 15 Renfield St. son of Wm. JamesThomson, Flesher, 25 Monteith Row Archd. Hay, Power Loom Manufacturei Clyde Factory, Dalmarnock.
1866-67	William Arneil, Hairdresser, 96 Glassfoi Street. William MacLean, Accountant, West George Street. William Watson, Bootmaker, Glasgow. James Smith, Confectioner, Queen Stree John Stewart Mair, Lace Merchant, 10 Argyle Street. Wm. Brown Torrance, Agent, 55 Hutche son Street. Alex. M'Laren, Merchant, 8-12 Buchana Street. Alex. Begg, Manufacturer, 263 Argyle St. Matthew Forsyth, Grocer, 69 Taylor St. James Craig, Wine Merchant, 4 Carlto Place. James Craig, jun., Wine Merchant, 26 St. Vincent Street.

APPENDIX.

Year of Membership.	Names of Members.
1866–67	William Blackburn Craig, Drysalter and Oil Merchant, Glasgow.
	Michael Wright Fleming, Warehouseman, 97 Montrose Street.
	Thomas Struthers, Upholsterer, 96 Buchanan Street.
	William Sim, Granite Merchant, Glasgow.
1867-68	Allan Houston M'Lellan, Merchant, Glasgow.
	James Morton, M.D. and Surgeon, 109 Bath Street.
	Alex. Buchanan, Letterpress Printer, Glasgow.
	William Miller, Bishopbriggs.
	Walter Bannerman, Wright, Gordon Street.
	John Buchanan, Custom House Officer, Glasgow.
	Rev. Gilbert Johnston, Shettleston.
	Wm. Johnston, Sugar Refiner, Glasgow.
	John Johnston, Merchant, Glasgow.
	James Downie, Manufacturer, 12 Montrose Street.
	John Gartshore, Manufacturer, So. Hanover Street.
	James Couper, Yarn Merchant, Smith's Court.
	Daniel Brown, Confectioner, 60 Queen St.
	Alex. Pollock, Grocer, 87 Gallowgate.
1868–69	Wm. Taylor, Starcher, Stirling Road.
	Samuel Macfarlane, Merchant, West George Street.
	Wm. Reid, Surgeon, 2 Morris Place, Monteith Row.
	Henry Morrison, Iron Turner, Glasgow.
	Andrew Mitchell, Draper, Cowcaddens St.
	James Hutton, C.A., Glasgow.
	William Calder Salmon, Shuttlemaker, Duke Street.
1869-70	James Robson, Teacher of Music, 94 Montrose Street.
	James Forbes, Letter Carrier, 5 Shamrock Street.
	David Cherry, Maltman, 76½ Kirk Street, Calton.
	Robert Miller, Bookseller, 186 Trongate.
	William Cherry, Maltman.
	James Murdoch, Photographer, 1 Quarry Street, Hamilton.
	Thos. Maltman, Warehouseman, Glasgow.

Year of Membership.	Names of Members.
1869–70	Hugh Andrew, Warper, 6 Glebe Street.
	James Winning, Cashier, 3 Cathkin Terr. Mount Florida.
1870-71	Alexander Laird, Warehouseman, Glasg.
	John Gilchrist Stewart, Clerk in Glasgo
	Archibald Arnott, Clerk, 221 St. Vinc Street.
	James Laird, 12 Strathmore Street, Brid end, Perth.
	Robert Walker, Warehouseman, Glasgo
	Robert Downie, jun., Dyer in Glasgow.
	James Thom, Manufacturer, Park Vi Factory, Glasgow.
	Thomas Taylor Brown, Calenderer, 2 Cochrane Street.
	Robert M'Connell, Bleacher, 209 No Woodside Road.
	John Macfarlane, Baker, 486 Duke Stre
	Robert Fisher Alexander, Oil Mercha Glasgow.
	William Alexander, Writer, Glasgow.
	James Alexander, jun., Oil Merchant Glasgow.
	Ernest Smith, Manufacturing Chemist Glasgow.
	Robert Asheton Napier, Engineer and I Shipbuilder, Glasgow.
	William Galloway, Manufacturer, 49 V ginia Street.
	Adam Elliott, Yetholm, near Kelso.
	Samuel Wilson, Merchant, 61 Oswald St
	James Barr, Manufacturer, 54 Gord Street.
	Alex. Fullarton Barr, Manufacturer, Gordon Street.
	William Burn, Auctioneer and Valuat 9 Royal Exchange Place.
	James Downie, jun., Yarn Merchant, Ingram Street.
	John Shaw Thomson, Manufacturer, Ingram Street.
	Thos. Crawford, Manufacturer, 9 Freder Street.
	Robert Murdoch, Banker, City of Glasg Bank, Virginia Street.
	Thomas Robinson Johnstone, Mercha 19 West Nile Street.
	James Findlay, Manufacturer, 68 Gord Street.
	Thomas Lucas Paterson, Merchant, Ne hall House, Dowanhill Gardens.

APPENDIX.

Year of Membership.	Names of Members.
1-72	William Scott Paterson, Merchant, Glasgow, and residing at Dowanhill there.
	Robert Muir, Sewed Muslin Manufacturer, Ingram Street.
	David Hennedy, Commission Merchant, 14 Queen Street.
	Alexander Robb, Merchant, 203 Crown St.
	Robert Fyfe Easton, Calenderer, 82 Mitchell Street.
	William Duncan, Merchant, 124 St. Vincent Street.
	William Drysdale, Banker, Helensburgh.
	Alexander Wilson Clark, Umbrella Manufacturer, 95 St. Vincent Street.
	John Christie Reid, Chartered Accountant, 8 Princes Square.
	Thomas Millar Fergusson, Merchant, 89 Mitchell Street, residing at Aytoun House, Dowanhill.
	Andrew Paterson, Manufacturer, 4 St. John's Terrace, Hillhead.
	Rev. John Brown Johnston, D.D., Minister U.P. Church, Govan.
	John Hunter, Manufacturer, 5 Ardine Terrace, Crosshill.
	James Wallace, Bleacher and Finisher, Burnbank (East), Glasgow.
	George Black, Writer, Glasgow.
	Alexander Findlay, Pianoforte Maker, 110 West Nile Street.
	Stephen Mason, Manufacturer, Glasgow.
	William Houston, Merchant, 23 Royal Exchange Square.
	George Younger, Yarn Merchant, 1 North Court, Royal Exchange.
72-73	William Robb, Merchant, 8 Ingram Street.
	George Patrick, Warehouseman, 84 Great Hamilton Street.
	Robert Wilson Bryson, Commercial Clerk, 342 Duke Street.
	David Yuill, Gardener, Bluevale, Glasgow.
	Henry Bruce, jun., Insurance Agent, Renfield Street.
	James Campbell, 153 Renfield Street.
	Hugh Watson, 45 Drygate Street.
	Ebenezer Steel, Annfield Terrace, Partick.
	William Newlands, 6 Lynedoch Crescent.
	David Stobo, Engineer, Glasgow.
73-74	James Millen, Cashier, Glasgow.
	John Millen, Coalmaster, Glasgow.
1873-74	Alexander Woodrow, jun., Lithographer, Glasgow.
	Peter Burn Wilson, Merchant, Glasgow.
	James Yuill, Saddlers' Ironmonger, Glasgow.
	John Couper, Yarn Agent, Glasgow.
	James Couper, Yarn Agent, Glasgow.
	Thomas Keith, Potter, 80 St. James' Road.
	David Alexander Black, Accountant, 14 Princes Square.
	David Henderson Anderson, Manufacturer, Glasgow.
1874-75	John Wilson, jun., Engraver, Glasgow.
	Robert Thomson Dodd, Photographer, Glasgow.
	Walter Macfarlan, Ironfounder, Glasgow.
	James Fleming Millar, Cashier, Glasgow.
	David Paterson, Drysalter, Glasgow.
	James Wilson, West India Merchant, 30 John Street.
	William M. Mair, Warehouseman, 83 Sauchiehall Street.
	Robt. Alexander Mair, Accountant, 79 St. Vincent Street.
	Charles Stewart Mair, Grain Merchant, 83 Sauchiehall Street.
	Adam Kidd, Manufacturer, 56 Brunswick Street.
	James Thomson Stewart, Commission Merchant, 75 Bath Street.
	Andrew Lindsay, Pentographer, M'Neil St.
	Thorburn Alston, Gilder, 26 Taylor Street.
1875-76	John Murray, 3 Tennant St., Townhead.
	Robt. Brodie, Writer, 87 St. Vincent Street.
	James Young, Manufacturer, 64 Gordon Street.
	John Ebenezer Young, Manufacturer, 64 Gordon Street.
	Robert Bannerman, Merchant, 19 Newton Street.
	Walter Bannerman, jun., Merchant, 13 Jane Street.
	Humphrey Ewing Crum-Ewing, Merchant, 68 George Square.
	William Johnson Govan, Manufacturer, 15 Renfield Street.
	Albert Harvey, Muslin and Tapestry Manufacturer, 63 Ingram Street.
	John Birkmyre Wingate, Manufacturer, 5 Royal Exchange Square.

APPENDIX.

1875-76 Alex. Wilson Smart, Manufacturer, New Burnside Mills, 103 Brook Street, Mile-end.
James Alexander Campbell, LL.D., Merchant, Glasgow.
Thomas Clavering, Merchant, 21 St. Vincent Place.
Samuel James Harvey Easton, Warehouseman, 68 Queen Street.
Samuel Fyfe Easton, Merchant, Gordon St.
Alex. Grant, Cotton Spinner and Manufacturer, Broad Street, Mile-end.
Robert Walker, of Letham Hill, Manufacturer, Glasgow.
George Smith, Shipowner, 200 Argyle St.
Jas. Anderson, Manufacturer, Atlantic Mills, Glasgow.
Wm. Horatio Scott, Merchant, 19 Great Western Road.
Innes Wright Scott, Merchant, 12 Prince's Terrace.
Wm. Fleming, Warehouseman, at Messrs. Arthur & Co.'s, Queen Street.
Gilbert Taylor, Merchant, Messrs. Henry Monteith & Co.'s, So. Frederick Street.
James Thom, jun., Manufacturer, Parkview Factory, Upper Suspension Bridge, Glasgow.
Robt. Innes Steel, Warehouseman, 6 Regent Park Terrace.
Alex. Ferguson Steven, Merchant, Glasgow.
Robert Muir Steven, Lithographer, 30 Montrose Street.
Thos. Watson, Merchant, 9 Belhaven Terr.

1876-77 David Todd, 5 Doune Terrace.
William Smith, Confectioner, Helensburgh.
John Pollock, Student, 87 Gallowgate.
John Ewing, Clerk, 18 Albert Drive, Crosshill.
Peter Ferguson, Brushmaker, 33 Hope Street.
Wm. MacLean, jun., 98 West George St.
David MacLean, Accountant, 98 West George Street.
Ebenezer MacLean, 10 Somerset Place.
Peter Steven, 210 Renfrew Street.
Andrew M'Onie, Engineer, 1 Scotland St., Tradeston.
John Abercromby Bruce, 80 Buccleuch St.
Angus Mitchell, Manufacturer, 42 Miller St.
James Marshall, 8 Somerset Place.

1876-77 Jas. Henderson, Wright and Builder, Broomhall, Partick.
Andrew Steven, 7 Radnor Street.
Cauvin Spittal Alston, Deputy Governor Glasgow Prison.
John Millar, Calico and Muslin Printer, Royal Exchange Square.
Adam Turnbull, Chemist and Aerated Water Manufacturer, 76 Dundas Street, Kinston.
Charles Smith, Seedsman, 36 Howard St.
Alex. B. Stewart, Merchant, 5 Buchanan S.

1877-78 Wm. Rae, Wood Carver, 202 North Woodside Road.
John Forsyth, Gas Surveyor, 5 Northumberland Street, Govanhill.
David Sandeman, Woodlands, Lenzie.
James Grierson, 61A Robertson Street.
Wm. Harper Minnoch, jun., 6 Woodside Crescent.
William Murray Alston, Civil Engineer, Burnbank Gardens.
Andrew Jackson Kirkpatrick, 10 Woodside Place.
John Marshall Easton, 70 James Watt St.
James Alexander Duncan, 65 Hamilton Drive.
Robert Duncan, 65 Hamilton Drive.
Robert Murray, Grain Merchant, 58 Buccleuch Street.
John Thomson Murray, Gas Inspector, Armadale Street, Dennistoun.
Richard Sandeman, Blair Villa, Lenzie.
Boswell Sandeman, 11 John Street.
Francis Sandeman, 11 John Street.
William Campbell Seton, Calenderer, 2 High Street.
John Moffat, Produce Agent, Kinsimb South-west Coast of Africa.
John Auchinvole, 113 Ingram Street.
John Wallace, Bleacher and Finisher, Busbank, East.
Frederick James Easton, 81 Buchanan St.
Robert Andrew Knox, Park Quadrant.
James Campbell, of Tullichewan.
James Anderson Napier, 24 St. Vincent
John Gourlay, C.A., 24 George Square.
James Young, Greenhead Cottage, Uddingston.

1878-79 William Meikle Gemmell, 367 Duke Street

APPENDIX.

Year of Membership.	Names of Members.
1878-79	James Cunningham, 24 Springfield Place, Leeds.
	John Brown, Teacher of Music, 214 West Regent Street.
	Daniel Brown, jun., Restaurateur, 214 West Regent Street.
	David Robertson Brown, Restaurateur, 214 West Regent Street.
	Francis Hamilton Brown, Chemist, 214 West Regent Street.
	David Thomson Murray, Clerk, Caledonian Railway Co., 3 Tennant Street.
	Charles James MacLean, Writer, 188 West Regent Street.
	John Paterson Paton, Insurance Broker, Royal Exchange.
	James Newlands, 6 Lynedoch Crescent.
	Joseph Findlay Newlands, 6 Lynedoch Crescent.
	Alexander M'Leod, Grocer, 491 Sauchiehall Street.
	George Thomson, Flesher, Gt. Hamilton St.
	Robert Harvey Wright, Tinplate Worker, 156 Gallowgate.
	John Parker, Accountant, 58 West Regent Street.
	James Dunn, 20 Park Circus.
	Robert Ness, Schoolmaster, 77 Hill Street, Garnethill.
	Henry Sinclair, Manufacturer, 5 Gloucester Street.
	Arthur Burns, Confectioner, Kyle Street.
1879-80	James Connell, Janitor, Greenside Public School, Glasgow.
	George Lyle, 37 Abercorn Street.
	William Purdon, Engineer, 48 Harvie St., Bridgeton.
	Peter Salmon, Printer, 233 Duke Street.
	Thomas Hodge, Merchant Draper, Main Street, Anderston.
	Robert Hutcheson, Merchant, 54 Union St.
	Councillor John Filshill, Confectioner, Glasgow.
	John Scott Strang, Accountant, 48 Jane Street.
	John Paterson, Insurance and Property Agent, Shettleston.
	Thomas Newstead, 59 Main St., Shettleston.
	James Thomson, Huddersfield.
	David Crawford, jun., Dunterlie Villas, Barrhead.
1879-80	James Wilson, Letterpress Printer, 68 John Knox Street.
	Michael Wilson, Bookbinder, 21 Castle St.
	Alexander Pollock Cubie, Power Loom Tenter, 162 London Road.
	Thomas Jenkins, Purveyor, Woodlands, Crosshill.
	Robert Anderson, Manufacturer, 16 Princes Square.
	John Macfarlan, Factory Manager, 2 Jane Place, Darnley Street, Pollokshields.
1880-81	Alexander Andrew, Superintendent of Police, Glasgow.
	James Barclay, S.S.C., Edinburgh.
	Robert Buchanan Barclay, Board of Supervision, Edinburgh.
	John Collins, Merchant, Bowling, near Glasgow.
	Archibald M'Neill Allardyce, Plumber, 20 Clyde Terrace.
	Robert Gilchrist Paterson, Manufacturer, 4 St. John's Terrace, Hillhead.
	John Smith, Merchant, Glassford Street.
	Thomas Brown, Merchant, 51 Cochrane St.
	John Melville Leggatt, Warehouseman, 2 St. James Street, Greenhead.
	Robert Leggat, Lithographer, 38 Sauchiehall Street.
	John Miller, Joiner, 116 Rottenrow.
	Thomas Foggo Marr, Wholesale Stationer, 29 East Ingram Street.
	William Liddell, Resident Medical Officer, Govan Parochial Board, Merryflats.
	Lawrence Rutherford Inglis, Warehouseman, 19 Gardner Street.
	James Scott, Clerk, 26 Robertson Street.
	Thomas Murdoch, Wholesale Grocer, 87 Meadowpark Street, Dennistoun.
	Adam Gemmell, Stationer, 229 George St.
	John Ritchie, Warehouseman, 29 Ingram Street.
	Major Charles Atkinson Logan, The Royal Scots Regiment, 10 Belmont Crescent.
	Alexander Ferguson, Printer, 7 Hopetoun Place.
	John Henderson, Assistant Treasurer, School Board, 20 West Graham St.
	Robert Reid, C.A., 40 St. Vincent Place.
1881-82	William Smith, jun., Warehouseman, Torwood, Helensburgh.

APPENDIX

Year of Membership.	Names of Members.
1881-82	James Craig, Surgeon, Linden Cottage, Partick.
	Arthur Davidson, Auctioneer, 43 Argyle St.
	James Carrick, Letterpress Printer, 62 Argyle Street.
	Robert M'Connell, Bleacher, 20 Windsor Terrace.
	Thomas M'Connell, Wright, 20 Windsor Terrace.
	William M'Connell, 20 Windsor Terrace.
	John M'Connell, 20 Windsor Terrace.
	David Valentine Wyllie, Architect, 74 Hutchison Street.
	John M'Culloch, Engine Fitter, 374 Springburn Road.
	Angus Mitchell, jun., Power Loom Manufacturer, Burnbank Factory, Hamilton.
	John M'Pherson Mitchell, Power Loom Manufacturer, Burnbank Factory, Hamilton.
	William Clarke, 81 Meadowpark Street.
1882-83	William Finlayson, Wholesale Woollen Cloth Merchant, 15 Hutchison Street.
	James Muter, Draper, 20 High Street.
	Robert M'Dougall, Accountant, 57 West Nile Street.
	The Rev. Archd. Browning Drysdale Alexander, Langbank.
	Robert Douie Urquhart, Advocate, Edinburgh.
	William Gemmell, Cashier, 143 Main Street, Bridgeton.
	James Paterson, Manufacturer, St. Marnock Street, Mile-end.
	George Stewart, Manufacturer, 113 Ingram Street.
	John Hutcheson Kerr, Aberdona, Clackmannanshire.
	Charles Chalmers Bryce, Merchant, 141 West George Street.
	William Wilson, Clerk, 26 Taylor Street.
	Robert Wilson, West India Merchant, Bantaskin, Falkirk.
	James Wilson, jun., Bantaskin, Falkirk.
	Gilbert Taylor Wilson, Bantaskin, Falkirk.
	Alexander Taylor Brown, Draughtsman.
	John Hunter Brown, 51 Cochrane Street.
	Thomas Herbert Brown, 51 Cochrane St.
1883-84	William Sturgeon, 97 Kenmure Street, Pollokshields.

Year of Membership.	Names of Members.
1883-84	Robt. Paterson, Schoolmaster, John Street Public School.
	John Caldwell, Flesher, 212 Main Street, Bridgeton.
	Charles Edward Clark, Writer, West George Street.
	Hugh Graham, Commission Merchant, 19 New City Road.
	James Sloan, Merchant, 7 Royal Bank Place.
	Alexander Rankin Horn, Banker, Clydedale Bank Ltd., 96 Trongate.
	William Taylor, Bank Accountant, 14 Crownpoint Road.
	John Anderson, Drysalter, 136 Buchanan Street.
	Malcolm Macfarlane, M.A., Teacher, Grammar School, Inveraray.
	George Sloan, Shipowner, 140 Hope Street.
	James Cowan Paterson, Accountant, Glasgow.
	Robert Smith Paterson, 13 Holyrood Crescent.
1884-85	Adam White, Chemical Merchant, 138 West George Street.
	John Marshall, Warehouseman, 114 Hospital Street.
	James Gourlay Macpherson, Merchant, Queen Street.
	George Gibson, jun., Merchant, 77 Queen Street.
	Adam Knox, Engineer, 47 Crownpoint Rd., Mile-end.
	James Waddell, Bank Agent, 419 Gallowgate.
	James Alexander, Yarn Merchant, 78 Mill Street.
	James Legate, 1 West Garden St., Burnbank Gardens.
	James Frew, Portioner, 15 Royal Terrace, Crosshill.
	John Fulton, Merchant, 23 Herriet Street, Pollokshields.
	Alexander Smith Barr, Yarn Salesman, 13 Westmuir Street, Parkhead.
	Robert Wardrop Forrest, Doctor of Medicine, 319 Crown Street.
	Robert Baird Galbraith, Merchant, 35 Glassford Street.
	James Hamilton, Provision Merchant, 4 Argyle Street.

APPENDIX.

Year of Membership.	Names of Members.
1884-85	Alexander Smith Caldwell, Butcher, 101 Kingpark Place, Greenhead Street.
	George William Younger, Yarn Merchant, 166 Ingram Street.
	Robert Tannahill Younger, Advocate, Edinburgh.
	John Stevenson Stewart, Warehouseman, 21 Buchanan Street.
	Ninian Bannatyne Stewart, Warehouseman, 21 Buchanan Street.
	William Finlayson, jun., 67 Roslea Drive.
	William Yuill, 19 Meadowpark Street, Dennistoun.
	James Claude Gordon Laird, 28 Cochrane Street.
	Charles Allardyce, 63 Abbotsford Place.
	Archibald M'Neil Allardyce, 63 Abbotsford Place.
	William Alexander Campbell, Warehouseman, 137 Ingram Street.
	Matthew Pearce Campbell, Warehouseman, 137 Ingram Street.
	James Mann, Warehouseman, 21 Glassford Street.
	John Graham Couper, Warehouseman, 21 Glassford Street.
	Edmond Baird Paterson, Writer, 20 Lynedoch Street.
	John Thomson, Rector, Deaf and Dumb Institution, Langside.
	William Alexander Smith, Yarn Merchant, 6 South Hanover Street.
	David Walker, Draper, 65 Candleriggs.
	James Gardner Aitken, 42 Miller Street.
	David Cooke, 42 Miller Street.
	Alexander Allan, 42 Miller Street.
	John Scott Stout, Shoemaker, 38 Gallowgate.
	Andrew Graham Service, Iron Merchant, 27 St. Vincent Street.
	Robert Forrester Graham, Warehouseman, 123 Argyle Street.
	George Halliday, Warehouseman, 123 Argyle Street.
	Thomas Mills Wilson, Merchant, 42 Glassford Street.
	Thomas Macfarlane, Warehouseman, 39 Miller Street.
	William John Tillie, Warehouseman, 39 Miller Street.
	Andrew Arthur, Warehouseman, 78 Queen Street.
1884-85	James Arthur, Warehouseman, 78 Queen Street.
	Thomas Glen Arthur, Warehouseman, 78 Queen Street.
	Matthew Arthur, Warehouseman, 78 Queen Street.
	William Ogilvie, Warehouseman, 78 Queen Street.
	John Robert Kay, Warehouseman, 78 Queen Street.
	Robert Kedie, Warehouseman, 21 Buchanan Street.
	James Robert Sloan, Manufacturer, 7 Royal Bank Place.
	Robert Gilchrist Finlay, jun., Manufacturer, 12 South Frederick Street.
	Thomas O'May, Officer of the Incorporation of Weavers, 2 St. Andrew Square.
	Robert Eason, Stationer's Assistant, 674 Gallowgate.
1885-86	Henry Bowie Fyfe, Writer, 133 St. Vincent Street.
	William Elder Allan, Teacher, 130 South Portland Street.
	Robert M'Nish, Tea Merchant, 68 York St.
	James Laughland, Warehouseman, 67 Mitchell Street.
	Alexander Hannah, Warehouseman, 3 South Hanover Street.
	John Robertson, Bleacher and Finisher, Rutherglen.
	John Service, Warehouseman, 67 Mitchell Street.
	Robert George Munsie, Yarn Salesman, 10 Berkeley Terrace.
	Hugh Brown, Merchant, 9 Exchange Sq.
	Robert Megget Knox, Engineer, 47 Crownpoint Road, Mile-end.
	John Sinclair Knox, 10 Clayton Terrace, Dennistoun.
	George Caldwell, Flesher, 101 Greenhead Street.
	Thomas Alexander Paul, Merchant, 112 Wellington Street.
	Robert Telford, Commercial Traveller, 7 Union Place, Farme, Rutherglen.
	William Graham Young, Physician, 22 Monteith Row.
1886-87	William Scouller Macalister, 383 Duke Street.

APPENDIX.

Year of Membership.	Names of Members.
1886-87	David Brown, jun., House Factor, 69 Clyde Street, Calton.
William Alexander Caskie, M.D., Largs.
Robert Wyllie, Biscuit Manufacturer, 354 Paisley Road.
Thomas Mason, 21 Clyde Place.
John Dawson, at George Younger & Co., 166 Ingram Street.
Ebenezer James Mozart Allan, Music Publisher, 130 South Portland Street.
James Buchanan Muir, 62 Waddell Street.
Ebenezer Brown Fleming, Commission Merchant, 185 West George Street.
Alexander White Tod, Manufacturer, 76 Wilson Street.
James Taylor Drysdale, Drysalter, 124 Renfield Street.
1887-88	William Brown Watson, Manufacturer, Bernard Street Mills, Glasgow.
Walter M'Lintock, jun., 112 Parson Street.
William Stewart Ramsay, Manufacturer, 134 Queen Street.
William Buchanan, 67 Alexandra Parade.
James Mitchell Watson, Manufacturer, Bernard Street Mills, Glasgow.
William Morison Paterson, Manufacturer, St. Marnock Street.
Archibald Speirs, House Factor, 74 Canning Street.
James M'Dougall, 88 Warroch Street, Anderston.
James Burns Kidston, jun., Writer, 50 West Regent Street.
1888-89	John Buchanan, 6 Norfolk Street.
James Buchanan, 22 Robertson Street.
Andrew Brock, 43 Moir Street.
David Dreghorn, Kinning Park.
Benjamin Chesney, 22 Caledonia Road.
James Peebles, 13 Wellpark Street.
William Adam, 5 Main Street, Anderston.
John Whitehead Wilson Drysdale, 183 Fordneuk Street.
Alexander Kyd, 13 Oswald Street.
William M'Queen, Weaver, 52 Weaver St.
1889-90	William Hadyn Allan, 111 New City Road.
William Craighead, 51 Whitevale Street.
William Kidston, Writer, 50 West Regent Street.
Archibald M'Kinnon, 139 Greenhead St.

Year of Membership.	Names of Members.
1889-90	Thomas Swan, 32 Polmadie Road.
Alexander Nisbet Paterson, 4 St. John Terrace, Hillhead.
James Blakeston Stewart, 33 Lacrosse Terrace, Hillhead.
William Hopper Stewart, 33 Lacrosse Terrace, Hillhead.
John Lauder Stewart, 33 Lacrosse Terrace, Hillhead.
James Jamieson, 7 Fergus Place, Kirkcaldy
William Allan, 117 Golfhill Terrace, Dennistoun.
William Fleming, 138 Duke Street.
1890-91	John M'Skimming, 4 Bute Mansions, Hillhead.
Thomas James Menzies, Stranraer Academy, Stranraer.
Thos. Calder M'Leod, 59 St. Vincent Street
Robert Dougall M'Ewan, 22 Montrose St.
1891-92	Andrew Gibb, 30 South Street, Greenwich
John Ernest Kerr, Aberdona, Clackmannanshire.
John Logan M'Culloch, 15 Castle Street.
James M'Kechnie, 52 James Orr Street.
Hugh James Craig, 1 Hamilton Terrace East, Partick.
John Boyd Wallace, 66 Huskisson Street, Liverpool.
Alexander Waddell, Eastbourne Place, Shawlands.
John Waddell, Invereck, Kilmacolm.
Andrew Miller Wilson, 7 Park Terr., Govan
William Russell, 3 Park Terrace, Langside
Thomas Orr, Maxwell Street.
1892-93	George Sutherland, 80 Grant Street.
John Allan M'Lean, Havanna, Cuba.
James Morrice, 10 Cecil Street, Manchester
William Cecil Easton, Redholm, Helensburgh.
Duncan Turner Easton, Redholm, Helensburgh.
James Hamilton, 19 Wilson Street.
Alexander Clark, 1 Newhall Terrace, Bridgeton.
Alexander Buchanan, 51 M'Aslin Street.
William Macfie, 26 Bishop Street, Rothesay
James Place, 21 Seytoun Avenue, Langside
David Logan, 6 Garnet Terrace, Mount Florida.

APPENDIX.

Year of Membership.	Names of Members.
1892-93	Alexander Norrie Woodrow, 75 Glassford Street.
	John Gray, 3 West Scotland Street.
	Alexander Gartshore, 43 Virginia Street.
	William Swan, 32 Polmadie Road.
1893-94	David Crosby Wright, 155 Reidvale Street.
	William Yuille Orr, Maxwell Street.
	John Fraser Orr, M.D., 1 Berlin Terrace, Pollokshields.
	Samuel Leckie, 35 North St. Mungo Street.
	And. Docherty, 7 Firpark Terrace.
	Francis Gilchrist Cuzen, 286 London Road.
	Wm. Arthur Liddell, 13 Argyle Place, Partick.
	David Dunn, Merchant, 64 Robertson St.
	William Miller Findlay, 125 Buchanan St.
	James Baillie, 26 Montague Street.
	John Buchanan, 10 Steven Street.
	William Hewat, 22 Queen Mary Avenue, Crosshill.
	John M'Culloch, 421 Gallowgate.
1894-95	Wm. Houston, 125 Buchanan Street.
	Wm. Mitchell, Hazelwood, Langside.
	John Andrew Downie, 57 Ingram Street.
	David Sinclair Brown, 46 Main Street, Bridgeton.
	Jas. Allan, 13 John Street.
	James Johnston Fisken, 78 Queen Street.
	Archd. Love Holmes, 13 John Street.
	George Galloway Pomphrey, 137 Ingram Street.
	Edwin Connell Wilson, Bantaskin, Falkirk.
	Robert Alexander Reid, 125 Buchanan St.
	John Bogle Smith, 134 Ingram Street.
	Alex. Davie Smith, 134 Ingram Street.
	William Barr, 88 Gt. Clyde Street.
	Hugh Watson, jun., 93 Annfield Street.
	William Gardiner, 10 St. James's Terrace, Hillhead.
	Jas. Robertson, jun., Writer, 35 St. Vincent Crescent.
	Geo. Stevenson M'Nish, 1 Colebrooke Place, Hillhead.
	John Stevenson M'Nish, 1 Colebrooke Place, Hillhead.
	David Jamieson Graham, Glen Ter. Distillery, Langholm.
	Archd. Cameron Wallace, 183 West George Street.
	And. Davie Manson, 104 Hydepark Street.
1894-95	Joseph Paton Maclay, 123 Hope Street.
	Wm. Paton Maclay, 104 Hydepark Street.
	Robert Downie, jun., 111 Finlay Drive, Dennistoun.
	John Buchanan Rae, 818 New City Road.
	Colin Campbell, 123 Hospital Street.
	John Gemmell, 15 Newhall Terrace, Greenhead.
	Henry Drysdale Winning, 10 Campsie Crescent, Langside.
	Arthur Mayer Macintyre, 8 Lindsay Terr., Partick.
	James Marshall Downie, Woodside, Lenzie.
	James Speirs Cherry, Merrylee Villa, Shawlands.
	William Cherry, Merrylee Villa, Shawlands.
	Gavin Speirs Cherry, Merrylee Villa, Shawlands.
	James Mitchell Alexander, 5 Doune Terr., Kelvinside.
	David Duff Alexander, 5 Doune Terrace, Kelvinside.
	William M'Dougall, 83 South Portland St.
	John Dalrymple Johnston, 6 Fitzroy Place, Sauchiehall Street.
	Wm. Johnston, 6 Fitzroy Place, Sauchiehall Street.
	William Maclay, 93 Hope Street.
	William Stuart Service, Writer, Glasgow.
	Walter Darling Noble, 21 Glassford Street.
1895-96	John George Augustus Baillie, Writer, 76 Albert Drive, Crosshill.
	John Hewat, 22 Queen Mary Avenue, Crosshill.
	William Hewat, 22 Queen Mary Avenue, Crosshill.
	Henry Alston Hewat, 22 Queen Mary Avenue, Crosshill.
	James Alexander Millen, 47 Commerce St.
	Andrew Robertson, Trearne Cottage, Wellshothill, Cambuslang.
	Robert Fairlie Young, Dunkeld, Buchanan Drive, Cambuslang.
	John Reid, 61 Henderson Street.
	Jas. Booth, 21 Granville Street, St. George's Road.
	Hugh Brown, jun., 9 Clairmont Gardens.
	Laurence Robertson Brown, 9 Clairmont Gardens.
	William Desbrasey Woodburn, 22 Eldon Street, Greenock.

APPENDIX.

Year of Membership.	Names of Members.
1895–96	George Smith, jun., 75 Bothwell Street.
	Robert Workman Smith, 3 Clairmont Terr.
1896–97	David Wright M'Culloch, 66 Evelyn Street, Dennistoun.
	Harry Lumsden, Writer, 207 Ingram St.
	Duncan T. Kirkpatrick, 5 Park Terrace.
	Thomas A. Kirkpatrick, 5 Park Terrace.
	James Docherty, Coats Ltd., Paisley.
	Peter M'Auslin Carrick, 13 Battlefield Gardens, Langside.
	Allan MacDougall, 149 West George Street.
	William Gray, 44 Maxwell Drive.
	Stanley Pearson Crossland, Glenville, Gledholt, Huddersfield.
	John Caldwell, jun., 228 Meadowpark St.
	James Milne, 15 Castle Street.
	Hugh Austin Stirling, Solicitor, 133 St. Vincent Street.
	Nicol Paton Brown, 8 Doune Gardens.
1897–98	Geo. Ferrier Anderson MacNaughton, The Manse, Carsphairn, Kirkcudbrightshire.
	Robt. Mathers Mann, 21 Glassford Street.
	John Lyle, 10 Fordneuk Street.
	Henry Alexander Reid, 108 West George Street.
	Hubert Victor Kirkpatrick, 5 Park Terrace.
	Charles L. Wollheim, 48 West Regent St.
	John M. Steven, 115 Stirling Road.
	William D. Steven, Superintendent, India General Steam Navigation Co., Calcutta.
	Peter A. Steven, 2 Hampton Court Terrace.
	William Boyd, jun., C.A., 112 Bath Street.
	John Hunter, 5 Langside Terr., Langside.
1898–99	Daniel Wright, 11 Bannatyne Avenue.
	James Thomson Mitchell, 137 Ingram St.
	John Stevenson Downie, Public School, Newton Mearns.
	Thomas Brown, 8 Pentland Place.
	Thomas Macnair, 27 St. Vincent Place.
	Allan Taylor, 143 Crownpoint Road.
	James Wylie Smith, 49 Jamaica Street.
	Wm. Peebles, 5 Dunchattan Street.
	Wm. R. Danskin, 81 Pollok Street.
	John S. Houston, 125 Buchanan Street.
	James M'Allister, 541 Duke Street.
	Charles Chalmers Bryce, 223 West George Street.

Year of Membership.	Names of Members.
1898–99	Francis Legate, 1 Queensborough Dri Hyndland.
	Alex. Buchanan Selkirk Legate, 1 Quee borough Drive, Hyndland.
	John M'Kenzie, 103 Burnside Street.
	Jas. F. Bannerman, 108 West George St
	Thomas Scott, 153 Queen Street.
1899–1900	Jas. A. Reid, Writer, 172 St. Vincent St
	William Brodie, Writer, 77 St. Vinc Street.
	James MacDougall, 27 Caird Drive, Parti
	Frederick L. MacLeod, 59 St. Vinc Street.
	William Anderson, Lynorne, Blairgowri
	John Barr, 17 Battlefield Gardens, La side.
	Thomas Kirkpatrick Monro, 10 Clairm Gardens.
	Conal A. Wilkie, 72 Tobago Street.
	William Frame, 5 Walmer Terrace.
	Herbert F. Stockdale, Technical Coll
	Alexander Kidd, 239 Ingram Street.
	John Eadie, 69 Eglinton Street.
	Alexander Laird, jun., 113 King's P Place, Greenhead.
1900–01	David Marshall, 22 Montrose Street.
	Wm. Albert Harvey, 16 Westbourne Gd
	George Thomson Harvey, 16 Westbou Gardens.
	Wilson Harvey, 16 Westbourne Garder
	Thomas Harvey, 16 Westbourne Gardc
	James Thomson Caldwell, Bellafield Hou Uddingston.
	Robert Hamilton, Lochend, Glengarno
	James Howie Young, 92 Union Street.
	Reginald Mollison Young, Farmer, Cri larich.
	Harry Adamson Young, 24 Belhaven T
	John Erskine Young, jun., Lieut. R.S. 24 Belhaven Terrace.
	John Robson Young, 53 Mill St., Bridget
	Geo. Robson Young, 8 Clairmont Terra
	Robert Frew Young, 8 Clairmont Terra
	James E. Houston, 1 Seytoun Aven Langside.
	John M'Kenzie, jun., 103 Burnside Str
	Thos. Watson Macpherson, 62 Queen St
	John George Gunn Wright, 10 New B lington Street, London.
	John Aiken Danskin, 8 Ardgowan Stree

APPENDIX.

Year of Membership.	Names of Members.

-02 Jas. Gourlay, 11 Crown Gardens, Dowanhill.
John Wm. Gourlay, C.A., 180 Hope Street.
A. Rodger Reid, 1 Derby Crescent, Kelvinside, N.
Robert A. M. Reid, 1 Derby Crescent, Kelvinside, N.
R. M. Maclay, C.A., 209 West George St.
William MacLean, 3 Grosvenor Crescent, Kelvinside.
John Fraser, 31 West Street, Calton.
Archibald Robertson, 51 James Street, Calton.
Hugh Reid, 13 Victoria Buildings, Shettleston.
John M'Lea Wilkinson, Liberal Club, Glasgow.
Robertson Buchanan Stewart, 146 Argyle Street.

-03 Gilbert Innes, 21 Glassford Street.
James Filshill, 420 Gallowgate.
Jas. C. Webster, 103 West George Street.
David Wilson, D.L., D.Sc., of Carbeth, Killearn.
Lord Inverclyde, Castle Wemyss, Wemyss Bay.
Andrew Walker, 14 Montrose Street.
James C. Campbell, 9 Lynedoch Crescent.
John Graham Dow, 207 Ingram Street.
William Taylor, 16 St. Vincent Place.
W. M. Dickson, Glenroy House, Princes Town, Trinidad.
H. Taylor Brown, 111 French Street.
John Reid, Hydepark Locomotive Works, Springburn.
Arthur Kay, 78 Queen Street.
Herbert Ogilvie, 78 Queen Street.
David Couper, Bridgend Mills, Dalry.
Thos. Couper, 21 Glassford Street.
William Hammond Couper, 21 Glassford Street.
Jno. Graham Couper, jun., C.A., The Hollies, Langbank.
Jas. Hammond Couper, 21 Glassford Street.
Robert Suttie, 10 Princes Square, Buchanan Street.
Herbert Dunn, 20 Park Circus.
Bannatyne Dunn, 20 Park Circus.
Angus Rew, 56 Petershill Road.
David Crabb, 36 North Frederick Street.
Thomas Mason, jun., Polmadie.

1902-03 Robert Wylie Mason, Polmadie.
Andw. S. Strang, 201 Greenhead Street.
Hugh Yuill, D. & J. Anderson's, Bridgeton.
William Ritchie, 77 Queen Street.
Stewart Porteous Auchinvole, 113 Virginia Place.
William Hislop Manson, M.A., Avenue Villa, Mansionhouse Road, Langside.
James Muir Watson, 13 Bellgrove Street.
Malcolm W. Lindsay, 2 West Regent St.
Alex. Wilson Smart, jun., C.A., 98 High Street, Paisley.
Lewis A. Smart, Birkbeck Bank Chambers, Holborn, London, E.C.
John M'Clure Brodie, B.L., 23 Belhaven Terrace, Kelvinside.
Thomson Brodie, C.A., 23 Belhaven Terrace, Kelvinside.
Archd. Campbell Holms MacLean, Lieut. The Royal Scots, Aldershot.
H. J. Thomson, 147 Bath Street.
Walter Wilfrid Blackie, B.Sc., 17 Stanhope Street.
John Edward Lyle, 10 Fordneuk Street.
Walter Muir Watson, Airedale Shed, Silsden, York.
James Wilson, ter., Mayfield, Falkirk.
John Ross Wilson, Mayfield, Falkirk.
Tom Taylor Wilson, Mayfield, Falkirk.
Robert Wilson, jun., Mayfield, Falkirk.
Cecil Guy Wilson, Mayfield, Falkirk.
George H. M'Kay, 40 Dumbarton Road.
Henry A. Kidd, 571 Sauchiehall Street.

1903-04 James Dunn Dunn, 20 Park Circus.
Thomas Walker M'Intyre, 21 Bothwell St.
John Wishart, 39 St. Vincent Place.
James Andrew, Writer, 160 West George Street.
Arthur Yuill, 93 Candleriggs.
Thomas Forrest, 1 Moray Place.
William Forrest, 114 Dixon Avenue, Crosshill.
James Dick Forrest, L.D.S., 114 Dixon Avenue, Crosshill.
Robert Wardrop Forrest, M.B. & C.M., 114 Dixon Avenue, Crosshill.
Robert Oswald Blyth, 1 Montgomerie Quadrant.
Robert Johnston Galbraith, 4 West Regent Street.
Charles Galbraith, 35 Glassford Street.

D*

APPENDIX.

Year of Membership.	Names of Members.
1903–04	Chas. Alexander Mackinlay, 28 Dobbie's Loan. George Francis Newlands, Writer, 135 St. Vincent Street. Alexander Fyfe, M.A., 16 Montgomerie Quadrant. Henry Halcro Fyfe, 198 West George St. John Dunn, Baker, 29 Bellgrove Street. Robert Dick, 19 Waterloo Street. Archd. Montgomerie Craig, 7 Robertson Lane. Rev. Wm. Muir, B.D., St. Andrew's U.F. Manse, Blairgowrie. Cecil Ogilvie, 78 Queen Street. James H. Parker, C.A., 89 West Regent St. John Turner, 27 King Street, Liverpool. Geo. Lambie Reid, Windsor Place, Shettleston. Hugh Young Reid, 13 Victoria Buildings, Shettleston. Adair Campbell, 137 Ingram Street. Robert Glassford Alexander, 11 Belmont Crescent. J. Cecil Arthur, Fullarton, Troon. Andrew J. Guthrie, 29 West George Street. William Geo. Black, Writer, 88 West Regent Street. John Knox, jun., Silsden, York. William Knox, Silsden, York. Alexander Macindoe, 104 West George St. Joseph Gunn Mowat, 50 Wellington Street. James Gemmell Bissett, Netherpark, Largs.
1904–05	Robert Headrick, 21 Bothwell Street. Andrew Docherty, 8 Miller Street. James Walker Downie, 4 Woodside Cres. Andrew Marshall Downie, 4 Strathmore Gardens, Hillhead. Robert Cleland Gourlay, Caledonia Engine Works, Paisley. Robert James Gourlay, Bank of Scotland, St. Vincent Place. William Holt Woodburn, 17 Carlton Place. Arthur Blackburn Craig, 41 St. Vincent Pl. Rev. William Carmichael, U.F. Church, Crossknowe, Torrance. John Comrie Maclay, 5 Waterloo Street. Kenneth Maclay, 21 St. Vincent Place. Rev. Edward T. S. Reid, St. Cuthbert's Church, Hawick. James Shaw, 101 St. Vincent Street. David Simson Morton, 309 Dobbie's Loan.

Year of Membership.	Names of Members.
1904–05	David Cooke, 631 Alexandra Parade. James Cook, 93 Hutcheson Street. George Buchanan Marshall, 703 Cathcart Road. Robert Downie, jun., 111 Finlay Drive, Dennistoun. John P. Kinghorn, 105 West George Street David Rennie Macalister, 106 Cowcaddens Street. David Wright, 57 Reidvale Street. James Russell, 32 Fortis Green Road, East Finchley, London. Frederick Taylor, 49 Jamaica Street. Thomas Cunningham Todd, 30 Gordon Street. Arthur Herbert Graham, 107 Buchanan Street. John Henry Weston, 17 West Register St. Edinburgh. John Connell, 5 West Scotland Street. William Eglinton Russell, 32 Fortis Green Road, East Finchley, London. John Russell, Woodend, Lethington Avenue, Langside. John Fleming, 138 Duke Street. Thomas Tod, 26 Queen Street. Frederick William Hirst, Mountjoy Road, Huddersfield. John Taylor, 40 Queen Square, Strathbungo. James Manuel Webster, 103 West George Street. Arthur Andrew Maclay, Thornwood, Langside. David Baird, 139 Greenhead Terrace. Harry Baird, Mossbank, Gallowflat, Rutherglen. George Paterson, 376 St. Vincent Street. Walter Wardlaw Fyfe, 16 Montgomerie Quadrant, Kelvinside. John Erskine Fyfe, 16 Montgomerie Quadrant, Kelvinside. Alexander S. T. Gray, 3 Maxwell Terrace, Pollokshields. D. Macfarlane Macleod, 47 Morningtor Road, Bow, London, E. Donald Fraser Macnair, 41 St. Vincent Pl. James Archibald Holmes, 13 John Street
1905–06	James Watson M'Ewan, 9 Eglinton Drive James M'Kenzie Copland, 111 French St. Bridgeton.

APPENDIX.

Year of Membership.	Names of Members.
1905–06	David Whitelaw Kidston, C.A., 102 Hope Street.
	John Alexander Christie, Union Bank of Scotland, Ingram Street.
	Andrew Thomson Reid, Hydepark Locomotive Works.
	William Ferguson, 40 West Nile Street.
	Thos. Binnie, jun., 207 Hope Street.
	Thomas Adam, 27 Union Street.
	Andrew Baird, 93 Hutcheson Street.
	James Lindsay, 166 Gt. Hamilton Street.
	Edward Alston, 23 Sandyford Place.
	Charles Frederick Alston, 74 East Twelfth Street, Oakland, California.
	James M'Skimming, 6 Hamilton Drive, Pollokshields.
	Charles Scott M'Skimming, 6 Hamilton Drive, Pollokshields.
	William Kilpatrick Hutton, M.D., 11 Beaumont Gate, Dowanhill.
	James Johnston, 405 Cathcart Road.
	Alexander Burrell, 114 John Street.
	Charles Andrew Hislop, The Croft, Brookfield, Johnstone.
	Thomas Greenlees, jun., 22 Montrose St.
1906–07	Andrew Paterson Hamilton, Solicitor, 100 West Regent Street.
	John Hamilton, 1 North Park Terrace.
	William Miller, 186 Trongate.
	John Baird Walker, 24 George Square.
	William Alexander Burnet, 24 George Sq.
	John George Stevenson, Solicitor, 147 St. Vincent Street.
	Robert Stewart M'Nicol, 7 Royal Bank Pl.
	John Dawson, c/o Wm. Graham, jun., & Co., 7 Rua da Princeza, Lisbon.
	Wilson Dawson, 22 Montrose Street.
1906–07	Thos. Wyllie, 31 Clifford Street, Ibrox.
	Robert Wyllie, jun., 29 West George Street.
	Alexander Govan, Argyll Motors Ltd., Alexandria.
	Thomas Laurie Hendry, 34 West George St.
	Daniel Rippon Kilpatrick, 7 Royal Bank Place.
	Robert Shaw Paterson, c/o Messrs. Leisler Bock & Co., 55 West Regent Street.
	James Adam, 51 Buchanan Street.
	William Allan Lambie, 111 French Street, Bridgeton.
	James Pollock Morton, Renfield Weaving Factory, Pollokshaws.
	Cauvin Spittal Alston, 190 West George St.
	William Bogle Alston, Eastvale Place, Kelvinhaugh Street.
	Chas. Edward Hamilton, 1 North Park Terrace.
1907–08	Jas. Golder Macfarlane, 39 Miller Street.
	John Fraser Orr, Writer, 180 West Regent Street.
	John Graham, 29 Somerville Drive, Mount Florida.
	Robert Baxter, 37 St. Monance Street, Springburn.
	James Carruthers, 5 Balmano Street.
	Alexander M'Kenzie, 49 Cadogan Street.
	Robert Murray, 21 Park Street, Kinning Park.
	Charles Main Murray, 151 Whitehill Street, Dennistoun.
	John Thomson Murray, jun., 151 Whitehill Street, Dennistoun.
	Robert Wright, 87 Meadowpark Street.
	Nathaniel Martin Donaldson, 52 Cochrane Street.

HONORARY MEMBER.

Admitted May, 1907.

The Right Honourable Sir Henry Campbell-Bannerman, G.C.B., LL.D., M.P., Prime Minister and First Lord of the Treasury, son of a Member.

Lightning Source UK Ltd.
Milton Keynes UK
UKOW042023070313

207323UK00001B/16/P